Home Economics Teacher's

Survival Guide

Margaret F. Campbell   Robert C. Campbell

THE CENTER FOR APPLIED
RESEARCH IN EDUCATION
West Nyack, New York 10995

Library of Congress Cataloging-in-Publication Data

Campbell, Margaret F.
    Home economics teacher's survival guide / by Margaret F. Campbell,
Robert C. Campbell ; illustrations by Robert M. Baumbach.
      p.   cm.
    ISBN 0-87628-401-2
    1. Home economics—Study and teaching (Secondary).   2. Teachers—
Aids and devices.   I. Campbell, Robert C.   II. Title.
TX165.C34   1993   93-3822
640′.712—dc20   CIP

© 1993 *by* The Center for Applied Research in Education
All rights reserved.
Permission is given for individual teachers to reproduce the science
worksheets and illustrations for classroom use. Reproduction of these
materials for an entire school system is strictly forbidden.

Printed in the United States of America

10 9 8 7 6 5 4 3

ISBN 0-87628-401-2

ATTENTION: CORPORATIONS AND SCHOOLS
The Center for Applied Research in Education books are available at quantity
discounts with bulk purchase for educational, business, or sales promotional use.
For information, please write to: Prentice Hall Career & Personal Development
Special Sales, 240 Frisch Court, Paramus, New Jersey 07652. Please supply: title
of book, ISBN number, quantity, how the book will be used, date needed.

**THE CENTER FOR APPLIED RESEARCH
IN EDUCATION**
West Nyack, NY 10994
A Simon & Schuster Company

On the World Wide Web at http://www.phdirect.com

Prentice-Hall International (UK) Limited, *London*
Prentice-Hall of Australia Pty. Limited, *Sydney*
Prentice-Hall Canada Inc., *Toronto*
Prentice-Hall Hispanoamericana, S.A., *Mexico*
Prentice-Hall of India Private Limited, *New Delhi*
Prentice-Hall of Japan, Inc., *Tokyo*
Simon & Schuster Asia Pte. Ltd., *Singapore*
Editora Prentice-Hall do Brasil, Ltda., *Rio de Janeiro*

ABOUT THE AUTHORS

MARGARET F. CAMPBELL, a graduate of The Pennsylvania State University, has taught junior and senior high school home economics for over 18 years. She is currently Coordinator of Home Economics in the State College Area School District, State College, Pennsylvania, where she has had extensive experience in curriculum development and staff training. Her recent interests include serving as co-chair for her school's Middle States Evaluation, implementing total quality management strategies in her department as a result of a comprehensive program review, and involving her staff in an in-depth inservice program of cooperative learning and Dimensions of Learning teaching strategies.

Mrs. Campbell is the author of *Home Economics Curriculum Activities Kit* (The Center for Applied Research in Education, 1990), and she is a coauthor of *Computer Applications Activities Kit: Ready-to-Use Lessons & Worksheets for Secondary Students* (Prentice Hall, 1989) and *Computer Literacy Activities Kit: Levels I and II* (Prentice Hall, 1987).

DR. ROBERT C. CAMPBELL has had 35 years of experience as an elementary teacher, high school mathematics teacher, assistant superintendent, and superintendent of schools. He founded Educational Computer Consultants, a group of professionals who worked with school districts to introduce computers successfully into the curriculum during the 1980s. Recently he served as a consultant to home economics departments involved in a comprehensive curriculum review process and as director for a Pennsylvania Department of Education grant involving technology in a private elementary school consortium.

He coordinated the writing of *Home Economics Curriculum Activities Kit* (The Center for Applied Research in Education, 1990), was a coauthor of *Computer Applications Activities Kit: Ready-to-Use Lessons & Worksheets for Secondary Students* (Prentice Hall, 1989), and served as editor and project director for the writing of *Computer Literacy Activities Kit: Levels I and II* (Prentice Hall, 1987).

FOREWORD

While many educational materials for home economics education tackled curricular and programmatic issues in recent years, few have done so with the insightfulness and forthrightness of the Campbell's *Home Economics Teacher's Survival Guide*. This resource features practical approaches to teaching that have been gleaned from an accumulation of over 100 years of teaching experience by Margaret and her colleagues and associates. These time-tested, practical ideas contain necessary-to-know information for those aspiring to the ranks of home economics teachers as well as for those pursuing professional enhancement. Margaret is especially strong in encouraging the integration of new technology for increased productivity and in promoting public relations and political involvement of home economics teachers for program success.

Margaret Campbell's success in program leadership in a highly academically oriented school district attests to her credibility in addressing the issues of this practical guide. Her integration of management skills presents a thoughtfully developed foundation for new teachers and a refreshing approach for professional renewal of experienced teachers.

Home economics educators will find this resource to be a valuable reference item containing the keys to promote program and professional effectiveness.

Susan F. Weis, Ph.D.
Professor-in-Charge
Home Economics Education
The Pennsylvania State University

ABOUT THIS RESOURCE

The *Home Economics Teacher's Survival Guide* is a book of ideas designed to help you survive the rigors of being a secondary school teacher. The ideas relate to the short-range demands of teaching five periods a day and the long-range demands of developing an outstanding home economics program, getting along with people, and preparing students for life in the twenty-first century. The detailed practical information in the *Guide* will quickly build your knowledge about teaching home economics if you are a beginning home economics teacher. If you are an experienced home economics teacher, you will find that the *Guide* adds depth to your repertoire of teaching, management, planning, and people skills.

THE GUIDE AT A GLANCE

The ideas in the *Guide* focus on three areas of a home economics teacher's responsibilities: (1) teaching strategies for survival and success, (2) managing your job and staying sane, and (3) coping with contemporary issues. It is important to recognize that these three areas overlap and that, if we are to survive, sooner or later we must direct our efforts toward self-improvement in each area.

Part One, Teaching Strategies for Survival and Success, focuses on the more immediate responsibilities of teaching such as getting ready for tomorrow's teaching assignment. For example, Chapter 1, "Tricks of the Trade," is a compilation of "nuts and bolts" ideas with practical application in the classroom. Ideas range from a year's worth of bulletin boards to focusing on special-event days and using experts in the classroom. Chapter 2, "How to Manage a Home Economics Lab," contains practical suggestions to better manage a foods and sewing laboratory. Chapter 3, "So You Need a Sub and the Sub Needs . . . ," is a field-tested collection of ideas to make substitute teachers' lives easier and more productive. It includes an emergency substitute teacher's kit with lesson plans and student activities. "Teaching Strategies for the Twenty-first Century" are presented in Chapter 4. Cooperative learning, Tactics for thinking, Dimensions of learning, and Practical reasoning are described. Sample lesson plans are included with directions for how to use these approaches systematically in the home economics classroom. Addresses for accessing additional information about these exciting teaching methods are listed.

Part Two, Managing Your Job and Staying Sane, focuses on the management skills you need to survive increasing job demands. Chapter 5, "Knowing Where to Find It," contains hundreds of addresses and telephone numbers for curriculum resources, departments of education, and unusual consumer information. Chapter 6,

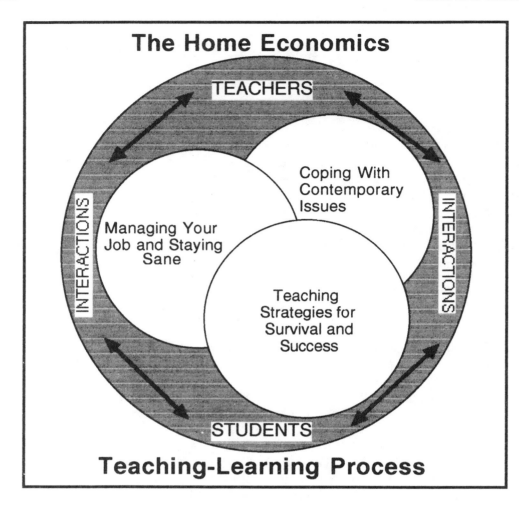

The Home Economics

TEACHERS

INTERACTIONS

Coping With
Contemporary
Issues

Managing Your
Job and Staying
Sane

INTERACTIONS

Teaching
Strategies for
Survival and
Success

STUDENTS

Teaching-Learning Process

"Managing Your Time," sets up a time management system for the workplace and gives suggestions for setting up a life-cycle time management program to enhance your personal life. Chapter 7, "Getting the Home Ec Message Across," begins with a review of writing skills needed by home economics teachers. The chapter features a collection of tips and examples for memos, letters, reports, courses of study, lesson plans, and student activity sheets. Chapter 8, "New Technology in the Home Ec Classroom," describes how home economics teachers can use word processing, database management, desktop publishing, and telecommunications to increase personal and departmental productivity. It also gives suggestions for using microcomputers in the instructional program.

Part Three, Coping with Contemporary Issues, is an insurance plan to be used in every school if home economics is to survive as a respected subject. This plan suggests ways in Chapter 9, "Reviewing and Updating Your Program," to cope with the demands of keeping your program up to date. Directions and reproducible forms to use to complete a comprehensive curriculum review are included. Chapter 10, "Selling Your Program Through Public Relations," contains a list of 100 public relations ideas for home economics teachers and a wealth of reproducible public relations materials. Chapter 11, "Politics and Your Program's Survival," explains how you can be politically savvy, get what you need, and keep what you have. Chapter 12, "Getting Along with People," presents a step-by-step strategy to apply on the job, at home, and in the classroom to get along better with difficult people. A personal growth plan to develop seven habits of effective people and the personal characteristics of principle-centered leadership is outlined.

HOW TO USE THIS RESOURCE

The *Home Economics Teacher's Survival Guide* is every home economics teacher's companion. The ideas it contains are useful at the middle school, junior high school, and senior high school levels. The areas of responsibility represented by the three parts of the book are interrelated, but do not need to be used in any set order. One approach is to read the *Guide* from cover to cover, to get a sense of its magnitude, and then to go back to pick and choose from those areas that seem to be of the most immediate concern. Or you may choose to read chapters at random based upon what strikes your fancy.

In the pressure to do the urgent, such as get ready for tomorrow's classes, we sometimes forget to do the important. It is essential you recognize that the long-range survival of your home economics program may depend upon how well you:

Use teaching strategies for the twenty-first century

Keep your program up to date

Apply public relations techniques

Employ political savvy, and

Get along with others.

Home Economics Teacher's Survival Guide is a useful resource that will help you and your program survive if you consider the ideas found in all three parts of the book.

ONE FINAL WORD

Never before have home economists faced such an exciting challenge. The needs of the individual and family seem to grow each day, while the resources to do our jobs get smaller. We have prepared a resource guide that contains information and ideas you need to survive the changes that are occurring in our schools and society. We wish you good fortune in using these ideas to survive as a teacher and grow as a person as you prepare young people to lead successful, happy lives in the twenty-first century.

Margaret F. Campbell
Robert C. Campbell

CONTENTS

*Pages in italics are reproducible pages.

*Pages in italics are reproducible pages.

*Pages in italics are reproducible pages.

*Pages in italics are reproducible pages.

*Pages in italics are reproducible pages.

*Pages in italics are reproducible pages.

*Pages in italics are reproducible pages.

PART THREE: COPING WITH CONTEMPORARY ISSUES

Chapter 9.   REVIEWING AND UPDATING YOUR PROGRAM   231

*Pages in italics are reproducible pages.

*Pages in italics are reproducible pages.

*Pages in italics are reproducible pages.

PART ONE

TEACHING STRATEGIES FOR SURVIVAL AND SUCCESS

- *Tricks of the Trade*
- *How to Manage a Home Economics Lab*
- *So You Need a Sub and the Sub Needs . . .*
- *Teaching Strategies for the Twenty-first Century*

HOME
ECON
OMICS
EDUCA
TION FOR
LIVING

1

CHAPTER 1
TRICKS OF THE TRADE

A POTPOURRI OF IDEAS

This chapter contains a collection of ideas to help make you a more effective teacher with less effort. Although referred to as "tricks," the ideas represent good teaching and efficient classroom management. Divided into two main groups, "Classroom Aids and Suggestions" and "Resources Outside the Classroom," the ideas in this chapter give you immediate applications—many that require only as much time as it takes to make copies.

CLASSROOM AIDS AND SUGGESTIONS

BULLETIN BOARDS

Bulletin boards can add zing to your program. Here are some pointers and a start-up kit of ready-to-use ideas.

Pointers for Bulletin Boards

1. What bulletin boards can do:

sell your program	generate interest
amuse	direct discussion
encourage involvement	increase awareness
focus information	encourage further study

2. Where to get ideas:

shopping malls	television
store window displays	posters
inside store displays	magazine and newspaper advertisements
Forecast magazine	fellow teachers
textbook illustrations	billboards
song titles or lyrics	sign boards

If you are energetic, contact the schools in your area and start a regional home economics bulletin board exchange.

3. Materials to use:

magazine and newspaper illustrations	advertisements
photographs	forms
brochures	3-D objects
fabric swatches	wrapping paper
yarn, string, tacks	empty packages
envelopes	computer graphics
product information	sample products

Comb neighborhood garage and yard sales for old magazines, posters, photographs, and advertisements.

Ask local store owners to give you advertising and display materials when they are finished with them.

4. Some helpful hints:

Keep it simple.

Use Velcro® dots to hang large or heavy objects on a bulletin board. Use them to hang posters you want to use again.

Use a personal computer to generate letters, banners, titles, slogans, and labels.

Use large, colorful illustrations and lettering.

Add three or four pinches of dash, such as fabric, textured paper, notions, 3-D objects, photos of students—anything with eye-catching appeal.

Start a vertical file to store your successful ideas for future recycling or modification.

Reproducible masters are provided here to give you a ready-to-use bulletin board start-up kit:

HOME ECONOMICS EDUCATION FOR LIVING

© 1993 by The Center for Applied Research in Education

© 1993 by The Center for Applied Research in Education

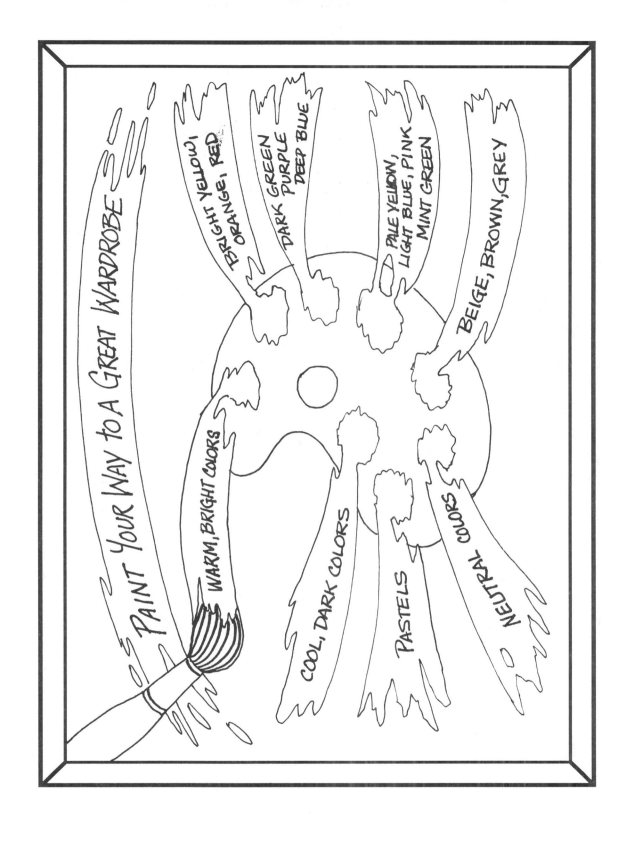

© 1993 by The Center for Applied Research in Education

SUCCESSFUL PARENTING IS MORE THAN GOOD LUCK!
IT'S GIVING...

SECURITY

AFFECTION

RECOGNITION

FAITH

GUIDANCE

LOVE

INDEPENDENCE

PROTECTION

ACCEPTANCE

© 1993 by The Center for Applied Research in Education

CREDIT

ARE THE CARDS FOR YOU?

POWER CREDIT

FUN IN USE CARD

BANK IN YOUR POCKET 278134792

PHONE

INSTANT MONEY CARD

$

EZ

PAY DAY CREDIT

GOLD BANK CARD

BUY IT CARD

$ HOW MUCH DO YOU PAY FOR CREDIT?

$ DO YOU KNOW YOUR RIGHTS?

$ DO YOU KNOW YOUR LIMIT?

$ WHAT DO YOU DO IF YOU LOSE A CREDIT CARD?

© 1993 by The Center for Applied Research in Education

© 1993 by The The Center for Applied Research in Education

NUTRITIOUS SNACKING

AROUND THE CLOCK

12 1 2 3 4 5 6 7 8 9 10 11

PICTURES OF NUTRITIOUS FOODS

PICTURES OF NUTRITIOUS FOODS

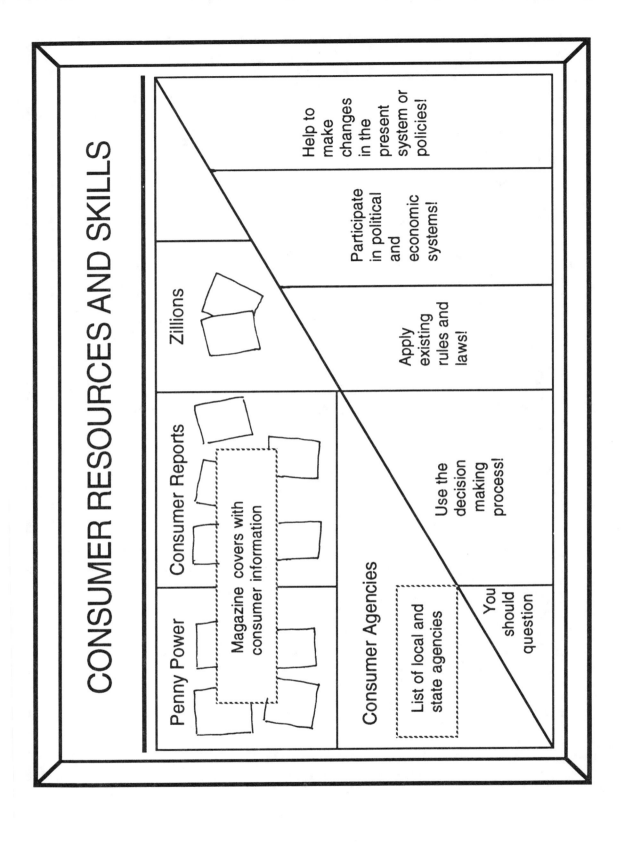

CONSUMER RESOURCES AND SKILLS

Penny Power

Consumer Reports

Zillions

Magazine covers with consumer information

Consumer Agencies

List of local and state agencies

You should question

Use the decision making process!

Apply existing rules and laws!

Participate in political and economic systems!

Help to make changes in the present system or policies!

© 1993 by The Center for Applied Research in Education

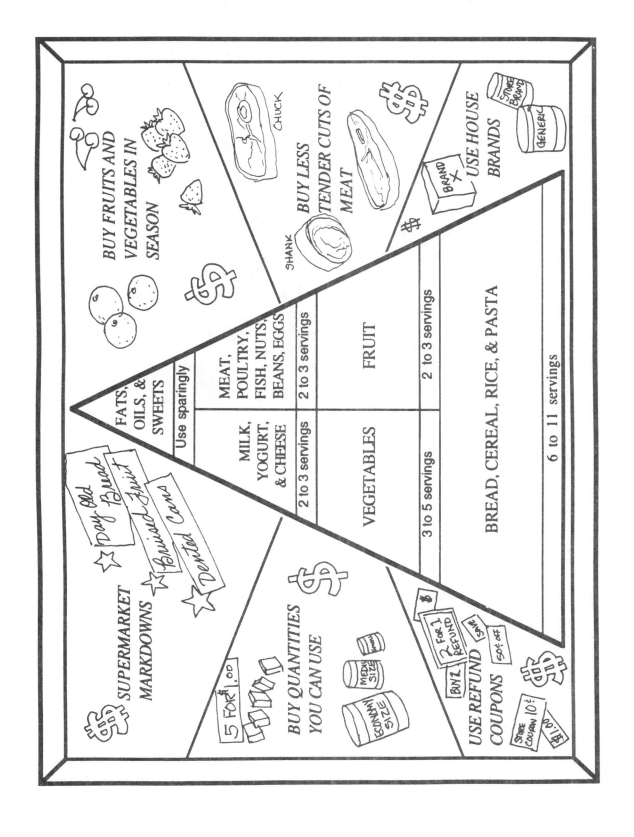

BUY FRUITS AND VEGETABLES IN SEASON

BUY LESS TENDER CUTS OF MEAT

CHUCK

SHANK

USE HOUSE BRANDS

STORE BRAND

GENERIC

BRAND X

FATS, OILS, & SWEETS

Use sparingly

MEAT, POULTRY, FISH, NUTS, BEANS, EGGS

2 to 3 servings

FRUIT

2 to 3 servings

MILK, YOGURT, & CHEESE

2 to 3 servings

VEGETABLES

3 to 5 servings

BREAD, CEREAL, RICE, & PASTA

6 to 11 servings

SUPERMARKET MARKDOWNS

Day Old Bread

Bruised Fruit

Dented Cans

BUY QUANTITIES YOU CAN USE

5 FOR $1.00

ECONOMY SIZE

MEDIUM SIZE

USE REFUND COUPONS

2 FOR 1 REFUND

SAVE 50¢ off

BUY 2

STORE COUPON 10¢

$1.00

© 1993 by The Center for Applied Research in Education

* Understand Cooking Terms

* Read the Recipe

* Measure Accurately

*Use Fresh Ingredients

*Use tools Effectively

*Focus on Safety and Sanitation

*Use Correct Time and Temperature

PROGRAM FOR BAKING SUCCESS

© 1993 by The Center for Applied Research in Education

© 1993 by The Center for Applied Research in Education

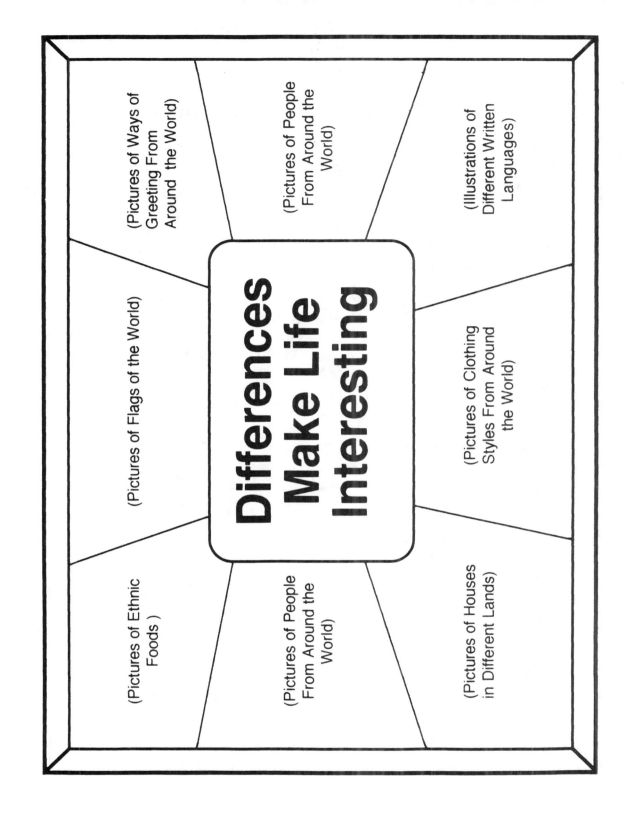

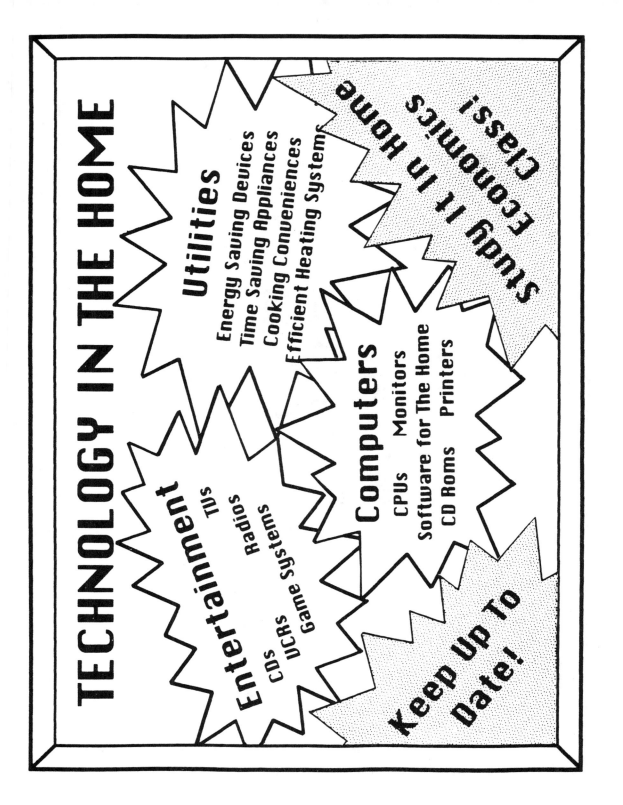

TECHNOLOGY IN THE HOME

Utilities
Energy Saving Devices
Time Saving Appliances
Cooking Conveniences
Efficient Heating Systems

Entertainment
TVs
Radios
CDs
VCRs
Game Systems

Computers
CPUs   Monitors
Software for The Home
CD Roms   Printers

Study it in Home Economics Class!

Keep Up To Date!

© 1993 by The Center for Applied Research in Education

© 1993 by The Center for Applied Research in Education

Suggestions from the Home Economics Students

ENVIRONMENTAL AWARENESS
BEGINS IN THE HOME...

(3 x 5 cards with student ideas)

...AND CONTINUES BEYOND!

(3 x 5 cards with student ideas)

FOCUS ON SPECIAL EVENTS

Add interest to home economics activities by focusing attention on the special days, weeks, or months. For example, use these commemorative days as themes for bulletin boards, display cases, and content of lessons.

Start a vertical file of materials for those events you identify as having special importance for home economics. Here is a starter list of commemorative events.

Annual Special Events/Commemorations

September

Be Late for Something Day   National Courtesy Month
Dr. Cookie Week   National Grandparent's Day
Hot Breakfast Month   National Hispanic Heritage Week

October

Consumer Information Month   National Pasta Month
Halloween   National Pie Day
International Microwave Month   United Nations World Food Day
National Fashion Week

November

Child Safety and Protection Month   Sandwich Day
Homemade Bread Day   Thanksgiving
National Family Bread Making Month

December

Christmas   Underdog Day
Hanukkah   Unicef Anniversary
Make Up Your Mind Day

January

Birth Defects Prevention Month   National Hobby Month
Chinese New Year   National Oatmeal Month
Human Resources Month   National Soup Month

February

American Heart Month   National Develop Your Self-esteem
Black History Month   Month

February, *continued*

Canned Food Month
Great American Pies Month
Human Relations Month
Levi Straus's Birthday
National Cherry Month

National Embroidery Month
National Grapefruit Month
Presidents' Day
Shape Up with Pickles Time
Susan B. Anthony's Birthday

March

American Chocolate Week
Easter (sometimes)
Mental Retardation Month
National Frozen Food Month
National Nutrition Month
National Pancake Week
National Peanut Month

National Procrastination Week
National Teenager's Day
National Women's History Month
Passover (sometimes)
Save Your Vision Week
St. Patrick's Day

April

Blame Someone Else Day
Cancer Control Month
Easter (sometimes)
Egg Salad Week
Home Improvement Time
Keep America Beautiful Month

Month of the Young Child
National Anxiety Month
National Consumer's Week
National Humor Month
Passover (sometimes)
Publicity Stunt Week

May

National Barbecue Month
National Egg Month
National Physical Fitness and
   Sports Month

Older Americans Month
Revise Your Work Schedule Month

June

Dairy Month
Flag Day
National Fresh Fruit and
   Vegetable Month

National Papaya Month
Turkey Lover's Month

Check the calendar each year to ascertain the exact dates for the special days and weeks listed.

MONEY-SAVING IDEAS

In times of tight budgets and diminishing resources, it is important to save money wherever you can. Some money-saving ideas to consider include:

- Requisition paper towels and trash liners from your building custodian rather than purchase them with home ec funds.
- Order in bulk through your cafeteria or a food service supplier.
- If your computer software fails, write to the publisher and inquire about replacement cost. Many publishers will replace damaged software at less than the cost of purchasing a new copy.
- Stock up on advertised specials.
- Ask for a school discount for everything you purchase locally.
- Solicit quotations from at least three sources for items of equipment over $25.00. Let the vendors know you are soliciting quotations and will give your business to the firm giving the lowest price for the item(s) you are purchasing.
- Start a file of money-off coupons. Have an aide—if you have one—check local papers in your school library.
- Order sewing patterns directly from the manufacturer to take advantage of their sizable discount.
- Have students bring some ingredients from home if they want to make recipes that are more exotic or expensive than your budget can stand.
- Get fabric store discount cards for your students before they purchase materials for class projects.
- Save sewing patterns to exchange with another teacher in your district or with a friend in a neighboring district.

CLIP ART FILE

Set up a clip art file of graphics and illustrations that you can cut and paste on student activity sheets or other handouts to make them more interesting and eye catching. You can find ideas for this file in *Forecast* magazine, noncopyrighted government publications, textbooks and copyrighted materials if you get permission to duplicate commercial clip art publications, computer clip art collections, state curriculum guides, publications of home economics professional organizations, and instructional units you have collected from other schools and colleagues.

You can organize your clip art file by course or by topic. Remember that you can enlarge or reduce the size of the artwork on most copy machines to prepare a variety of sizes for each item you want to keep in the file. Schools with the proper computer hardware and software can scan the images and save them electronically for use at a later time. Here, too, you must be careful not to infringe on someone's copyright.

THINGS TO SAVE

Beginning teachers need to start a file for food labels, product claims, product nutrition information, ingredient lists, and product preparation. These clippings are useful in consumer comparison activities, nutritional analysis activities, truth in advertising claims, and so forth.

These materials can be used on bulletin boards to add interest and realism. They can be used in packets of materials for small-group activities or in cooperative learning activities. You can include them as original material to be analyzed in unit tests. Or you can use them as visual aids when you introduce a lesson or unit.

HELP FOR SHOPPING AND OTHER CHORES

Ask your principal to relieve you of extra-duty assignments to compensate you for the time you spend shopping for supplies and materials, doing laundry, setting up and tearing down labs, and preparing sample products.

WELCOME BACK!

Use the sample "Welcome Back!" page to make students feel special and provide them with information about what they missed during an absence.

HOME ECONOMICS

Welcome Back!

I missed seeing your smiling face. While you were gone we completed the following assignments. See me if you have questions.

© 1993 by The Center for Applied Research in Education

DATE DUE: _____

ADJUSTMENTS FOR DIFFERENT READING LEVELS

It has been said that all teachers are teachers of reading and writing. Home economics teachers can help students develop better reading and writing skills by varying assignments to match their abilities and developing specialized learning activities.

Some Adjustments You Can Make

1. Check the reading level and *Fog Index* of basic texts when you select them. Ask a reading specialist to help you with this. Supplement them with other materials written at several different reading levels.
2. Set up a resource center of free and inexpensive materials, newspaper and magazine articles, product information, audio tapes, home economics–related magazines, videos, materials on loan from the community or school library, and so forth.
3. Develop a list of key vocabulary words for each unit of study. Distribute the list. Have students write definitions; use them to solve crossword and word-search puzzles, to complete activity sheets, to write reports, or to complete any type of activity that demonstrates they recognize, know the meaning of, and are able to use the key vocabulary in a sentence.
4. Develop student activities that use information age technology. Use tele-conferencing, videocassettes, television programming, electronic news, E-mail, on-line computer services, and personal computer software to teach content.
5. Relate classroom readings and writing activities to practical real-life applications and vocational goals.
6. Provide audio tapes for students with limited reading skills. For example, these tapes can be used for directions on how to complete an activity like following a recipe, basic information about a classroom discussion topic, or test questions.

PUZZLES

Kids of all ages love puzzles. Crossword and word-search puzzles are adaptable to classroom use. They are particularly useful to build vocabulary, to reinforce learning, to challenge the imagination, to motivate students to learn more, and to provide for individual differences.

Puzzles can be very helpful to a substitute. If something doesn't go right, they can be used as a fall-back position. For example, if the lesson plan you left doesn't take the entire class period, a couple of puzzles related to the lesson can be used. If any students finish early, they can be given a puzzle or two to complete. Make it a habit to include several puzzles related to current subject matter in your substitute teacher information.

Puzzle making has been made easy with the advent of inexpensive computer software. Once you have established an objective for a puzzle, you simply decide the clues and the answers, type them into the computer, and print out the puzzle ready to use! Check the advertisements and product reviews in *Electronic Learning* and *Forecast* for titles of puzzle-making software.

A Starter Kit of Puzzles

This kit will get you started with a supply of puzzles to use in various places in the curriculum.

HUMAN RELATIONS

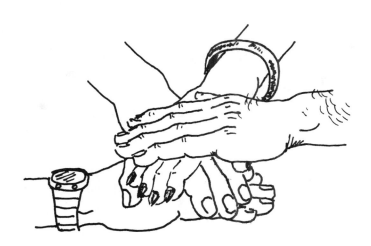

HUMAN RELATIONS

Across

5 Something confided, as a secret
7 An action
12 A careful plan or method
13 Meeting a goal or purpose
18 Style of living that reflects attitudes and values of an individual or group
19 To act in accordance with current customs
20 A belief or quality considered worthwhile or desirable
21 Positive, not destructive
22 Quality of being faithful to a person, custom or ideal
23 A preconceived preference or idea
24 The totality of qualities and traits of an individual

Down

1 A marriage partner
2 An act of abusive behavior
3 Relations between persons
4 An objective
5 An exclusive group of friends who tend to remain aloof
6 A strong subjective response to a person or event
8 A turning point, for better or worse
9 Strong affection for or attachment to another person based on personal ties
10 A body of ceremonies or rites
11 To reach a stage of responsible behavior
14 Settlement of a disagreement with a solution agreeable to both parties
15 Period of life between puberty and physical maturity, the teen years
16 Respect for different opinions
17 A person, group, or event considered to typify or conform to an unvarying manner

© 1993 by The Center for Applied Research in Education

Human Relations

© 1993 by The Center for Applied Research in Education

COOKERY TERMS

COOKERY TERMS

Across

4 To cut or remove from a larger piece
5 Cover a food with flour or sugar
7 Cut into small squares
8 Cut into very small cubes
10 Fry small amounts of food in hot oil while stirring
11 Mix solid shortening with flour
12 Remove excess fat with a sharp knife
14 Remove the core of a fruit
15 Spread a liquid coating on food
18 Mix well with a spoon or electric beater
19 Cover with a coating of crumbs
21 To cut or chop into very small pieces
22 Rub shortening on the surface of a cookie sheet
25 Cut away the skin or thin layer of a fruit or vegetable
28 To mix two or more ingredients
30 Cook over steam rising from boiling water
31 Combine two or more ingredients
32 Cut into small pieces

Down

1 Work dough by folding, turning, and pressing
2 Form a standing edge on a pie crust
3 To remove dough from the side of a bowl
5 Cook in hot fat that completely covers the food
6 Cut food into long, thin strips
9 Rub orange peel against a grater to get fine particles of rind
13 Soak in a seasoned liquid to add flavor
14 Soften and blend until smooth
16 Put flour through a sifter or fine sieve
17 To crush, as with potatoes
20 Make thin, straight cuts through outer fat on meat
23 Mix with a circular motion of a spoon
24 Brush liquid over food while it is cooking
25 Cook gently in water below boiling point
26 To cut away the skin or rind of a fruit or vegetable
27 To crush or pulverize
29 To combine or blend into one mixture

© 1993 by The Center for Applied Research in Education

COOKERY TERMS

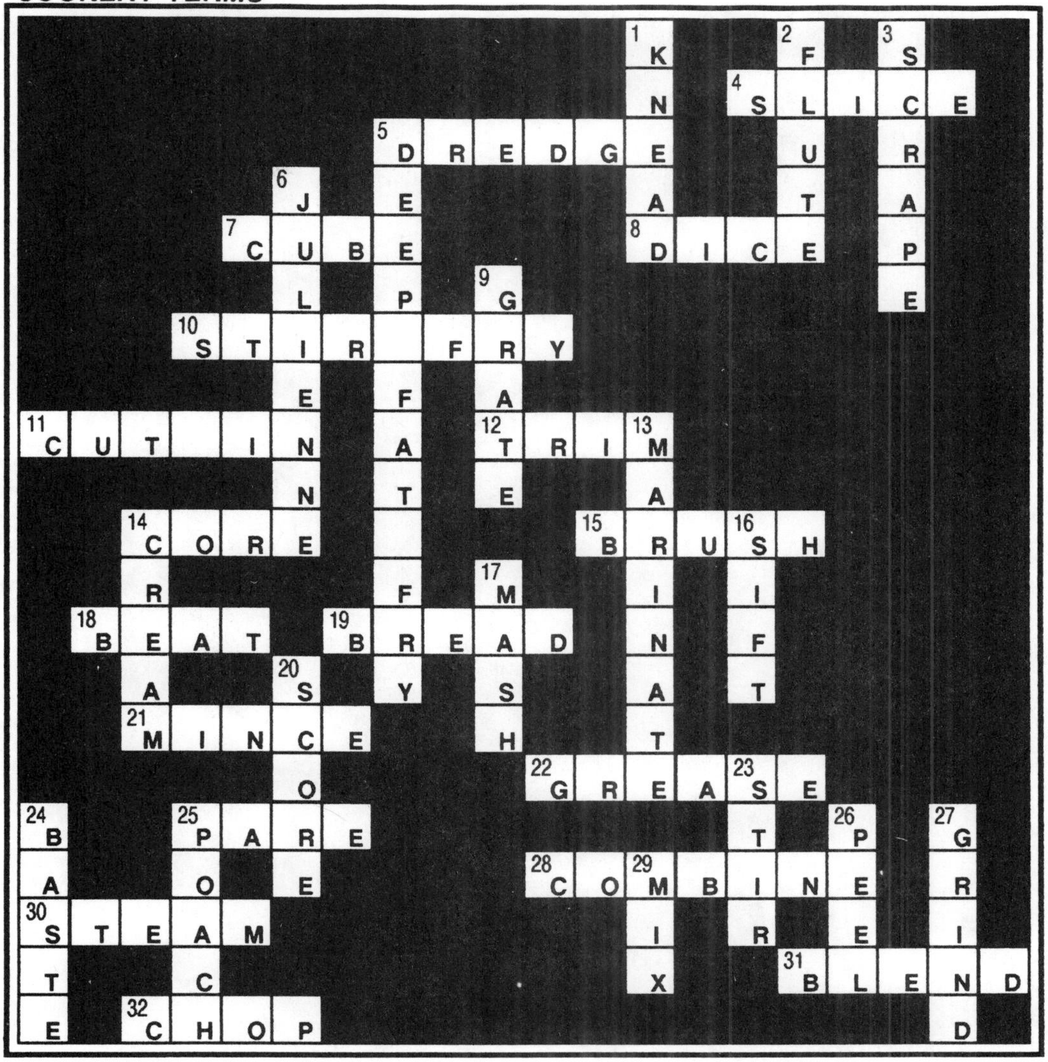

1 KNEAD
2 FLUTE
3 SCRAPE
4 SLICE
5 DREDGE
5 DEEP FAT FRY
6 JULIENNE
7 CUBE
8 DICE
9 GRATE
10 STIR FRY
11 CUT IN
12 TRIM
13 MARINATE
14 CORE
14 CREAM
15 BRUSH
16 SIFT
17 MASH
18 BEAT
19 BREAD
20 SCORE
21 MINCE
22 GREASE
23 STIR
24 BASTE
25 PARE
25 POACH
26 PEEL
27 GRIND
28 COMBINE
29 MIX
30 STEAM
31 BLEND
32 CHOP

© 1993 by The Center for Applied Research in Education

CONSUMER MATTERS

CONSUMER MATTERS

Across

3 Place where goods or services are sold
6 Money that comes from any source
7 Person who selects merchandise to sell in a department store
9 Booklet that displays items for sale by mail
10 Choices
12 Sale price from manufacturer or distributor
15 Difference between income and expenses
16 Event to sell items at less than regular price
18 A spending plan
19 Cost of food item per pound, quart, or other standard unit
20 Using property in exchange for specified rent
21 Large grocery store

Down

1 Degree or grade of excellence
2 Put an article for sale on reserve
4 Amount borrowed to purchase real estate
5 A store that sells a general line of merchandise
8 Asking price to consumer
11 Duties or work performed for another
12 Statement by manufacturer that product will operate as specified
13 Group of stores that sell merchandise at less than retail
14 Amount that expenses exceed income
17 Return of part of the amount paid for a product

© 1993 by The Center for Applied Research in Education

CONSUMER MATTERS

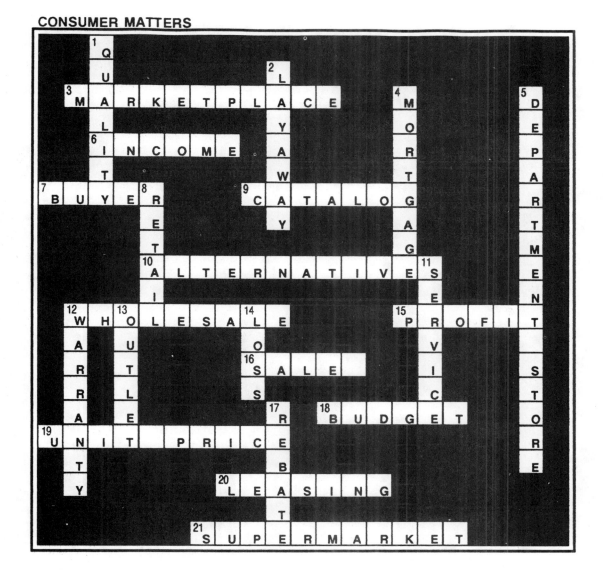

© 1993 by The Center for Applied Research in Education

SEWING

SEWING

Across

1 Shears that cut a zigzag edge
3 A 36-inch rule to measure
5 A plan to be followed to make a garment
6 Control speed of sewing machine
7 Toothed closing device
11 Cup worn to protect finger that pushes a needle
13 Lightweight cardboard piece of equipment to pin fabric to prevent slipping
14 Machine part to aid in sewing straight, even seams

Down

1 Metal rods used to fasten fabric
2 Tool to take out seams and remove stitches
4 Used with carbon paper to mark line on fabric
8 Invention to automatically sew stitches
9 Machine attachment to permit stitching close to a raised edge
10 Person who does custom sewing
12 Treatment to shrink fibers in thread

© 1993 by The Center for Applied Research in Education

SEWING

© 1993 by The Center for Applied Research in Education

HOUSING

HOUSING

Across

1 Private living space
5 Payment made by tenant to occupy the property of another
9 Single-family unit attached to other units on its sides
12 Factory-built house moved to the home site by truck
15 Goods and service establishments in community
16 Difference between amount still owed on real estate and what it could be sold for
17 Detailed plans for a building
18 Charge for a loan

Down

1 A condition of being secluded for personal space
2 Home that provides living space for one family
3 Separate living unit in a building
4 An apartment or townhouse that is purchased rather than rented
6 Protection from the elements
7 A building divided into two living spaces
8 To reconstruct a living space
10 To furnish a living space
11 First decision to make when choosing a home
12 Amount owed for real estate purchased
13 Repairs
14 Person who designs buildings

© 1993 by The Center for Applied Research in Education

HOUSING

© 1993 by The Center for Applied Research in Education

Crossword puzzle grid with the following answers:

Across:
- 1. PERSONAL SPACE
- 5. RENT
- 9. TOWNHOUSE
- 12. MOBILE HOME
- 15. FACILITIES
- 16. EQUITY
- 17. BLUEPRINT
- 18. INTEREST RATE

Down:
- 1. PRIVACY
- 2. SINGLE FAMILY
- 3. APARTMENT
- 4. CONDOMINIUM
- 6. SHELTER
- 7. DUPLEX
- 8. REMODEL
- 10. DECORATE
- 11. LOCATION
- 12. MORTGAGE
- 13. MAINTENANCE
- 14. ARCHITECT

RESOURCES OUTSIDE THE CLASSROOM

HOW TO KEEP AWARE OF WHAT IS NEW

Changes are occurring at ever-increasing speed. If your program is to keep up to date, you should have a plan to find out what is happening that impacts upon home economics education. Some tips are:

1. Join the American Home Economics Association (AHEA), read its publications, and attend meetings.

2. Read *Forecast, What's New in Home Economics, Consumer Reports, Dairy Council Nutrition Network,* and *Nutrition Newsletter* regularly.

3. Join the Association of Supervision and Curriculum Development (ASCD) or find out who in your school or school district belongs. Ask to borrow their copy of the organization's publications.

4. Read *The Kappan,* publication of the professional fraternity, Phi Delta Kappa.

5. Write to AHEA for a description of the Teacher of the Year Award winners' programs.

6. Keep in regular contact with the home economics specialists in your state department of education.

7. Develop a good relationship with sales representatives.

8. Periodically contact regional information centers like The Penn State Nutrition Center, University Park, Pennsylvania 16802; the county agricultural extension office; and local utility companies about what is new.

9. Attend national issue forums to determine social trends and directions that impact on the home economics curriculum.

10. Read a national newspaper. For example, you will find *USA Today* has a home economics–related article in every issue.

SET UP A TEACHER'S EXCHANGE
FOR IDEAS/MATERIALS

Contact local home economics–related organizations, your school district's community/adult education division, and neighboring school districts about sharing units of instruction, audiovisual materials, computer software, and instructional games.

HOW TO REQUEST NEW TEXTBOOKS

Many school districts have a textbook adoption policy that includes a formal evaluation process. Here are two forms to customize your school's selection process to home economics. The first form is a summary of the process used to arrive at a recommendation; the second provides documentation for the appropriateness of the selection.

NEW TEXTBOOK REQUEST FOR HOME ECONOMICS DEPARTMENT

Summary

A. Evaluator(s)/Building

_____   _____

_____   _____

_____   _____

_____   _____

B. Statement of Need

_____

_____

_____

_____

_____

C. Textbooks Considered

Title	Publisher	Cost
_____	_____	_____
_____	_____	_____
_____	_____	_____
_____	_____	_____

D. Textbook Recommended

Title	Publisher	Cost
_____	_____	_____

© 1993 by The Center for Applied Research in Education

EVALUATION CRITERIA FOR TEXTBOOKS

Complete the following evaluation checklist for the home economics content areas being considered.

Evaluator: _____ School: _____ Date: _____

A. General Information	Good	Fair	Poor
1. The textbook contains current, accurate information.	___	___	___
2. The presentation of material is varied throughout the text.	___	___	___
3. The information is useful and practical without being trivial.	___	___	___
4. Each chapter contains appropriate study questions.	___	___	___
5. Illustrations are effectively used to create visual interest.	___	___	___
6. The content matches the curriculum.	___	___	___
7. The content is consistent with the instructional objectives for the course in which the book will be used.	___	___	___
8. The reading level is appropriate.	___	___	___
9. The textbook is sensitive to issues of sexism, racism, cultural diversity, age, handicap, etc.	___	___	___
10. The textbook makes an important contribution to the curriculum that is not being made by the present collection of textbooks.	___	___	___

B. Clothing and Textiles Subject Matter Evaluation

	Good	Fair	Poor
1. Basic clothing construction steps are clearly explained.	___	___	___
2. Sewing techniques for a variety of fabrics are included.	___	___	___
3. Information about fashion design is presented.	___	___	___
4. Wardrobe planning and selection principles are explained.	___	___	___
5. The proper care of clothing techniques are discussed.	___	___	___
6. A consumer decision-making process is applied to the planning and selection of a wardrobe.	___	___	___

© 1993 by The Center for Applied Research in Education

	Good	Fair	Poor
C. Foods and Nutrition Subject Matter Evaluation			
1. The textbook discusses the relationship of food choices to nutrition for total well-being.	___	___	___
2. The instructions for food preparation are clearly and completely written.	___	___	___
3. Management skills are included for all areas of food preparation.	___	___	___
4. Instructional material is included that requires students to use higher-level thinking skills.	___	___	___
5. Up-to-date information about new equipment and preparation techniques is included.	___	___	___
D. Housing and Home Furnishings Subject Matter Evaluation			
1. There is a balance of information between housing and interior decorating.	___	___	___
2. Energy and environmental issues are addressed.	___	___	___
3. Alternate forms of housing accomodations for individual and family living are discussed.	___	___	___
4. The foundation concepts of line, design, and color are explained, not assumed to be known.	___	___	___
5. The effect of "family" on housing and home furnishing choices is investigated.	___	___	___
6. Home management principles are explored.	___	___	___
E. Child Development Subject Matter Evaluation			
1. Various child growth and development and learning theories are compared.	___	___	___
2. All elements of child growth and development are analyzed.	___	___	___
3. The development and adaptations of handicapped children are explained.	___	___	___
4. Current child-related issues and legislation are discussed.	___	___	___

© 1993 by The Center for Applied Research in Education

F. Family Relations Subject Matter Evaluation   Good Fair Poor

    1. Communication skills needed for a variety of family situations are explored.   —— —— ——

    2. Information about all phases of the life cycle is included.   —— —— ——

    3. Attention is given to alternative family structures.   —— —— ——

    4. Current government regulations and legislation relating to the family are discussed.   —— —— ——

    5. Information about balancing work and family is included.   —— —— ——

    6. How to manage family resources is discussed.   —— —— ——

    7. Information about needed parenting skills is included.   —— —— ——

© 1993 by The Center for Applied Research in Education

GRANTS

Locating Sources of Grants

If you have an idea to improve your program, but no money to fund it, consider making application for a grant. To locate sources of funding, it is important to identify your need clearly because most agencies have specific objectives and selection criteria. To start a search, contact your state department of education about possible sources of state and federal funding. Are there corporate, family, or private foundations located in your community? Would your parent/teacher organization or a local professional organization help you with funding? Check with your local library for information on funding sources. Ask if they have a copy of *The Foundation Directory.*

It is also possible to "piggyback" another agency's project. Check to see if there are agencies in your community receiving funding for a project that interfaces with your program. For example, if you are interested in starting an "Understanding Young Children" course that needs a child care center for your students to get "hands-on" experience, contact agencies who are operating child care centers in your community to see if they are interested in a location in your part of town.

How to Apply

Once you have identified possible sources of funds for your project, write for an application. Read the application and directions carefully to make sure you are eligible.

Most applications will require the following type of information:

1. An introduction to establish your credibility to carry out the project. It should explain the project, outline other activities that are related to the proposed project, and describe the school and its goals and philosophy. Include letters or statements of outside support for the project.
2. A problem statement based upon a needs assessment translated into a set of project goals.
3. A statement of project objectives with a description of the activities to be carried out to achieve the objectives.
4. An evaluation statement that describes the methods to be used to measure the accomplishment of the objectives.
5. A realistic budget.

Keep in mind that funding agencies are interested in the grantee developing the skills to be self-sufficient by the end of the funding period. You can demonstrate your intentions by requesting funds to employ a consultant to work with your staff on site or have staff members attend conferences or seminars to be trained in the skills they need to become self-sufficient.

Your proposal should represent the best work you are capable of. It should be prepared exactly as per the directions. It should be neatly typed with no misspelled words or typographical or grammatical errors. Layout is important. Provide ample white space, and generally, double space unless space is so tight you must use single spacing. Be brief, but not so brief as to leave out necessary information.

Remember, most grants are competitive. To be selected, your proposal must capture the reader's attention from the outset. The opening paragraph of your accompanying letter has to make the reader want to know more. Your letter should make it clear you are offering the agency the opportunity to do something worthwhile with its money.

BRINGING THE EXPERT TO CLASS

Every community has experts who will come into your classroom if invited. They can provide your students with firsthand experiences. The list of possibilities includes graduates of culinary schools, financial planners, representatives of human resource organizations and social agencies, bankers, businessmen and businesswomen, nearby college and university staff, local tradespeople, entrepreneurs, and small-business persons.

It is important to use an organized approach to involving experts in the classroom if you want to ensure a good experience for both your students and the visitor.

Guest Speaker Procedures

Here are some procedures you will find helpful.

1. Set up criteria for selection. Make sure your speakers represent diversity, including both sexes and different racial and ethnic backgrounds. Is the person well known in the community or respected in his or her profession? Has anyone else in the department used the person? If so, what was their evaluation? Does the person relate well to young people? Is he or she sincerely interested in coming into the school or doing it out of a sense of community obligation? Is the person an interesting speaker?

2. Carefully identify what you want the speaker to do. Make your initial contact via the telephone. State your name, school, and purpose of call immediately. Briefly describe the course and the outcomes the guest's visit could make to the class. Be prepared to be flexible about dates. Always make arrangements as far in advance as possible. Make sure you have checked the activity schedule to avoid conflicts with assemblies, pep

rallies, or fire drills. Let the person know you will be in touch about a week prior to the visit to work out the details.

3. Meet with the guest prior to the class visit to go over your expectations. Ask what the speaker would like to do. Identify any equipment or materials needed. Come to an agreement about what the speaker will do. Follow up the conference by sending the speaker an outline of what will be done during the class. Alter this procedure by letting capable students do the interviewing after establishing the goals in class.

4. Have students help identify the questions to ask the speaker. Set this up as a small-group activity. Break the class into groups of three or four students to develop a list of questions to ask the speaker. See the following sample worksheet, "Guest Speaker Planning Worksheet," for the small groups to use.

5. Have students use the "Guest Speaker Summary" sheet to record the important information they gleaned from the speaker's presentation. It is also important to have them evaluate the speaker by completing the rating section at the bottom of the form. See the reproducible master for the "Guest Speaker Summary" that follows.

6. Always give guest speakers the "red carpet" treatment. Arrange to meet them at the main office and escort them to your classroom. It is important to introduce a speaker appropriately. Give name, organization, special qualifications, and topic to be discussed. At the conclusion of the presentation, thank the speaker and present him or her with a memento of the visit. Presentation of a certificate of appreciation like the example given in Chapter 10 is an effective way to do this. Finally, have your guest escorted back to the main office or building exit. Don't overlook the opportunity to let your students handle these matters. Not only does it give them an opportunity to practice good social skills, it gives the guest an additional opportunity to interact with your students.

7. Following the visit, send the guest a thank you note. Be sure to mention one or two key contributions the speaker made, and express your hope he or she will come back again. This is also an opportunity to let your students participate by writing the note.

Name: _____ **Date:** _____

GUEST SPEAKER PLANNING WORKSHEET

    It is important for us to make maximum use of our time with the guest speaker. We have outlined what we want him or her to discuss with us. Make a list of questions you would like to ask to supplement what he or she tells us in class.

1. _____

   _____

2. _____

   _____

3. _____

   _____

4. _____

   _____

5. _____

   _____

6. _____

   _____

7. _____

   _____

8. _____

   _____

© 1993 by The Center for Applied Research in Education

Name: _____ *Date:* _____

GUEST SPEAKER SUMMARY

Name and position of speaker _____

_____

In complete sentences, state five or more main points of information presented by the speaker.

I agree with

I disagree with

I was surprised that

I would rate this speaker   10   9   8   7   6   5   4   3   2   1   because

_____

_____

_____

_____

_____

_____

© 1993 by The Center for Applied Research in Education

USE OF HOME ECONOMICS FACILITIES
BY OUTSIDERS

There is good news and bad news about letting outsiders use home economics facilities. The good news is, outsiders get to see something of what is going on in the home economics program. The bad news is, outsiders don't always treat the facilities and equipment responsibly. To eliminate the bad news:

1. Meet with the person using the facilities to review your standards and expectations for cleanliness and storage of equipment.
2. Demonstrate how to use the clothes washer and dryer so that all towels, cloths, and aprons are washed, dried, and put away before they leave.
3. Set up a message center where both parties can leave messages.

OUTCOME-BASED EDUCATION

If your school is getting involved with OBE (Outcome-Based Education), don't reinvent the wheel. Home economics is a subject area where considerable OBE development has already been completed.

An excellent resource is the Minnesota Department of Education's "Model Learner Outcomes for Home Economics Education." It is a set of knowledge and process outcomes for consumer housing, consumer textiles and clothing, home and family resource management, work/career, and technology. The learner outcomes are organized to be used with the Minnesota Home Economics Curriculum Examples, a practical reasoning approach to teaching home economics.

For information, call your state department of education and ask to borrow a copy of the *Minnesota Secondary Home Economics Resource Management Curriculum Examples*. If your state department has a resource center affiliated with VEIN, the Vocational Education Information Network, it probably has copies for loan. If not, contact the Minnesota Department of Education, Capitol Square, 550 Cedar Street, Saint Paul, Minnesota 55101, or the Minnesota Curriculum Services Center, 3554 White Bear Avenue, White Bear, Minnesota 55110; telephone: (800) 652-9024.

CHAPTER 2
HOW TO MANAGE
A HOME ECONOMICS LAB

LIFE IN THE LAB CAN BE HECTIC

In addition to writing lesson plans, attending committee meetings, and correcting papers, home economics teachers get to run laboratories. Lab sessions happen almost daily because they are integral parts of many courses, not just occasional occurrences. They require supplies that can't be ordered by mail or delivered to the classroom door by United Parcel Service. Many of the supplies are perishable and must be acquired at the last minute. Some labs require that money be collected from students before the items can be purchased. To complicate matters further, home economics departments frequently do not have aides.

Operating a successful lab program almost seems like a full-time job. In this chapter there are techniques to help ease the lab chores in the foods and sewing laboratories. You will find:

- Suggestions to simplify marketing tasks.
- Reproducible masters to help students plan foods lab activities.
- Ground rules for the foods lab.
- Important information about kitchen safety.
- Suggested ways to provide for the handicapped student.
- Information about a suggested home studies program.
- Ideas for the sewing laboratory.

IDEAS FOR THE FOODS LAB

Marketing

Doing the marketing for a foods laboratory is not the favorite pastime for home economics teachers. Here are some things to do to ease the burden.

1. Have the students determine the ingredients each kitchen needs for the laboratory experience. This can be done on a weekly basis several days prior to the laboratory lesson. Use a form like the following "Market Order List." Give it to students in each kitchen and have them indicate their kitchen's grocery needs as they prepare for the lab session. Have a central location for students to turn in their requests.

2. If you have a print shop in your district or school, have these forms made up into pads. If you don't, make photocopies or dittoes.

3. After you collect the forms, have one person make a tally for each class. Use the master list titled "Master Marketing List" to simplify the process. You may rearrange the list to better correspond to the layout of the store where you do your marketing.

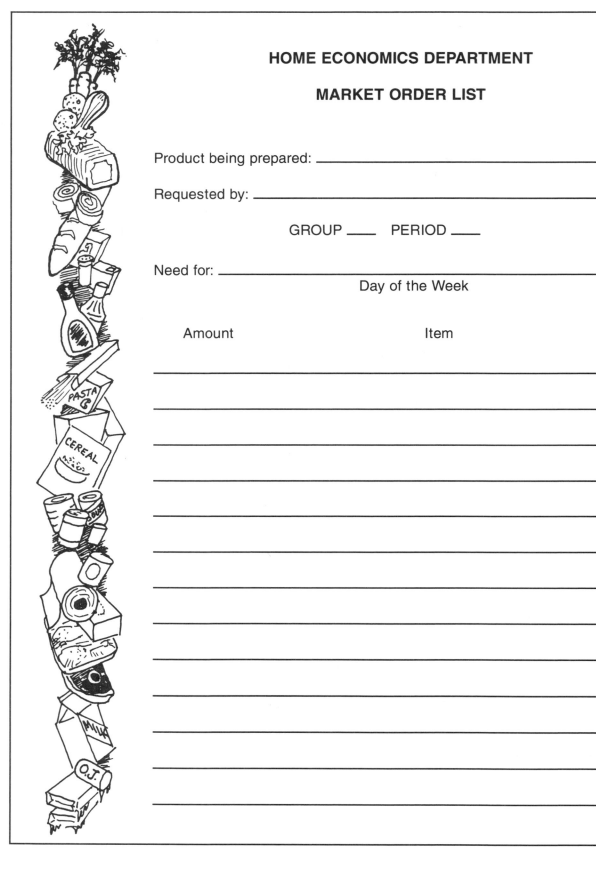

HOME ECONOMICS DEPARTMENT

MARKET ORDER LIST

Product being prepared: _____

Requested by: _____

GROUP ____ PERIOD ____

Need for: _____
Day of the Week

Amount   Item

_____

_____

_____

_____

_____

_____

_____

_____

_____

_____

_____

_____

© 1993 by The Center for Applied Research in Education

MASTER MARKETING LIST

FRESH PRODUCE:

_____   _____   _____

_____   _____   _____

BAKED PRODUCTS:

_____   _____   _____

_____   _____   _____

BAKING SUPPLIES:

_____   _____   _____

_____   _____   _____

**SALAD DRESSING
SEASONINGS
CONDIMENTS:**

_____   _____   _____

_____   _____   _____

PASTA PRODUCTS:

_____   _____   _____

_____   _____   _____

CEREAL PRODUCTS:

_____   _____   _____

_____   _____   _____

CANNED GOODS:

_____   _____   _____

_____   _____   _____

PAPER PRODUCTS:

_____   _____   _____

_____   _____   _____

MEAT PRODUCTS:

_____   _____   _____

_____   _____   _____

DAIRY PRODUCTS:

_____   _____   _____

_____   _____   _____

FROZEN FOODS:

_____   _____   _____

_____   _____   _____

MISCELLANEOUS:

© 1993 by The Center for Applied Research in Education

PRELIMINARY TO FIRST HANDS-ON
LAB SESSION

It is important that students know how to measure accurately, use knives properly, interpret a recipe, and practice good sanitation and safety before beginning their first hands-on cooking or baking experience. You need to teach these skills thoroughly in a first-level course and quickly review them at the beginning of other cooking or baking courses. You can teach these concepts through a demonstration or discussion. Have the students complete an activity sheet like those provided as you conduct or discuss the information. Have the students file the information in their notebook or file folder for future reference.

REPRODUCIBLE MASTERS FOR HANDOUTS
AND STUDENT ACTIVITY SHEETS FOLLOW

SANITATION INFORMATION SHEET

It is important to practice good sanitation when preparing food products. They are easily contaminated if prepared or stored in unsanitary conditions. Contaminated foods cause food poisoning. Food poisoning causes gastrointestinal discomfort that lasts from a few hours to several days and ranges from mild to severe.

Food poisoning is best prevented by following procedures to keep the kitchen facilities, equipment, utensils, food, and persons as clean and free of bacteria as possible. This is called practicing "good sanitation." Good sanitation is achieved by paying careful attention to personal hygiene and work habits.

Personal Sanitation Procedures

1. Keep your hands clean at all times. Wash them with hot soapy water before you begin food preparation and after coughing or sneezing or handling raw meats, fish, poultry, or eggs.

2. Use separate towels to dry hands and dishes. Never drape the dish towel over your shoulder.

3. If you have an open cut or sore on your hand, use plastic gloves when handling food.

4. Tie your hair back or cover it with a net or hat.

5. Wear clean clothes. Avoid loose garments that can accidentally touch food. Roll up long sleeves.

6. Wear an apron.

7. If a utensil or dish towel falls on the floor, do not use it again until it is washed.

8. Use a separate spoon for tasting, not the one you use for stirring.

Kitchen Sanitation Procedures

1. Wash counter tops and other work surfaces before beginning to cook.

2. Keep work surfaces clean by wiping up spills as they occur.

3. Thoroughly clean utensils and cutting boards with hot soapy water after each use.

4. Wash pots, pans, bowls, and dishes with hot soapy water as soon after use as possible. Keep soiled things away from the food preparation area.

5. Wash tools and utensils used on raw foods before using them on cooked foods.

6. Dispose of all food wastes properly. Remove garbage and trash at least once a day. Keep garbage container clean.

7. Change dish cloths and towels frequently.

8. After food preparation, clean all equipment, utensils, and tools, including work surfaces and floors.

© 1993 by The Center for Applied Research in Education

SANITATION

Food poisoning is prevented by keeping the kitchen _____, _____, utensils, food, and your _____ as clean and free of _____ as possible. This is called practicing "good sanitation." Good sanitation is achieved by paying careful attention to _____, _____, and _____ habits.

Personal Sanitation Procedures

1. Keep your hands clean at all times. Wash them with hot soapy water before you begin food preparation and after coughing and sneezing or handling raw meats, fish, poultry or eggs.

2. Use separate towels to dry hands and dishes. Never drape the dish towel over your shoulder.

3. If you have an open cut or sore on your hand, use _____ _____ when handling food.

4. Tie your _____ back or cover it with a net or hat.

5. Wear _____ clothes. Avoid loose garments that can accidentally touch food. Roll up long sleeves.

6. Wear an _____.

7. If a utensil or dish towel falls on the _____, do not use it again until it is _____.

8. Use a separate spoon for _____, not the one you use for stirring.

Kitchen Sanitation Procedures

1. _____ counter tops and other work surfaces before beginning cooking.

2. Keep work surfaces _____ while working by wiping up _____ when they occur.

3. Thoroughly clean utensils and _____ boards with hot soapy water after each use.

4. Wash _____, pans, bowls, and _____ with hot _____ water as soon after use as possible. Keep soiled things away from the food _____ area.

5. Wash tools and utensils used on _____ foods before using them on cooked foods.

6. Dispose of all food _____ properly. Remove garbage and trash at least _____ a day. Keep garbage container _____.

7. Change dish cloths and towels _____.

8. After food preparation, clean up all _____, _____, and tools, including all work surfaces and _____.

© 1993 by The Center for Applied Research in Education

© 1993 by The Center for Applied Research in Education

Name: _____ Date: _____

KNOW YOUR KNIVES

Pictured below are the most commonly used knives. Name the knife in the space provided and list examples of the foods you would typically cut with the knife.

Knife	Food
 a. _____	
 b. _____	
 c. _____	
 d. _____	
 e. _____	
 f. _____	
 g. _____	
 h. _____	

KNOW YOUR KNIVES ANSWER SHEET

Knife	Food
a. _____ French knife	All vegetables
b. _____ Butcher knife	Large pieces of uncooked meat
c. _____ Carving knife	Meat roasts and whole roasted fowl
d. _____ Bread knife	Bread, rolls, and cakes
e. _____ Utility knife	All purpose; can be used for almost anything
f. _____ Paring knife	Fruits and vegetables
g. _____ Grapefruit knife	Citrus fruits
h. _____ Cleaver	Cut bone and meat and section poultry

© 1993 by The Center for Applied Research in Education

© 1993 by The Center for Applied Research in Education

Name: _____ **Date:** _____

SLICE IT RIGHT!

Place a good knife in the hands of someone who knows the proper cutting techniques, and that person will save enough time in a year to take a week's vacation! Watch your teacher closely during the cutting demonstration. In the space provided, write a description or draw a picture of each type of cut and list three examples of foods normally cut with each procedure.

a. Chop or Mince

Description _____

_____

Picture

Three examples of foods

1. _____ 2. _____ 3. _____

b. Slice

Description _____

_____

Picture

Three examples of foods

1. _____ 2. _____ 3. _____

c. Peel

Description _____

_____

Picture

Three examples of foods

1. _____ 2. _____ 3. _____

---

d. Cube or Dice

Description _____

_____

Picture

Three examples of foods

1. _____ 2. _____ 3. _____

e. Julienne

Description _____

_____

Picture

Three examples of foods

1. _____ 2. _____ 3. _____

f. Section

Description _____

_____

Picture

Three examples of foods

1. _____ 2. _____ 3. _____

g. Carve

Description _____

_____

Picture

Three examples of foods

1. _____ 2. _____ 3. _____

© 1993 by The Center for Applied Research in Education

SLICE IT RIGHT! ANSWER SHEET

To cut into small pieces.
onion, garlic, celery

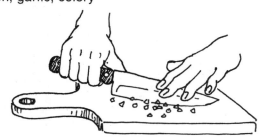

a. Chop or Mince

To cut food into flat pieces.
cucumbers, zucchini, carrots

b. Slice

To cut away the skin or a thin layer of the outside of fruits and vegetables.
apple, pear, onion

c. Peel

To cut into small squares.
apples, cheese, bread

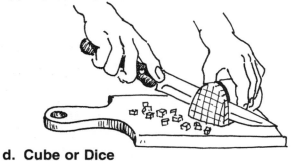

d. Cube or Dice

To cut food into long, thin strips.
cheese, carrots, bell pepper

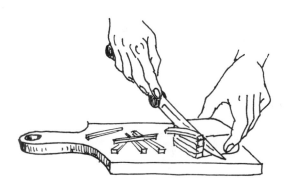

e. Julienne

To cut food into its natural sections.
orange, grapefruit, garlic

f. Section

To divide into pieces by cutting or slicing.
roast beef or pork, roast chicken and turkey

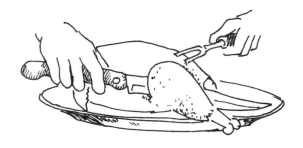

g. Carve

© 1993 by The Center for Applied Research in Education

ACCURATE MEASUREMENT

The key to cooking and baking good products is accurate measurement. A pinch of this and a dash of that will not produce reliable results time after time. It is important you learn to measure liquid and dry ingredients accurately. Study the information below to learn the best way to measure accurately.

How to Measure Liquid Ingredients

Liquid ingredients are measured in a liquid measuring cup. Place the cup on a level surface, and fill it to the desired level. Check the measurement from eye level.

How to Measure Dry Ingredients

Stir dry ingredients first to break up any lumps. With the measuring spoon, scoop up a heaping spoonful and level it with a straight-edged spatula.

Flour will pack when it stands. Therefore, many recipes call for sifted flour. Sift the flour onto paper and then carefully spoon it into a dry measuring cup to overflowing. Remove the excess with a straight-edged spatula. Never tap the cup to level the flour because this will cause it to pack.

Sugar does not require sifting unless it is lumpy. Confectioners' sugar tends to get lumpy and will require sifting before measuring. Measure confectioners' sugar as you do flour. White sugar is simply spooned into the measuring cup to overflowing and then leveled with a straight-edged spatula. Brown sugar may be lumpy. Crush it with a rolling pin and then pack firmly into a dry measuring cup, leveling with a straight-edged spatula.

How to Measure Shortening

Shortening should be brought to room temperature before measuring. Press solid shortenings into a dry measuring cup. Level the shortening with a straight-edged spatula and remove it from the cup with a rubber spatula. For requirements less than ¼ cup, use a measuring spoon.

© 1993 by The Center for Applied Research in Education

ACCURATE MEASUREMENT

The key to cooking and baking good products is accurate measurement. A pinch of this and a dash of that will not produce reliable results time after time. It is important you learn to measure liquid and dry ingredients accurately. Watch your teacher demonstrate measuring techniques and complete the information below. Keep this activity sheet in your lab folder for future reference.

How to Measure Liquid Ingredients

Liquid ingredients are measured in a _____ measuring cup. Place the cup on a _____ surface, and fill it to the desired level. Check the measurement from _____ level.

How to Measure Dry Ingredients

Stir dry ingredients first to break up any _____. With the measuring spoon, scoop up a _____ spoonful and level it with a straight-edged _____.

Flour will _____ when it stands. Therefore, many recipes call for _____ flour. Sift the flour onto _____ and then carefully spoon it into a _____ measuring cup to _____. Remove the excess with a straight-edged spatula. Never _____ the cup to _____ the flour because this will cause it to pack.

Sugar does not require _____ unless it is lumpy. Confectioners' sugar tends to get _____ and will require sifting before measuring. Measure _____ sugar as you do flour. _____ sugar is simply spooned into the measuring cup to overflowing and then leveled with a straight-edged spatula. _____ sugar may be lumpy. Crush it with a rolling _____ and then pack firmly in a dry measuring cup, leveling with a straight-edged spatula.

How to Measure Shortening

Shortening should be brought to _____ _____ before measuring. Press solid shortenings into a dry measuring cup. Level the shortening with a straight-edged spatula and remove it from the cup with a _____ spatula. For requirements less than _____ cup, use a measuring spoon.

© 1993 by The Center for Applied Research in Education

LAB PLANNING PROCEDURES

Food preparation requires planning, and it is a skill students may have had little opportunity to practice in the real world. The use of a lab planning sheet accompanied by appropriate instruction in planning strategies will help them learn to use planning skills in their daily lives. Two lab planning methods are described. Reproducible masters are provided for a "Lab Planning" form to help students prepare for laboratory experiences.

Laboratory Planning Method 1

Directions

1. Assign students to their jobs—manager, assistant manager, first cook, and so on. There are as many jobs as there are students assigned to the kitchen. The function of the manager is to divide the tasks needed to complete the recipe into as many parts as there are people assigned to the kitchen. For example, if there are three students per kitchen, the recipe tasks are divided into three parts, four students four parts, and so on.

2. The form provides a way to distribute the washing and drying tasks by noting who is responsible and when they are responsible.

3. To make certain students get the opportunity to do all four jobs, use a rotation sheet. You assign the jobs for the first lab session. Then have the students complete the form for as many sessions as are indicated on the form. The jobs should be parceled out equally. A reproducible master for "Job Rotation Schedule" is provided.

4. Review the task for the day. Distribute the lab planning sheets, and let the students begin working.

5. Redistribute the completed lab sheets the day the food is prepared and let the students follow their assignments to complete the recipe.

6. Have the students complete the evaluation section of the form. Check the forms and discuss any differences between your evaluation and theirs. You assign the bonus point for outstanding work.

LAB PLANNING SHEET

Kitchen _____ Period _____

Product Being Prepared _____

Read the recipe/instructions carefully before making plans.

Manager _____	**Ass't Manager** _____
Write plans.	Help manager write plans and first cook complete market order.
***Wash	***Dry
Second day plan:	Second day plan:

© 1993 by The Center for Applied Research in Education

First Cook _____

Complete market order.

- -

Second day plan:
***Wash

Second Cook _____

Act as host or hostess and coordinate cleanup.

- -

Second day plan:
***Dry

Planning	4	3	2	1
Preparation	4	3	2	1
Cleanup		3	2	1

Product	3	2	1	
Serving		2	1	Total _____
Cleanup	3	2	1	20
Bonus Point			1	

© 1993 by The Center for Applied Research in Education

JOB ROTATION SCHEDULE

Job	Lab 1.	Lab 2.	Lab 3.	Lab 4.	Lab 5.	Lab 6.
	Student Name					
Manager						
Ass't Manager						
First Cook						
Second Cook						

© 1993 by The Center for Applied Research in Education

Laboratory Planning Method 2

Directions

1. Assign students to kitchens and to their respective jobs: head cook, assistant cook, hostess or host, and cleanup coordinator.

2. If you are just beginning lab experiences, establish guidelines regarding job responsibilities and cleanup. A reproducible master, "Job Descriptions," is provided.

3. Review the laboratory assignment for the day.

4. Distribute "Foods Lab Planning Sheet" and briefly go over it to make certain students understand the assignment for the day.

5. Have students complete the "JOB ROTATION SCHEDULE" during the first lab session. The purpose of the schedule is to make certain all students get to serve in all capacities.

FOODS LAB PLANNING SHEET

Name	Job Assignment	Section #____
1.		Kitchen #:
2.		Prep Date:
3.		Product Being Prepared:
4.		
5.		Lab Absentees

Work Plan	Market Order _____
Time Plan Individual Duties	Amount Item

Utensils Needed	Place Setting

Evaluation

Planning	5 4 3 2 1	Preparation	5 4 3 2 1
Product	5 4 3 2 1	Cleanup	5 4 3 2 1

Comments:

© 1993 by The Center for Applied Research in Education

JOB DESCRIPTIONS FOR HOME ECONOMICS DEPARTMENT

Head Cook

Is responsible for cooking.

Gets out utensils.

Measures ingredients in the kitchen.

Assistant Cook

Helps head cook with the cooking responsibility.

Goes to the supply counter.

Returns all ingredients to their proper location.

Hostess or Host

Sets the table.

Serves the food.

Clears the table and gets rid of the garbage.

Cleanup Coordinator

Organizes kitchen cleanup.

Makes sure cleanup is completed satisfactorily.

Requests teacher to check the kitchen.

The following cleanup duties must be completed before the kitchens are checked by the teacher.

- Return all equipment to its proper place.
- Clean counter tops.
- Clean table.
- Clean and dry stove top, including chrome parts.
- Clean canisters.
- Clean and dry sinks.
- Remove garbage properly.
- Return all ingredients to the supply cupboards.
- Place dirty towels and sponges in washer.
- Sweep kitchen floor including under the table.

© 1993 by The Center for Applied Research in Education

JOB ROTATION SCHEDULE

Job	Lab 1.	Lab 2.	Lab 3.	Lab 4.	Lab 5.	Lab 6.
	Student Name					
Head Cook						
Ass't Cook						
Host or Hostess						
Cleanup Coordinator						

© 1993 by The Center for Applied Research in Education

Establishing Ground Rules for the Foods Laboratory

If students are to be successful in the foods lab, certain directions need to be given. If you implement a set of directions and then monitor their application so that each day's lab experience is conducted in a consistent manner, life will be much calmer for you and your students. See the following example of a list of directions in memo form that you can modify to fit your situation.

MEMO: DIRECTIONS FOR USING THE FOODS LABORATORY

MEMO TO: All Students

FROM: The Home Economics Department

RE: Directions for Using the Foods Laboratory

Many students use this lab everyday. If we are to work in an environment free of confusion, the equipment and supplies we work with must be organized. We have organized the equipment and supplies in a logical system. This system will be reviewed by your teacher. The following instructions will help keep the laboratory in good working order.

1. When removing a utensil from a cupboard or drawer, make a note of its exact location. Always return it to its proper place.

2. Bowls or measuring cups from your kitchen should not be used for refrigerator storage. Always use appropriate storage containers from your kitchen as listed on the inventory sheet.

3. Wear the clean aprons provided to protect your clothing and to maintain good sanitation.

4. Parts of appliances and utensils are always stored together. For example, beaters and electric cords are stored together, lids are stored with their saucepans, racks with broilers, and so on.

5. Everyone shares in cleanup unless permission has been received from the teacher or group members.

6. Wet dish cloths and towels should be placed in the laundry basket or washer.

7. Shoulder-length hair must be tied back. Ask the teacher for a rubber band.

8. For sanitary reasons, chewing gum is not permitted during food preparation.

9. Wash hands before handling food—every time!

10. Food products are not to be taken from the laboratory without permission.

© 1993 by The Center for Applied Research in Education

Keeping Track of Equipment

Equipment not normally found in a kitchen must be stored according to some plan if students are to locate items they need. One method to do this is to number every storage cupboard drawer and door. Then prepare a master alphabetized list of the equipment that is not a part of each kitchen's inventory. Make a note beside each item of the door or drawer number where it is located. Laminate the list; attach Velcro® dots and hang them in strategic locations throughout the lab. By using this procedure, you avoid the need for students to call out to ask where they can find something or move about the lab to ask where to find the piece of equipment they need.

Laboratory Safety

Home economics foods laboratories can be hazardous places. It is good teaching technique to review carefully kitchen safety and to provide students with a copy of suggested safety practices they should follow. You can duplicate the sample "Kitchen Safety Practices" to hand out to students.

KITCHEN SAFETY PRACTICES

The foods laboratory can be a hazardous place. You will be using electrical equipment, moving machinery, and working around very hot surfaces. Carefully review this list of suggestions, and practice them in your food preparation activities.

1. Dry hands thoroughly before connecting or disconnecting electrical appliances.

2. Use a rubber scraper to clean the sides of an electric mixer bowl when it is operating.

3. Turn the handles of pans so that they are over the work area or stove surface. Protruding handles can be bumped or caught on clothing, leading to severe burns.

4. Use a broom, dustpan, and damp paper towel to clean up broken glass.

5. Keep drawers closed at all times to avoid bumping them and spilling ingredients or food products.

6. Keep work surfaces clear of clutter. Return sharp knives to the correct block, if available.

7. Wash knives separately from other utensils.

8. Use dry pot holders when handling hot objects.

9. Practice proper knife safety. For example, cut away rather than toward yourself. Only use sharp knives. Call dull knives to the teacher's attention immediately.

10. When removing a lid from boiling food, tip it away from yourself to shield your face and hands from steam.

11. Avoid reaching across hot burners.

12. Avoid wearing loose, hanging clothing that may become entangled in the mixer or pot handles or catch on fire from hitting a hot burner or oven unit.

13. Avoid grease fires by using the correct-size pan and keeping heat low enough to prevent excessive splattering.

14. Drain food products well before lowering them into the deep-fat fryer.

15. Always know the exact location of the fire extinguishers and blanket.

© 1993 by The Center for Applied Research in Education

Providing for Students with Disabilities

Providing meaningful foods lab experiences for persons with disabilities takes some thought. These are some steps to take to plan, present information, and alter lab procedures.

Before the student with disabilities arrives in class you can:

1. Get to know the student via a parent/student/teacher conference. Focus on the student's disability to learn about his or her strengths and impairments.
2. Follow up to find out what the experts in your school system or community suggest the student is able to do in the foods lab.
3. If possible, arrange a private conference to familiarize the student with the lab. Review the types of things he or she will be doing and go over lab rules and procedures.
4. Get the school psychologist, learning specialist or parent to help you plan adaptations for four or five lab sessions for you to get the hang of it. Make adaptations to the lab manuals and worksheets. Be sure that the vocabulary used is at the appropriate level, that the print size is adapted for sight-impaired students, and that other necessary changes are made to accommodate the student.
5. Prepare the class for the arrival of a student with disabilities. Discuss the disability, what the student can and cannot do, what adaptations will be made, the importance of acceptance, and ways they can help. Have the students complete a lab experience while simulating the handicap. This can be very enlightening. For example, have them do the lab blindfolded, with one arm tied so it is not usable, while seated, or while wearing mittens.

There are adaptations you can make to equipment and facilities. Consider the following.

1. Choose appliances with push buttons or controls that are large enough to be grasped easily and are easy to turn.
2. Use treated nonstick pans and utensils so that students with disabilities can participate in cleanup activities. This will aid them in becoming accepted by classmates.
3. Use a microwave oven to eliminate some cooking steps—melting shortening, boiling water, for example.
4. Adapt too small handles by placing pipe insulation around the handle and then wrapping it with duct tape.
5. Mark measuring cups and spoons with large bright letters. Fingernail polish works well on most surfaces.
6. Place cutting boards on nonslip surfaces. Place a damp towel or dish cloth under cutting boards and bowls to prevent them from slipping.

7. Purchase a magnifying glass on an adjustable stand to help visually impaired students do such tedious jobs as cake decorating, for example. The science department may have one of these you can borrow.

8. Use wide-mouthed jars or containers so students can reach inside to scoop or grasp ingredients.

9. Use lightweight plastic, stainless, or aluminum flat-bottomed bowls with handles to help students stabilize them during mixing and pouring.

10. Make a counter board that can be attached to the arms of a wheelchair so the student can work at a comfortable level. Your local hospital or rehabilitation center will probably lend you a wheelchair tray.

Here are ways to adapt your teaching methods:

1. Use a cassette recorder to record recipes and directions. Include a verbal description of the foods lab and especially the kitchen work area to point out the location of stove, sinks, equipment, and supplies.

2. Buy boxes and packages of ingredients that are easy to open—flip tops, pull strings or perforated tabs, and so on.

3. Choose recipes that do not have time-consuming steps. For example, use a drop or bar cookie recipe rather than one needing a cookie cutter and use drop biscuits rather than cutout ones.

4. Consider eliminating some cooking steps by using convenience foods, ready-made pie crusts, instant pudding, packaged stuffing, and instant mashed potatoes.

5. Let severely disabled students complete just one or two tasks they are capable of doing to demonstrate to others that everyone is able to make a contribution and also to help the student build a feeling of self-worth.

Home Studies

The laboratory experiences that are part of most foods courses can be enriched and extended through a systematic program of home studies. Home studies encourage students to extend their skills by cooking or baking a product at home. The product is then eaten by family members who complete an evaluation sheet and return it to the teacher. See the "Home Studies Assignment" reproducible master.

Home studies can be included in courses as a requirement or as an extra-credit activity. If you require the activity, it is a good idea to permit parents or guardians to elect an alternative experience. With so many single-parent families and families where both parents work outside the home, it may not be appropriate for the student to be cooking or baking if no one is present in case of an accident or emergency.

Parents or guardians need to be informed about the Home Studies program. Here is a sample letter followed by a reproducible Home Studies Assignment master.

HOME STUDIES ASSIGNMENT LETTER
TO PARENTS OR GUARDIANS

PARK PLACE JUNIOR HIGH SCHOOL
Park Place, Michigan

Dear Parent or Guardian,

Your son or daughter is enrolled in the Home Economics Food and Nutrition course. The home study phase of this course requires your child to prepare one recipe from each unit of study. He or she can prepare more than one recipe and receive extra credit.

Enclosed is the form used in the home study assignment. Please note that you are requested to complete an evaluation of the product before your child returns the form to me.

If you prefer that your son or daughter not participate in this experience, please complete the section at the bottom of this letter and return it to me by September 20. I will give him or her an alternative assignment to complete the home study requirement.

Thank you for your cooperation.

Regards,

Rebecca Q. Underwood

_____

I prefer that my son/daughter not participate in the Home Studies Program at this time. Please assign him/her to an alternative activity.

_____
Parent or Guardian

© 1993 by The Center for Applied Research in Education

Name: _____ **Date:** _____

HOME STUDIES ASSIGNMENT SHEET

Course _____ Section _____

Unit of study _____

Name of recipe: _____

Recipe's source: _____

Steps taken to complete recipe:

_____

_____

_____

_____

_____

_____

Student evaluation:

_____

_____

_____

Parent or guardian evaluation:

_____

_____

_____

_____
Signature

© 1993 by The Center for Applied Research in Education

Alternative Student Evaluation Techniques:

Home economics with its many hands-on, cooperative learning experiences lends itself to alternative methods of student evaluation. Where the proof of one's skill lies in the quality of a product and the procedure used to produce the product, self-evaluation is a natural evaluation method. Periodical use of a "Laboratory Performance Checklist," like the reproducible one that follows, is a useful way to involve students in their own evaluation and the evaluation of the cooperative procedures they used to produce a product.

Name: _____   ***Date Due:*** _____

LABORATORY PERFORMANCE CHECKLIST

Kitchen # _____   Date of Lab _____

Product Prepared _____

© 1993 by The Center for Applied Research in Education

Personal/Group Work	Excellent	Good	Needs Improvement
I practiced proper sanitary procedures.			
My kitchen worked well together.			
Proper equipment was used.			
The recipe was followed correctly.			
Each person did assigned job.			
Kitchen was cleaned properly at end of period.			
I was conscious of the safety of others.			
I used safe techniques.			
Product Evaluation The product tasted good.			
The product looked good.			

STUDENT COMMENTS:

TEACHER COMMENTS:

I feel I earned a _____. I will work on _____

IDEAS FOR THE SEWING LAB

Obtaining Patterns, Fabric, and Notions

Getting patterns, fabric, and the notions needed for four or five sewing classes is no small task. A few simple procedures like these make the procurement tasks more manageable.

1. Select 20 to 40 pattern options from which students may choose. Base the selection upon current fashion, complexity of the pattern, and the cost involved in purchasing the fabric and notions needed.
2. Order the patterns by telephone from the manufacturer to save time and money. You will receive an attractive manufacturer's discount on direct orders.
3. Let the students take the pattern envelope out of class only to purchase the fabric and notions. In this way, the student who is late getting the necessary materials can still work with the pattern pieces to get ready for actual construction.
4. Don't overlook the use of kits for many projects to teach the basic skills. *Forecast* magazine is an excellent reference for kits sources. Preview a kit before buying it in large quantity.
5. If you order kits, charge students a little more for them to cover the cost of stuffing and to provide kits to those students who are economically disadvantaged.

Care of Equipment and Facilities

1. Clean and oil the machines according to the manufacturer's directions regularly.
2. Have all machines cleaned, oiled, and adjusted yearly.
3. Cultivate a business relationship with a local repair service so that you can get machines repaired on a 24-hour basis.
4. Assign students to machines so that you can monitor the way they take care of the equipment.
5. Have the industrial arts department fasten a large magnet on the end of a handle to pick up pins from carpeted floors.
6. Have students sit in their seats at the end of each period to inspect cleanup visually. This keeps your facility reasonably orderly at all times.

Student Licensing

Licensing students to operate a sewing machine or serger is an idea that has been around a long time. It can work, especially at the middle or junior high school levels. Basically the idea calls for the students to learn the parts of the machine, how to thread the machine, wind a bobbin, sew selected basic stitches, and demonstrate a minimum level of control of machine operation. The student completes a test and upon successfully demonstrating knowledge and skill is licensed to use the machine independently.

The following is a blackline master for a student license. Make copies of the master on your school's copy machine or send them to your district print shop. Have students provide you with a photo to paste in the space provided. Be sure to use rubber cement. If your school has a media center, ask them to laminate the cards for your. If you don't want to ask students for photos, fasten a copy of your department or school logo in the space before making copies of the license.

LICENSE

TO OPERATE A
SEWING MACHINE

PHOTO HERE

SIGNATURE_____

© 1993 by The Center for Applied Research in Education

CHAPTER 3

SO YOU NEED A SUB
AND THE SUB NEEDS . . .

WHAT'S IT LIKE TO BE A SUB?

Imagine you are playing the lead in the smash Broadway hit "A Day in the Life of Ms. Sub." The house lights dim, the curtain goes up, Act 1 . . .

Scene 1   It's 6 A.M.; the phone rings. It's Ms. Smith from Friendly High School wanting to know if Ms. Sub can substitute for Ms. Gourmet in home ec. Part of her says "Yes" and part of her says, "No." What to do? In a flash she thinks about getting her two children ready for school, finding her way to the school, and knowing where to park when she gets there and what she's going to wear and what the family will do for dinner. Already in a frazzle, she says "Yes" and is on her way.

Scene 2   She arrives at school and the parking lot is full. A Friendly student finally helps her find a space after what seems like hours of circling the lot. She makes her way through a maze of walls and strange people to the office where Ms. Smith hands her a huge ring of keys and a few sheets of paper with some notes scribbled on them. Between phone calls, student interruptions, and the principal calling for attention, Ms. Smith tries to give Ms. Sub directions to the home ec suite.

Scene 3   Undaunted, she runs her hand through her hair and makes her way through miles of corridor and hundreds of Friendly students who look like all-state linemen for the football team. Upon arrival at the home economics department, she's faced with finding which of the 30 keys on the ring opens the classroom door. She finally gets inside, throws her coat over a chair, glances at the sheets of paper that pass for lesson plans, and hears the bell ring for first period.

Scene 4   As the class arrives, she hears, "Yuk, a substitute! What's your name? How did you say you pronounced that? What's wrong with Ms. Gourmet? Did she die? Is she pregnant? Will she be back tomorrow?" Using the sketchy lesson plan, Ms. Sub tries to get some classroom order and start the lesson. Immediately there is a chorus of voices. "We did that yesterday! Oh, no, not that again! How boring! I have to go see my counselor. I don't have a pencil. I forgot my notebook. I don't want to work in that group."

91

And so it goes in the life of Ms. Sub and her co-subs all across America every day school is in session.

We know it's important to be prepared for a substitute teacher, but too frequently we are so wrapped up in doing the urgent, we don't get around to doing the important. In this chapter you will find directions for a system to make life easier for your substitute and more productive for your students. You will find:

1. A list of the organizational and procedural information to provide a substitute.
2. A day-at-a-glance idea to get the substitute off to a good start.
3. A model substitute's lesson plan when you have time to prepare for an absence.
4. Directions on how to organize an Emergency Substitute Teacher Kit.

The chapter concludes with a set of generic lesson plans for emergency situations—something you can pull out when the flu strikes at 4 A.M., your administrator stops you in the hall in the morning and tells you about an important meeting of the Curriculum Council you need to attend at 11 A.M., or your son falls and breaks a leg on his way to the school bus!

BASIC INFORMATION TO PROVIDE

If a substitute teacher has to search for your daily schedule, class lists, seating charts, or lesson plans, much valuable time will be wasted, and your students will be shortchanged. To improve communication with your substitute teacher and maximize learning, you need to set up a substitute information file.

A Substitute Information File

Keep a substitute information file in the school office if that is your school's policy or in an easy-to-find place in your classroom or the home economics department office. The information should be complete, up to date, and clearly marked "Substitute Information File." Following are things to include:

1. Your daily teaching schedule showing time and location for all of your classes and other assignments.
2. A sheet with the names and room numbers of your department head and other home economics teachers. If you are a single-person department, identify another teacher near your classroom who has agreed to help a substitute. This sheet can also identify where to find roll/grade book, seating charts, lesson plans, and special materials that may be needed.

3. A map of the school with the nearest bathroom, faculty lounge, principal's office, and faculty lunch room clearly marked. Be sure to mark your classroom. If you have assigned responsibilities in other locations, like a study hall, mark them in a different color.

4. An up-to-date list containing the names of two or three reliable students in each class.

5. A list of any special duties you are assigned and what that assignment involves, for example, hall duty, lunch duty, or bus duty.

6. A list of the important classroom or school rules the substitute needs to know. Some examples are hall passes, sitting in assigned seats, going to the counselor, and tardiness.

7. Special instructions for the care of equipment.

8. Discipline referral procedures.

9. Copy of student and teacher handbooks.

10. Your expectations for follow-up to the actual daily teaching assignment. Is the substitute to correct worksheets, lab manuals? Is he or she responsible for doing the daily laundry, picking up pins, seeing that all work areas are clean and orderly, tote trays stored properly?

GETTING YOUR SUBSTITUTE OFF TO A GOOD START

Anything you can do to get a substitute quickly acclimated will pay dividends. Attach a "My Day at a Glance" form to the front of the Substitute Information File. See the following reproducible master of a sample form.

MY DAY AT A GLANCE

WELCOME! Thank you for subbing for me today. Here are a few facts about my teaching assignment.

1. My teaching schedule is _____

   _____

   _____

   _____.

2. I teach in room(s) _____.

3. The daily bell schedule is _____

   _____

   _____.

4. See _____ in Room _____ for help.

5. Emergency lesson plans are in my Substitute Information File. Please choose one that most closely fits what you think the class subject matter is.

6. Here are the names of helpful students for the class listed.

   _____

   _____

   _____

7. My special duties, by day, are:

   Monday _____

   Tuesday _____

   Wednesday _____

   Thursday _____

   Friday _____

© 1993 by The Center for Applied Research in Education

OTHER WAYS TO HELP A SUBSTITUTE

1. Label your keys with some form of identification. If you cannot place a piece of tape on every key to indicate what it is for, color code them and leave the code list in the Substitute Teacher's File.

2. Print or type the names on your seating charts. Keep the charts current so the substitute is not reporting or calling upon students who are absent, have dropped the course, or have moved.

3. Keep your desk orderly. Clearing it at the end of each day is a good habit to develop for all occasions. An orderly work space makes it easier for a substitute and presents a positive model to students.

4. Keep some pencils, blank paper, and chalk in your desk.

5. Let students know how you expect them to behave for a substitute. It is school as usual. The same rules apply, the same lab procedures are to be followed, the same quality of product is expected.

6. Treat your substitute as a member of your team. If your absence is predictable, call them to discuss what you want them to do. If you will be out for several days, invite them to come in to review your plans. Don't forget to thank them.

A MODEL SUBSTITUTE TEACHER LESSON PLAN

What to Include

The single most important thing you can do for a substitute is to leave an easy-to-follow lesson plan with sufficient detail so classes can go on almost as if you were there. The plan might include a "General Information," "My Schedule," and "Lesson Plan" section. The "General Information" section describes attendance procedures, announcements, and opening exercises. The "My Schedule" section outlines your schedule for just the day or for the week. The "Lesson Plan" section typically contains three parts. First, some background about the unit, what the students have already studied and what they will do today. Second, an easygoing, chatty description of how to teach the lesson. Third, what follow-up you expect of the students and the substitute. For example, the students are to prepare their market orders for the next lab, and the substitute is to correct activity sheets or quizzes, do the laundry, or carry out other directives during a preparation period.

A SAMPLE LESSON PLAN

LESSON PLAN FOR PEGGY SMITH
MARCH 5, 199X

General Information

Our school does not have a homeroom period. Therefore, attendance, the pledge, and announcements take place at the beginning of first period. Students should be assembled by 8:15.

Attendance

There are two plastic packets of attendance cards on top of my desk. There is a card for each student. Put the cards together to take attendance. Remove the card for any student absent and place it in the plastic envelope with Velcro® on the back. If no students are absent, take a green card and the card with my name on it and place in the envelope with Velcro®. Place this envelope on the patch of Velcro® fastened to the outside of the classroom door. Collect the absentees' cards from my mailbox at the end of the day and put with the other cards. If you have a problem, students know the procedure; ask one of them to do it for you.

The Pledge and Announcements

Have students stand for the pledge and listen respectfully to the announcements that follow. The announcer will conclude with the statement, "This concludes today's announcements." Begin class.

The Lesson
Wednesday, March 5

Period 1—8:15 to 9:02. Lifeways, Room 32. Student folders and classroom materials are in the top drawer of the teacher's desk.

We are currently studying managing individual and family resources. We have already studied decision making, needs versus wants, and the beginnings of financial planning. Today, we start the personal budgeting process.

Begin class with a brief description of what students will do today. Show the video "Personal Budgeting." It runs about 30 minutes. At the conclusion of the tape, begin a discussion by asking several of the discussion questions on pages 13 and 14 of the discussion guide. You probably won't get through many of these questions today. Please mark the questions you used.

Conclude the lesson by having students summarize the purpose of a personal budget: Why is it important to budget financial resources?

© 1993 by The Center for Applied Research in Education

Period 2—9:06 to 9:53. Planning. Use this time to get ready for the rest of the day. Get the table setting/etiquette lesson ready for third period, "Baking with a Gourmet Touch." The white plastic bag with the tablecloth, napkins, and centerpiece is on the bookshelf in the sewing room (next door). Plates and flatware are in the foods room cabinets 56 and 57. Study the table setting/etiquette information and student handout (attached). Check the procedure for the Senior Foods classes visit to Super Saver Market across the street from the school.

.... continue for rest of classes...............................

Follow-Up

Please be sure to collect student packets at the end of Lifeways class and put them back in the drawer.

Get my mail at the end of the day and place on the top of my desk. Be sure to get the attendance cards.

See that all kitchens have been put back in order. This should have been done at the end of each period, but please make a final check before leaving.

THANK YOU VERY MUCH FOR SUBSTITUTING TODAY!!
I REALLY APPRECIATE YOUR WILLINGNESS TO HELP.

© 1993 by The Center for Applied Research in Education

AN EMERGENCY SUBSTITUTE TEACHER KIT

Life is full of surprises. We don't always know when we are going to be absent, and there are times we just don't have time to prepare special lesson plans. That's when an Emergency Substitute Teacher Kit can come in handy.

What Is the Emergency Kit?

The kit is a bag containing brief instructions and all the materials needed to present complete lessons for a day or two. You can use a plain paper bag, a plastic shopping bag, or a carry-all you picked up at a convention. The kit is most helpful when you follow a few guidelines to set it up. For example:

1. Write a brief friendly note of welcome that lists what is in the bag, how it is to be used, and the classes for which it is intended.
2. Put each lesson's materials in a separate envelope clearly marked on the outside.
3. If the lesson involves a video, make sure to note where the VCR and television receiver are located.
4. Provide examples of finished projects if this would help the substitute understand what to do.

What It Should Include

The Emergency Kit should include videos, textbook-type lessons, and projects. Here are some ideas.

Videos

Have an assortment of videos on several home economics topics. Label each with its name, length in minutes, and classes where it could be used. Include copies of a student activity sheet like the reproducible master provided here. Suggest the teacher show the video, have the students complete the activity sheet as they watch the video, and conclude the class with a class discussion.

Your department or school media center may have copies of videos that you can get on extended loan to place in the kit. You can, with permission, record various cooking and sewing programs and child development topics from your local PBS station. Half-hour segments where chefs demonstrate how to prepare selected recipes are generally accurate and do not subject the viewer to information overload. There are several sewing series carried by PBS stations. You can record selected segments and include the sample materials to have students practice what is taught in the video lesson. Your school's guidance department may have teen topic videos with accompanying study materials that they will lend you. There are many topics that lend themselves to use in human development classes. For example, teen pregnancy, career selection, drugs and alcohol, child abuse, marriage, and dealing with crisis are all topics around which an emergency lesson can be built.

VIDEO ACTIVITY SHEET

Your name _____ Name of video _____

This video is about _____.

Important points made in this video include _____

_____

_____

_____

_____

_____

_____

_____

_____

I would rate this video (excellent, good, fair, poor) because

_____

_____

_____

_____

© 1993 by The Center for Applied Research in Education

Textbook-Type Lessons

These lessons should be of the "stand-alone type." No prerequisites are needed to complete the lesson successfully. Look for ideas in your basic textbooks or major reference works. Select topics not generally included in the course. Make up a brief lesson plan. Identify the location of the books. Give the lesson a title. Indicate the pages to be read and any questions the students are to answer. Include a key to the location in the book of the answers to the questions. Write two or three thought-provoking discussion questions to bring the lesson to closure. Do this for each area of home economics for the classes you teach.

Newspaper and Magazine Articles

Another idea is to have a collection of newspaper and magazine articles about recent happenings or developments in home economics. Place these in a large envelope and staple a set of directions to the outside of the envelope. Suggest the substitute distribute the articles to pairs of students. Have the students read the article, identify which of the five areas of home economics the article discusses, and summarize the article by preparing a 30-second sound bite. Conclude the lesson by having students present the sound bites and discuss their significance.

Projects

There are some simple projects you can place in the kit. For a child development class, have students design a symmetry lesson where they cut several full-view pictures from magazines, cut each picture in half, and mount it on a sheet of drawing paper. Students draw the other half of one or more of the half pictures to show the young children the task. Include a sheet of directions and a sample in a large brown envelope. On the sheet of directions give the lesson a name, list the courses where it can be used, and tell the substitute where the magazines are located.

Package a simple needlepoint or cross-stitch project. Package pieces of fabric, thread, needles, and directions in a plastic bag. Include a set of directions for the substitute. This lesson may take more than a period. Be sure to tell the substitute to have students complete the project outside of class.

Although it is unlikely you will have more than one emergency, continue to change the activities in the kit. You never know when the spirit will move you to sub for yourself on a day that you aren't feeling particularly well but didn't stay home!

GENERIC EMERGENCY LESSON PLANS

Have a set of emergency lesson plans that are generic, that is, not based on any prerequisites. Here are two examples. Note that the lesson on decision making can be used in all five areas of home economics. To adapt it to each area, simply change the scenario for Activity 2.

For each lesson make copies of the student activity sheets. For the decision-making lesson, make a list of examples of teenage-type decisions the substitute can use as starters when students have trouble getting started. Keep them simple. You also need to make a transparency of the Decision Wheel. Place all the items, including the lesson plan, into a large envelope and mark on the outside, "Emergency Lesson Plan for _____."

Emergency Lesson Plan 1: Decision Making

Introduction

In this lesson students learn to use a seven-step decision-making process. To introduce the lesson, mention to students that good decision makers use a systematic process to arrive at a solution to a problem; decisions are influenced by facts, wants, and needs; decisions concerning similar problems change over time; and decisions made through the use of a systematic process are usually better decisions.

Activities

1. Introduce the decision-making process by describing a decision you recently made. Discuss the factors you considered before arriving at your decision. Did these factors center on certain topics such as time and money? Was your decision satisfactory? Why?

2. Establish the scenario that the students are going to purchase a portable CD player. Distribute the activity sheet "The Decision-Making Process." Use the transparency of the Decision Wheel or draw one at the chalkboard to explain the steps in the decision-making process. Have the students make notes on their activity sheet for each step of the process as you explain it. At the conclusion of this exercise, students should notice that people don't always agree with the final decision. Why is that so? Have the students practice making a decision by completing the activity sheet "Making Your Own Decision." When they have finished, let a few of them describe how they used the decision-making process to come to a decision.

Name: _____ **Date:** _____

THE DECISION-MAKING PROCESS

Every day there are decisions you must make. Many are small and may involve things like whether you are going to stay in bed an extra minute or two or eat breakfast. Others are much more important, such as what career you are going to pursue.

Fortunately, there are systematic processes we can use to help us make decisions. If we use a systematic process, we will almost certainly make better decisions. One example of such a process is shown below. It is called the Decision Wheel process.

Your teacher is going to discuss the Decision Wheel process and apply it to making a decision about purchasing a portable CD player. Follow along, and make notes in each part of the wheel.

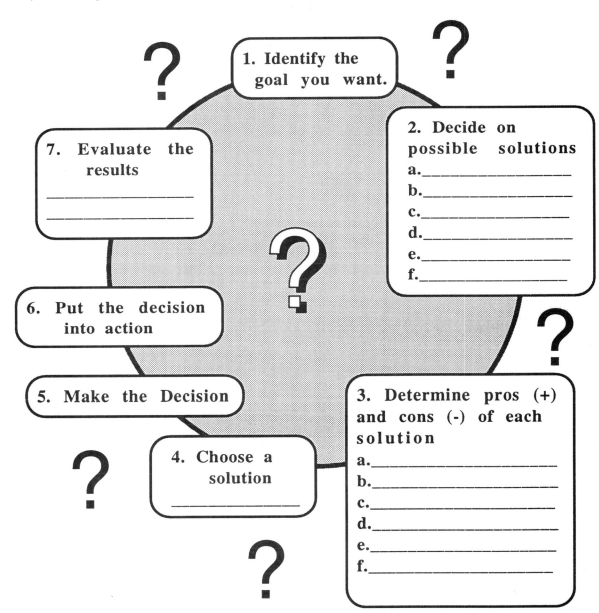

© 1993 by The Center for Applied Research in Education

© 1993 by The Center for Applied Research in Education

Name: _____ Date: _____

MAKING YOUR OWN DECISION

Your teacher has reviewed the decision-making process called the Decision Wheel. Now it is your turn to try to use the process. Think of a decision you might have to make. Keep it simple. For example, you might want to use as your problem whether or not to go to the movies, or deciding which sweater or jacket to buy, and so on. Complete each section of the wheel.

1. Identify the goal you want.

7. Evaluate the results
_____
_____

2. Decide on possible solutions
a._____
b._____
c._____
d._____
e._____
f._____

6. Put the decision into action

5. Make the Decision

4. Choose a solution
_____

3. Determine pros (+) and cons (-) of each solution
a._____
b._____
c._____
d._____
e._____
f._____

Emergency Lesson Plan 2: Herbs and Spices

Introduction

Begin class by explaining to students that they are going to learn about herbs and spices, the substances used in cooking to enhance or bring out the flavor of the other ingredients used in the recipe. Tell them they will:

- List familiar herbs and spices.
- Learn what the experts say about herbs and spices.
- Find recipes for a variety of foods and identify the herb or spice used.
- Learn the importance of herbs and spices in cooking.

Activities

1. Have students brainstorm a list of herbs and spices. List the correct ones on the chalkboard or an overhead transparency. Have a student volunteer write the list. Challenge the class to name 36. Possible spice responses include allspice, anise, caraway seed, cardamom seed, cayenne, celery seed, chili powder, cinnamon, cloves, coriander, cumin seed, curry powder, dill seed, fennel seed, ginger, mace, mustard, nutmeg, paprika, white and black pepper, sesame seed, turmeric. Possible herb responses include basil, bay leaf, chervil, Italian seasoning, marjoram, mint, oregano, parsley, poultry seasoning, rosemary, saffron, sage, savory, tarragon, thyme. (5 minutes)

2. Distribute the activity sheet "Liven It Up—What the Experts Say." Have the students fill in the blanks with the correct word—herb, spice, or seasoning blend—and list examples in the space provided. They can refer to the list generated by the class. Have them read "The Rules for Herbs, Spices, and Seasoning Blends." Discuss the information with the class when students are finished reading. (8–10 minutes) (See the answer sheet at the end of this chapter.)

3. Distribute the activity sheet "Importance of Herbs and Spices in Cooking." Have kitchen groups consult cookbooks to find a recipe that uses an herb or spice as an ingredient in each of the following categories: appetizers, hot and cold beverages, breads, cakes, cheese dishes, cookies, desserts, egg dishes, fish and shellfish, jams and jellies, meats, pastas, pickles, pies and pastry, poultry, rice dishes, salads and salad dressings, sandwiches, sauces (main dishes and dessert), souffles, soups, stuffings, vegetables, marinating. Allow each group to share one recipe idea. Collect all papers.

4. Conclude the lesson by discussing possible answers to the question, "Why are herbs and spices important in cooking?" (See the answer sheet at the end of this chapter.)

Note

If you are going to substitute tomorrow, this lesson can be extended by taking students to the library and having them research the history of a different herb or spice, its use in cooking, and any other interesting information about it. When they have concluded this work, let them give a short presentation about the herb or spice they researched. If the herb or spice is available in the home economics department, pass it around so students can see and smell it. Collect research notes.

Name: _____ **Date:** _____

LIVEN IT UP!

What the Experts Say

1. _____ are the leaves of plants used as seasonings. They can be used fresh or dried. The flavor of fresh _____ is not as concentrated as the dried. Examples are _____
_____.

2. _____ are dried roots, stems, and seeds of plants mainly grown in the tropics. Examples are _____
_____.

3. _____ are mixtures of dried spices and herbs that are usually powdered. Examples are _____
_____.

© 1993 by The Center for Applied Research in Education

© 1993 by The Center for Applied Research in Education

Name: _____   **Date:** _____

RULES FOR USING HERBS, SPICES, AND SEASONING BLENDS

1. Generally, use ¼ teaspoon for every four to five servings of food. You can always add more at the end if the food is not seasoned to your taste.

2. Cooking evaporates liquids and increases the strength of the herb or spice flavor. Add seasoning during the last hour of cooking.

3. Cold foods, such as salads, need more time to release the flavor of herbs and spices. Therefore, allow greater standing time for cold dishes.

4. Tie herbs and spices into a cloth bag if you do not like them floating in your food product.

5. Crush the leaves of herbs and spices before adding them to food. Fresh herbs should be finely chopped to release more flavor.

6. Store herbs and spices in tightly covered containers in a cool, dry place.

7. Herbs and spices dry out and lose their flavor. Herbs and ground spices have a shelf life of six months. Whole spices last about one year. Date herbs and spices when they are purchased.

8. Herbs vary in strength from strong to mild to delicate. The flavor of the food is a clue to the kind and amount of herbs to use. For example, since lamb is a strong flavor, it can take a strong flavored herb.

9. Don't confuse the word "spice" with the word "hot." Very few spices are hot.

IMPORTANCE OF HERBS AND SPICES IN COOKING

Consult several cookbooks to find a recipe for each of the categories listed that has an herb, spice, or a seasoning blend as an ingredient. List the recipe name, cookbook name, and page number in the space provided.

Food	Recipe Name	Cookbook Name	Page #
Appetizer			
Beverage			
Breads			
Cakes			
Cheese dishes			
Cookies			
Desserts			
Egg dishes			
Fish/shellfish			
Jams/jellies			
Meats			
Pastas			
Pickles			
Pies/pastry			
Poultry			
Rice dishes			
Salads and salad dressings			
Sandwiches			
Sauces			
Souffles			
Soups			
Stuffings			
Vegetables			

Why are herbs and spices important in cooking? _____

_____

_____

_____

© 1993 by The Center for Applied Research in Education

Student Activity Sheet Answers

Liven It Up! What the Experts Say

1. __(Herbs)__ are the leaves of plants used as seasonings. They can be used fresh or dried. The flavor of fresh __(herbs)__ is not as concentrated as the dried. Examples are _(parsley, oregano, chives, rosemary, marjoram, thyme)_ .

2. __(Spices)__ are dried roots, stems, and seeds of plants mainly grown in the tropics. Examples are _(cinnamon, nutmeg, cloves, allspice, ginger, pepper)_.

3. __(Seasoning blends)__ are mixtures of dried spices and herbs that are usually powdered. Examples are _(curry, chili powder)_ .

Importance of Herbs and Spices in Cooking

Why are herbs and spices important in cooking? *(Used imaginatively, they can transform an ordinary dish to a terrific one. They can give variety to menus and interest to meals. They enhance the flavor of other ingredients without adding calories or fat to the diet.)*

CHAPTER 4
TEACHING STRATEGIES FOR THE TWENTY-FIRST CENTURY

DIFFERENT APPROACHES AND DIFFERENT OUTLOOKS

People need new skills to succeed in the workplace, the family, the community, society, and the world as they prepare to enter the twenty-first century. But schools continue to place most of their emphasis on factual information and too little on process. They are organized as mass-production facilities to crank out one graduate after another. It is time to recognize that the same old approaches are not good enough.

We live increasingly in an interdependent world where individuals need to work cooperatively to complete tasks. Yet school tends to be where students must compete against each other to learn the most, to do the best job, and to get the highest grade. Or their learning experiences are individualistic, where they work on tasks with little or no concern about what others are doing. In this chapter you will learn about a system of teaching to change that focus. It is known as cooperative learning.

Research shows us that successful students have largely learned the how-to-learn skills, the content learning skills, and the reasoning skills outside the school curriculum. It is almost as if schools assume that all students were born with these skills or acquire them through some mysterious process like osmosis. Students who do not learn them drop out of school or function poorly in the workplace, the family, and community. In this chapter, you learn about *Tactics for Thinking,* a set of teaching strategies to teach thinking skills directly as an integral part of your home economics classes. You will also learn about another program to teach the thinking process called *Dimensions of Learning.*

Every person is called upon each day to make practical decisions. Although individuals may have some basic understanding of a decision-making process, they often do not make good decisions. In the home economics classroom, practical reasoning is a process to decide what to do in everyday home and family problems

110

based on the knowledge and information available to solve those problems. In this chapter you will learn how you can incorporate practical reasoning instruction as part of your regular program.

COOPERATIVE LEARNING

Introduction

Although recent changes in society, the family, and the workplace have increased the need to work cooperatively, schools still spend a disproportionate amount of time instructing students in classrooms dominated by competition and individual enterprise. Schools have been places where people sit in fixed rows, fiercely competing with others, and too infrequently interacting with them. By contrast, students find real-life situations dominated by teamwork, effective communication, coordination of activities, and division of labor. To achieve these skills, cooperative learning advocates suggest, with the backing of mountains of research, that between 50% and 60% of classroom experiences be structured in the cooperative learning mode. The remainder of the student's school experiences should be divided between competitive and individual structured lessons.

Home economics teachers decide the teaching strategies to use when they develop their lesson plans. They decide whether students are to be in competition with each other, learn on their own without interacting with others, or work together cooperatively.

In the competitive structure, students work to be the best. They are graded on a curve, work to finish first, work to get more answers right than others, and so on. Most students view school as a competitive place.

In the individualistic structure, students work by themselves to learn the knowledge, skills, and attitudes of home economics. Individual goals are assigned according to a timetable, and their efforts are evaluated by comparison to a fixed set of standards.

In the cooperative learning structure, students work together to learn and share skills, knowledge, and attitudes of home economics. Students work in small groups to learn the information and then see that other members in the group are successful learners also. Evaluation is based on a criterion-referenced set of standards.

Because of the very nature of home economics education with its emphasis on the ability to work cooperatively to build and maintain successful careers, families, marriages, friendships, and communities, cooperative learning belongs in the home economics classroom. What follows is a brief introduction to cooperative learning. It will not instruct you in how to use cooperative learning techniques successfully in your classroom but will show you why cooperative learning belongs in your classroom and suggest ways for you to go about learning more.

What Cooperative Learning Is

Cooperative learning requires face-to-face interaction among all students. It takes place when students realize that attainment of their own learning goals is dependent on other students learning their goals. Then they have positive interdependence—the feeling that they need each other to complete the group's task, or the understanding that they "sink or swim" together. It is achieved through mutually understood goals, appropriate division of tasks and available resources, assignment of roles, and the distribution of joint rewards.

In a cooperative learning lesson, each individual is responsible for learning the subject matter of the lesson. The learning situation is structured to maximize the achievement of each individual student. Each student's level of mastery is determined so that others can provide support and assistance as needed.

Cooperative learning promotes the appropriate use of interpersonal and small-group skills. Through these skills, students can successfully collaborate.

Finally, cooperative learning provides ample time for students to process how well their groups are functioning and how to use group process skills personally to help everyone within the group work effectively.

How the Cooperative Learning Classroom Differs

Cooperative learning groups differ from traditional learning groups in the following ways:

1. Cooperative groups foster positive interdependence while traditional groups do not.
2. Cooperative groups are heterogeneous while traditional groups are often homogeneous.
3. Leadership is shared in cooperative groups but is assumed by one person in traditional groups.
4. Group skills are taught in cooperative groups but are assumed and ignored in traditional groups.
5. Each individual is held accountable in a cooperative group but may not be in a traditional group.
6. Individuals learn group processing procedures in cooperative learning groups but do not in traditional groups.
7. The teacher is an observer and facilitator in a cooperative learning situation but performs the role of director in traditional situations.

The Teacher's Role

The teacher's role in cooperative learning is one of classroom manager and group process consultant. Cooperative learning experts suggest five major sets of strategies to structure cooperative learning situations:

1. Clearly specify the lesson's objectives.
2. Appropriately place students in learning groups before the lesson is taught.
3. Precisely explain the goal and task of the lesson.
4. Monitor group process to provide task completion assistance or increase interpersonal and group skills.
5. Evaluate achievement and assist students to discuss how well they collaborated.

Within these major sets of strategies, 18 steps structure the cooperative learning process:

1. Specify academic and collaborative skills objectives.
2. Determine the size of the group. Most cooperative learning groups range from two to six members.
3. Assign students to groups. Most experts recommend heterogeneous grouping, although homogeneous groups may be appropriate for certain learning tasks.
4. Arrange the room for face-to-face interaction and direct contact with materials.
5. Plan and distribute learning materials so that all members of a group will actively participate.
6. Decide upon group roles and assign to each individual member of the group. Over the course of time, all students should serve in all roles. Examples of roles include summarizer, recorder, encourager, researcher, observer, and corrector.
7. Explain the academic task so that students are clear about the assignment and understand the objectives of the lesson.
8. Be sure all students know they are responsible for learning the subject matter assigned to the group, making sure all other group members learn it, and making sure that all other class members learn it.
9. Determine the ways and means to assess each student's level of performance.
10. Determine procedures to foster intergroup cooperation.
11. Establish the criteria for acceptable work, and make certain these are communicated clearly at the beginning of the lesson.
12. Specify and clearly communicate the desired collaborative behavior.
13. Monitor students' behavior.
14. Provide students with assistance to complete tasks as needed.
15. Intervene when necessary to see that collaborative skills are being appropriately practiced.

16. Provide clear closure to the lesson.
17. Evaluate student learning, preferably with a criterion-referenced system.
18. Provide time for all students to assess how well their group functioned.

A Cooperative Learning Lesson Examined

Let's take a look at an introductory lesson in nutrition to examine the elements of a cooperative learning lesson and how such a lesson would be taught. The lesson uses a structure called "Jigsaw." Study the lesson plan carefully to see the elements and teacher strategies that make this a cooperative learning lesson. In particular, pay close attention to the lesson's objectives, the steps the teacher needs to complete to get ready for the lesson, and the activities that involve every student.

NUTRIENTS AND A HEALTHY BODY

Concept: Balanced nutrition is necessary for good health.

Objectives

- The student will learn the names of the six nutrient groups.

- The student will describe how each nutrient group promotes a healthy body.

- The student will list several food sources for each nutrient group.

- The student will apply management skills needed to organize the group and maintain appropriate behavior.

- The student will practice the functioning skills needed to manage the group's efforts to complete the assignment and to work effectively with each other.

Teacher Preparation

1. Divide the class into heterogeneous groups of three.

2. Be prepared to have students move their chairs into their working area so that they can interact face to face and have easy access to the learning materials.

3. Decide the information about each nutrient group you want each student to know. Arrange the information for two nutrient groups on one information sheet. Label it as "1" and make a copy for each group and one for yourself. Do the same for the remaining groups labeling them "2" and "3."

4. Prepare a list of questions to use as a learning check at the conclusion of the lesson. Make certain every nutrient group is included in the learning check.

Activities

1. Introduce the lesson by having a general discussion of the importance of good nutrition to good health. Tell the students they are going to use a process known as cooperative learning to learn about nutrients. Describe what that is.

2. Assign students to their working groups and have them count off—student 1, student 2, and student 3.

3. Outline the procedure "Jigsaw." The jigsaw method is like solving a puzzle. Each student has one piece of information. It, together with the information other students have, forms the whole. The task for the day is to see that every student in the class learns the information about all six nutrient groups. Students work alone to learn the information on his or her sheet. They then pair up with someone who learned the same information to decide how to teach it to the other members of their group. When this task is finished, they each return to their group and teach the information to their classmates. Their task is to see that every member of the group can demonstrate mastery of the information by answering questions posed by themselves, others, and the teacher.

© 1993 by The Center for Applied Research in Education

4. Describe where each group is to work and distribute the information sheets to the appropriate students—information sheet 1 to student 1, information sheet 2 to student 2, and so on.

5. Have students master the information on their sheets using appropriate study skills such as underlining and outlining. Provide about 6 minutes.

6. Call time and have students pair up with a like-numbered student to plan the teaching strategy, prepare any visuals or other materials to teach the information to others. Provide about 10 minutes.

7. When students are finished, have the original groups re-form in their group's space. Have them determine the order in which each student will teach his or her nutrient. During this phase it is important students practice good listening skills, take turns, ask clarifying questions, express support, share materials, praise, and check for understanding. The student making the presentation should check to see that the material has been mastered by all. Provide about 12 minutes. Monitor group process.

8. As a quick check for individual accountability, have students get together in their groups of 1's, 2's, and so on. Ask your accountability check questions making certain you do not call upon students who were assigned to the nutrient group to which the question refers.

9. If time is available, have the groups process how well they functioned today. If not, allow them to do this first thing tomorrow. Did they use appropriate social skills? Did they effectively collaborate to master the subject matter? Did they learn the subject matter? It is important to participate actively in the analysis of the process to provide students feedback about such things as whether you saw face-to-face interaction and ability to work positively toward a common goal.

10. Conclude the lesson by having students jot down two or three social or collaboration skills they practiced well and one they need to work on. Make the transition to the next lesson by pointing out why making food choices with the proper amount of nutrients is important to a healthy body. Tell them they will do a nutritional analysis of their personal eating habits.

© 1993 by The Center for Applied Research in Education

A Sample Cooperative Learning Lesson

Picture for a moment how to teach this same lesson using a traditional competitive or individualistic lesson structure. First, introduce the topic of nutrition in much the same way as described in the cooperative learning lesson. Then, present a lecture about the six nutrient groups and how they contribute to a healthy body. Have the students complete an activity sheet with missing information as the teacher presents a lecture on nutrients. The teacher should pause from time to time to ask clarifying questions and to make sure students complete the activity sheet. Students are permitted to ask questions when they don't understand something. At the end of the lecture, students are asked if there is anything they didn't complete on the activity sheet. If there is, that information is reviewed. When everyone has completed the activity sheet, bring the lesson to closure by discussing why making food choices with the proper amount of nutrients is necessary for a healthy body. Transition to the next lesson is made by telling students that tomorrow they will do a nutritional analysis of what they eat in a given 24-hour period.

There are many ways to teach this lesson traditionally. For example, a video about nutritional information and healthy bodies could be shown and then followed with an in-depth group discussion. Individual students could use a computer software program to complete a nutritional analysis. Following the lecture small groups could be assigned the task of analyzing a menu by completing a worksheet. A guest speaker could present the information to the class.

The following list shows some major differences between these competitive and individualistic structured approaches and the cooperative learning lesson.

Cooperative Learning	Competitive/Individualistic
1. Every student is actively involved in every segment of the lesson after the introduction.	1. Students may choose to tune out the lesson at almost any time.
2. Individual accountability was present. Students were checked to see they had learned their part, taught their part, and learned the whole concept.	2. No opportunity was present to check each individual's learning, although this probably would be done later via a quiz or test.
3. Students were involved in higher-order thinking skills. For example, they had to analyze group process.	3. The lesson was at the lower end of the taxonomy, of learning, that is, replication and comprehension levels.
4. Instruction and practice of the social and collaborative skills needed to work cooperatively to complete a task was built into the lesson.	4. Not present in lesson.

What Research Tells Us About Cooperative Learning

As teachers and parents, we continue to teach young people to be competitive and to be able to work independently, but we too often pay little attention to teaching them how to work cooperatively. Remember that cooperative learning lessons lead to:

- Greater achievement.
- Increased retention.
- More use of higher-level thinking/reasoning skills.
- Better attitudes toward school.
- Higher self-esteem.
- Increased ability to work constructively with others.
- Increased time on task.

Where to Get More Information

Here is a starter list of sources for more information about cooperative learning.

1. Write to the Cooperative Learning Center for a complete bibliography:

    Cooperative Learning Center
    150 Pillsbury Drive, S.E.
    Minneapolis, MN 55455
    (612) 624-7031

2. These books are good introductions to cooperative learning and may be ordered from the publisher indicated.

    From: Interaction Book Company, 7208 Cornelia Drive, Edina, MN 55435

    Johnson, David W., Roger T. Johnson, and Edythe Johnson Holubec (1988). *Cooperation in the Classroom.*

    Johnson, David W., Roger T. Johnson, and Edythe Holubec (1987). *Structuring Cooperative Learning: Lesson Plans for Teachers.*

    From: Prentice-Hall, Inc., Englewood Cliffs, NJ 07632

    Johnson, D. W., and R. T. Johnson (1987). *Learning Together and Alone: Cooperative, Competitive, and Individualistic Learning.*

    Johnson, D. W., and F. Johnson (1987). *Joining Together: Group Theory and Group Skills.*

    From: Resources for Teachers, 27134 Paseo Espada #202, San Juan Capistrano, CA 92675

    Kagan, Spencer (1989). *Cooperative Learning Resources for Teachers.*

A Final Word

It is important to understand that you should use all three structures—competitive, individualistic, and cooperative—in your classroom. Although current research findings about when to use competitive and individualistic lessons are incomplete, cooperative learning structures should be used approximately 50% to 60% of the time.

Integrate these structures into your daily lessons to teach students the skills to function in the three types of situations—competitive, individualistic, and cooperative—and you will help them hold jobs; achieve happy, stable marriages; and be contributing community members.

TACTICS

Introduction

People are being called upon in the workplace to work in quality circles and production teams, to participate in management decisions, and to undergo retraining. They must deal with different personal problems such as aging parents, AIDS, teen parenting, affordable housing, and health care, among others. They face changing community problems—decaying infrastructures, racial and cultural diversity, government burdened by debt, and increasing political pluralism.

Like most teachers, you probably believe schools share in the responsibility of teaching people the skills needed to deal with these problems. However, when you reflect upon how people learn to learn, learn cognitive information, and learn to reason and solve problems, you probably come to the conclusion that, for the most part, young people learn these things outside of school. You may also conclude that the teaching of these skills is serendipitous at best and nonexistent at worst in many schools. It is almost as if thinking skills are part of an invisible curriculum. This condition must change. Schools need to provide students direct and continuing instruction in how to use thinking skills in a variety of real-life situations.

Tactics is a systematic way for teachers to teach thinking skills at all levels K–12. Developed at the Mid-continent Regional Educational Laboratory, it is particularly relevant for home economics teachers because of their traditional role in teaching problem-solving skills for the family, home, workplace, and community.

What Tactics Is

Tactics is a program based upon the assumption that teaching thinking skills is a teacher-directed act, clearly recognizable and part of regular classroom instruction. *Tactics* does not rely on instructional materials to teach thinking. It relies on direct teacher interaction with students about the content being taught. The approach is not prescriptive, but a starting point for students and teachers to create additional ways to learn and apply thinking skills.

Tactics' skills are taught in the regular classroom as a way of teaching content. The program assumes you cannot separate the teaching of thinking skills from the teaching of content. Thinking and content are so inextricably linked that teaching thinking skills inevitably leads to improving a student's knowledge of content.

The Thinking Skills Tactics Teaches

Tactics contains 22 different skills divided among three major skill areas: learning-to-learn skills, content thinking skills, and reasoning skills.

The learning-to-learn skills are:

1. Attention control—a tactic for students to monitor and consciously control their level of attention.
2. Deep processing—a way for students to generate mental pictures, sensations, emotions, and linguistic information about a thought.
3. Memory frameworks—techniques for students to store and efficiently retrieve information.
4. Power thinking—a tactic for students to control their attitudes consciously so a learning situation is optimized.
5. Goal setting—a way for students to specify a direction for learning and to monitor their progress.
6. The responsibility frame—a process for students to monitor and control the extent to which they are assuming responsibility for their success in any activity.

The content thinking skills are:

7. Concept attainment—a tactic for students to learn the meaning of words by associating them with experiences.
8. Concept development—a process for students to learn concepts in a natural, easy, powerful way.
9. Pattern recognition—a way for students to recognize linguistic patterns and to use them to understand and organize information.
10. Macro-pattern recognition—a tactic for students to recognize and organize large blocks of information.
11. Synthesizing—a systematic process for students to restate and summarize information.
12. Proceduralizing—a procedure for students to break complex tasks into their component parts and then effectively learn the parts.

The reasoning skills are:

13. Analogical reasoning—a tactic for identifying how one set of concepts is similar to another set of concepts.

14. Extrapolation—the process to identify a general pattern from one type of information and see how it applies to other types of information.

15. Evaluation of evidence—a tactic to determine whether a claim is supported by an adequate system of proof.

16. Examination of value—the process to determine one's attitude toward some information and to identify the belief system supporting that value judgment along with an alternate set of beliefs that would support a different value judgment.

17. Decision making—the process for selecting among alternatives.

18. Nonlinguistic patterns—the process to recognize and create numeric, spatial, and sensory patterns.

19. Elaboration—the process of inferring information that is not stated.

20. Solving everyday problems—processes to systematically attacking problems of everyday life.

21. Solving academic problems—processes to solve different types of school-related problems.

22. Invention—a process to bring new products into existence.

Although this list of skills may seem overwhelming, the *Tactics* program offers you concrete suggestions of ways to integrate them into regular classroom activities. The program includes a teacher's manual and a collection of blackline masters. For each tactic, there is background information, a list of student objectives, a suggested strategy for introducing the tactic, and classroom examples of how to use the tactic. A set of blackline classroom activities accompanies the program. Home economics teachers will feel right at home with many of the suggested activities even though they may require some modification to fit the content being taught.

A Home Economics Example for Evaluation of Evidence

Let's take the tactic evaluation of evidence and examine how it could be taught in a home economics course as a regular part of the course's content. This is a particularly appropriate topic because you, as home economists, prepare individuals to make decisions about nutrition, clothing, household appliances, financial products, and health care. You also prepare individuals to make appropriate decisions about individual and family problems—balancing work and family, family crises, and career decisions. Evaluation of evidence is an important step in the process to make decisions about these matters.

Tactics suggests six steps to evaluate evidence. The individual must be able to:

1. Identify a claim as being unusual—something beyond what he or she knows or considers common knowledge.
2. Determine if the claim is reasonable.
3. Determine if an unreasonable claim can be supported in its present form.
4. Determine if support is presented for a claim.
5. Determine the reliability of the support for a claim.
6. Conclude that if the support is unreliable, the claim is unsubstantiated and rejected; if the support is reliable, the claim is substantiated and accepted.

Example

One way to teach students how to evaluate evidence is as follows. The home economics content for this example is part of a consumer unit for teaching students to analyze advertising or product claims whatever their source. The lesson uses a combination of cooperative learning and traditional strategies. More than one class period may be needed.

Rationale

Begin class by sharing with students the purpose of the lesson and how it will be accomplished. Tell them the purpose is to learn a systematic way to evaluate evidence so they can make better decisions about advertising claims and other decisions they are called upon to make. Discuss the concept of evaluation of evidence in the larger context of decision making. Suggest why it is important to be able to evaluate advertising claims and the promotional information provided by vendors. Tell the students this is an important step to make good consumer decisions. Give some personal examples of how you evaluated claims to decide to purchase an automobile, choose a diet plan, select a microwave oven, invest in the stock market, or select a child care center. Let students share their personal experiences.

Purpose

The next step is to share with students the purpose of the lesson and how to accomplish it. The purpose is to learn a systematic way to evaluate evidence, and they will use cooperative learning strategies.

Review

Briefly review the steps involved in the evaluation of evidence process: (1) being able to recognize a claim as unusual and beyond their present knowledge,

(2) determining if the claim is supported, and (3) determining if the support is reliable.

Materials/Equipment

Make a collection of newspaper and magazine advertisements, promotional literature, video tapes of television advertising, newspaper articles making claims, product labels, television newscasts where claims are made, or prepare a collection of written claims to include some that are vague, ambiguous, euphemistic, and meaningless.

Recognize and Rewrite

The next step is to teach students to recognize vague, ambiguous, euphemistic, and meaningless examples and to rewrite them so they are more precise or clear. Use the Jigsaw cooperative learning method.

Examining Claims

Begin this part of the lesson in a large-group setting. Use an overhead projector to show students representative claims of each type, and have them help you identify and restate them so they are more precise or clear. Prior to this, you will have prepared a collection of claims that includes one of each of the four types of claims and made as many copies as there are groups of students. For example, if there are six groups of students, you need six groups of claims. Label the vague claims "1," ambiguous claims "2," and so on. Following the large-group discussion/demonstration have the class get into their groups of four, distribute the sample claims, and have the students count off. Have the 1's take claim 1, 2's claim 2, and so on. Then, have students work independently to identify the type of their claim and to restate it to make it more precise or clear. Students pair up with a counterpart from another group to decide how they will teach the group to recognize the claim and restate it. Have them return to their group and go through the process of teaching it to their group. Check mastery by distributing an activity sheet that contains examples of each claim. Have students work individually to identify them and restate them. Use your typical process to determine how well each individual learned the material, collect papers, and go over the answers in class.

Unreliable Support

The next step in the lesson is to teach students five types of unreliable support: (1) overgeneralization, (2) oversimplification, (3) lack of credible source, (4) slanted information, and (5) appeal to emotion. Prepare an overhead transparency of consumer-related claim statements of all five types of unreliable support. Prepare a student activity sheet with similar examples that has spaces where the type of unreliable support can be identified and the claim can be "corrected." Conduct a large-group lecture/demonstration to teach students the types and how to change them so they are more precise, clear, or correct. Distribute the activity sheets and have students complete them individually or in pairs.

Differentiating

The final part of the lesson is to teach students to differentiate between supportable and unsupportable claims. They will synthesize all the information in the lesson and practice using the evaluation of evidence process. Collect or prepare a list that contains both supportable and unsupportable claim statements. This list should not be just consumer related because, at this stage, you want students to see this process can be used in a variety of situations.

Analyzing

This part of the lesson is conducted in a small-group cooperative analysis structure. Divide the class into groups of four or five students. Prepare claim analysis activity sheets—a sheet with a claim written at the top and a four-column chart below. Column 1 should provide space to write the claim; column 2, space to indicate if the claim is supportable; column 3, space to indicate if the claim is supported; and column 4, space to conclude if the support is reliable.

Sample column heads are shown here for illustrative purposes:

CLAIM ANALYSIS SHEET

The Claim	Is It Supportable?	Is It Supported?	Is Support Reliable?

Provide space at the bottom of the sheet to explain the analysis. The claim analysis sheets should include both supportable and unsupportable claims, examples of all four types of claims, and the five types of unreliable support. Make copies of the analysis sheets and arrange them into packets with a different packet for each group that contains one more claim than there are students in the group.

Have students report to their group's work station. Distribute the claim analysis sheets to each group. Have each student select a claim and independently analyze it. When students have finished this task, have them share the results with the rest of the group to get feedback regarding their accuracy. When all students have made their reports, the group should turn to the one remaining analysis sheet to complete it as a group and decide how to "teach" it to the rest of the class. Have groups make their presentations. Check individual mastery with a quiz, completion of a review activity sheet, or as part of a unit test later. Bring the lesson to a close by discussing how this process is used to make both wise consumer and other practical day-to-day decisions.

In isolation, this lesson may not seem that earth shaking in the overall scheme of your home economics classes. You might very well say, "I do that sort of thing all the time, what's the big deal?" The big deal is that *Tactics* provides you with a structure of what thinking skills to teach and makes suggestions of how, when, and where to teach them. It makes thinking a visible part of the curriculum.

Where to Get More Information

1. You can order *Tactics for Thinking* from

    Association of Supervision and Curriculum Development
    1250 N. Pitt Street
    Alexandria, VA 22314

2. You can request information about seminars and workshops sponsored by the Association of Supervision and Curriculum Development (ASCD). Write to them at the address given.

3. There is a national network of *Tactics* trainers who are affiliated with each state's branch of ASCD. They, too, sponsor seminars and workshops. Write to your state branch of ASCD for information.

4. Contact your state department of education or regional branch of the department—county office, Intermediate Unit, or Board of Cooperative Educational Services.

How to Get Started

It is important to remember, "Great oaks from little acorns grow." Teaching thinking skills is a process of becoming. It will take time, but it will provide great benefits for your students.

1. Get your department head, principal, superintendent, or someone to buy you a copy of *Tactics for Thinking*.

2. Go through the 22 skills and decide which most appropriately fit your curriculum and which are of most interest to you.

3. Keep your eyes and ears open to learn about *Tactics* seminars or workshops.

4. Talk with your peers, not necessarily home economics teachers, to see if anyone is interested in "buddying up" to try teaching thinking skills. It is helpful to have someone with which to discuss your ideas and help you evaluate your progress. This is the first step in setting up a network to involve your whole department or school in teaching *Tactics*.

5. Analyze your curriculum to see where the skills you selected might best fit.

6. From this point on, the procedure is simply a matter of systematically studying the *Tactics* manual to plan lessons and develop or modify materials to use. You will find that you can use many of the materials you already use and that what may be most different is the approach you use in class.

7. Over time, as you become more committed to teaching thinking skills directly, you will need to interface those you have selected with the content of your curriculum.

8. It is important to remember that thinking is not a process taught in isolation as a once and done deal. You need to provide students opportunities to practice the skills in many different situations and contexts over time so they independently apply the skills to practical everyday situations.

DIMENSIONS OF LEARNING

Dimensions of Learning is an instructional system developed over a period of two years at the Mid-continent Regional Educational Laboratory in Aurora, Colorado, involving more than 90 educators. It is a structured, yet flexible, approach home economics teachers can use to improve their curriculum, instruction, and assessment skills.

The *Dimensions of Learning* model shows you how to teach students directly five types of thinking: (1) positive attitudes and perceptions about learning, (2) acquiring and integrating knowledge, (3) extending and refining knowledge, (4) using knowledge meaningfully, and (5) developing productive habits of the mind. It is based on the assumptions that instruction must be both teacher directed and student directed, and assessment should focus on student's use of knowledge and complex reasoning rather than on recall of simple information.

What the Dimensions of Learning Are

The five dimensions are important because they are essential to successful learning. They are described as follows:

Dimension 1

Students' attitudes and perceptions affect their ability to learn. If they perceive the school environment as an unfriendly place, they will learn little. If they have a negative attitude toward classroom procedures, they will probably not get involved. For instruction to be effective, positive attitudes and perceptions about learning must exist.

Dimension 2

Students need to acquire new knowledge and then relate it to what they already know so it becomes a part of long-term memory, to learn successfully.

Dimension 3

Learning goes beyond acquiring knowledge to extending it, refining it, and analyzing it. Learners compare, classify, make inductions and deductions, analyze errors, create and analyze support, analyze perspectives, and create and apply abstractions.

Dimension 4

Learning is most effective when knowledge is used to perform meaningful tasks. *Dimensions* includes instruction in decision making, investigation, experimental inquiry, problem solving, and invention.

Dimension 5

Effective learners know how to regulate their behavior, think critically, and think creatively. *Dimensions* addresses the mental habits of being sensitive to feedback, being accurate and seeking accuracy, and working at the edge rather than the center of competence.

How Dimensions of Learning *Applies to Home Economics*

You will find ways in the *Dimensions of Learning* program to give structure to your efforts to teach students purposefully how to think. You will find concrete suggestions to improve existing lessons and to extend them into higher-level thinking skills. For example, you will learn how to help students extend and refine home economics knowledge through questioning, comparing, classifying, and analyzing errors. You will discover some new and interesting ways to teach the decision-making skills included in many home economics courses. Concrete, step-by-step instructions to teach investigation and problem solving are included. *Dimensions of Learning* is a perfect companion to *Tactics for Thinking*.

Where to Get More Information

1. Write to the Association of Supervision and Curriculum Development, 1250 N. Pitt Street, Alexandria, Virginia 22314; telephone: (703) 549-9110; fax: (703) 549-3891 for a list of publications.
2. ASCD can provide you with a list of the schools that were members of the Research and Development Consortium. The list along with the names of participants is included in the *Dimensions of Learning Teacher's Manual*.

How to Get Started

Order the following materials from ASCD at the address given:

1. *Dimensions of Learning Teacher's Manual,* 1992
2. *A Different Kind of Classroom: Teaching with Dimensions of Learning,* 1992
3. *Dimensions of Thinking,* 1988

PRACTICAL REASONING

What Practical Reasoning Is

Every day of our lives, we make decisions about perennial, practical problems. These decisions range from the simple, "What will I wear to school today?" to the complex, "Should I have a child at this stage in my career?" In practical everyday problem situations such as these, we often have difficulty recognizing that a problem exists. Or we find it harder to figure out what the problem is than to figure out how to solve it. These situations frequently deal with ethical and moral issues. There generally is no right solution, and the criteria to judge the best decisions are often not clear. Solutions depend as much on informal knowledge as on formal knowledge. Everyday problem solving frequently occurs in groups, as in the family, for example. Practical everyday problems are said to be ill structured. Schools spend more time teaching problem solving for structured situations than they do for ill-structured ones.

Home economists have traditionally taught decision making in many parts of their courses. In recent years several groups across the country became interested in preparing individuals to cope with practical, everyday ill-structured life problems. They called this decision-making process "practical reasoning" and defined it as the process of reaching conclusions about what to do in everyday home and family problems based on the knowledge available at the time. It is, they say, deciding what to do, what to believe, and what to value based on the knowledge that is available.

How Practical Reasoning Applies to Home Economics

The Division of Vocational Education in the Ohio Department of Education and the Ohio State University developed a secondary school curriculum model to teach critical thinking/problem solving in home economics. This work was aimed at the application of practical reasoning skills to the perennial problems of what to do regarding

- Creating a living environment.
- Economics and managing resources.

- Nurturing human development.
- Feeding and nourishing the family.
- Meeting personal and family textile needs.
- Coordinating work and the family.

A comprehensive curriculum guide for each of these areas of home economics was developed and is being used in Ohio secondary schools. The formal home economics subject matter curriculum begins after teacher-directed instruction in the practical reasoning process. Each perennial problem guide is broken down into a subset of practical problems, concerns, and validated homemaking skills to deal successfully with the perennial problem. A wealth of teaching strategies and instructional materials is provided.

A SAMPLE PRACTICAL
REASONING LESSON PLAN

This sample lesson plan is adapted from one of the introductory practical reasoning modules found in *Ohio Consumer/Homemaking Curriculum Guide Practical Action*. It should be noted that this lesson may require more than one class period.

Practical Reasoning—What's Best to Do?

Concepts

    I. Practical reasoning skills
        A. Gather adequate, reliable information.
        B. Question and test bases for decisions.
        C. Justify action with adequate, relevant, and morally defensible reasons.
        D. Collaborate with others to decide what's best to do.
    II. Characteristics of value principles, value claims, and factual claims
   III. Basic social values
   IV. Use of decision tests
        A. Universal test
        B. Role reversal test
        C. New cases test

Teacher Preparation

    1. Prepare a bulletin board "Controversy" from a collage of newspaper articles, editorials, Dear Abby letters, and letters to the editor to reflect

controversial issues facing families, individuals, and/or community. The board is more meaningful if the collage pertains to local issues. Over the collage add these questions: "Be impulsive? Follow others? Use habits, traditions? Use practical reasoning?"

2. Prepare copies of student handouts, "Energize . . . with Practical Reasoning," "Decide . . . with Practical Reasoning," and "Facts? or Value Claims?" for use in class. All are reproduced at the end of this chapter.

3. Make an overhead transparency of the "Practical Reasoning" blackline master.

Activities

1. Begin class by telling the students they are going to learn a problem-solving process to use in everyday practical problem situations. The process is called practical reasoning. The first step in the process is being able to identify the problem. Call students' attention to the bulletin board and via group discussion have them identify the controversial issues.

2. Discuss the meaning of controversy. Develop a list of criteria for identifying controversial issues. Include such things as "occur when many choices available," "reflect differing values," "require decision making and action," "consequences of actions uncertain," "often are practical 'what-to-do' problems." Place the list on the bulletin board.

3. At the chalkboard or overhead projector, have the students list some practical controversial issues or problems they face every day at home, school, or work. Lead into a discussion of how they can solve these issues. Be sure to include "by impulse," "by habit," "by tradition," "as others would solve them," or "by reasoning."

4. Move the discussion to an explanation of the components and skills involved in practical reasoning. Use the *Practical Reasoning Discussion Guide* to conduct a class discussion and complete the practical reasoning model at the overhead projector.

Practical Reasoning Discussion Guide

1. Explain that practical reasoning, not impulsive or irrational thinking, is needed to decide what is best to do about practical problems, the problems that affect the well-being of self and others—especially those in our family.

As you explain the practical reasoning process, use the transparency master "Practical Reasoning" so students can visualize the process. See the completed diagram for clarification as to how it should look when completed. Connect the 11 circles with arrows to denote people interacting and communicating together. Then write "COMMUNICATE" in the circles. Inside the first circle, write "FACTS" and "VALUES" at the top with the following beneath.

                    ALTERNATIVES
                    CONSEQUENCES
                 SITUATIONAL FACTORS
                        PERSONAL
                      ENVIRONMENTAL
                GOALS AND VALUES OF ALL

Connect the circles C and E with a long arrow, and label it as shown on the diagram, "Share Meanings" and "Negotiate Differences."

   2. Practical reasoning involves people communicating openly. As they communicate, they also create a trusting atmosphere. Describe this further by discussing open communication, trusting environment. As you conduct this discussion, write the words indicated on the transparency master. For clarification see the completed diagram at the end of this chapter.

   In practical reasoning, everyone interacts so the best decisions are made. The decision makers in families, individuals, and communities seek the "FACTS" and "VALUES" of those affected so the best decisions can be made. The facts and values particularly needed to solve practical, what-to-do problems include:

   • Alternative actions to solve problems.
   • Probable consequences to actions.
   • Personal and environmental situational factors.
   • Goals and values of all involved.

   Throughout this process of gathering and sharing facts and values, those who will be affected by the decision "SHARE MEANINGS," "QUESTION," "SCRUTINIZE," and "NEGOTIATE DIFFERENCES." Discuss what these terms mean.

   Gathering facts and values and clarifying meanings sometimes involves reading, talking with people, investigating, and comparing with people at work, at home, and in the community. Give examples of how this works in families, organizations, and the community.

   After adequate information is collected, the "SITUATIONAL FACTORS" and "VALUES" and "GOALS" can be used as the "CRITERIA" to evaluate the alternative actions.

   3. The potential decisions or alternative actions can be tested to determine if they are ethically justifiable. For example, we can ask ourselves:

   • What would happen if everyone made this choice? this decision? This is called the "UNIVERSAL TEST."

- How would I like to be the person affected by this decision? How would I feel? Would I want this action to be taken? This is the "ROLE REVERSAL TEST."
- In a similar situation, would this choice or action be best? This is the "NEW CASES TEST."

As you discuss these parts of the process, write the words on the transparency.

4. These communication and thinking skills are constantly interacting with our "ACTIONS." Most often we are not conscious of our processing all the information needed (possible alternatives, consequences, situational factors, and values) to make the best decision as we act. This interaction and intertwining of thinking, communicating, and action comprises practical reasoning. Becoming skilled in these processes can help us all make decisions we can be proud of—now and in the future.

As you discuss this information, draw the lines showing continuous interaction of people. Write in "ACTION." Conclude by labeling the completed diagram "PRACTICAL REASONING MODEL."

5. Have the students assemble into small groups to make a list of advantages and consequences of each problem-solving approach. Suggest they summarize their discussion ideas by listing the advantages and consequences for each of the ways to solve problems they identified earlier.

6. Distribute the "Energize . . . with Practical Reasoning" activity sheet reproduced at the end of this chapter and discuss the meanings and necessity for each communication and thinking skill in practical reasoning. Tell the students they will use practical reasoning to examine the practical problems they will discuss in the course. They should keep the checklist because they will periodically evaluate their progress toward using practical reasoning. Lead the students into a discussion of their thinking process.

- Do they typically use a decision-making process?
- Do they normally accept whatever anyone tells them?
- Do they question? Is questioning a "thinking habit"? Are they skeptical? Do they scrutinize?
- What do "skeptical" and "scrutinize" mean?

7. Explain that value principles can be criteria to help us judge what is best to do. Value principles are value claims that can be supported by factual claims. In our country, we have basic public policy affecting families and individuals.

8. Have the students complete the top part of the activity sheet "Facts? or Value Claims?" (reproduced at the end of this chapter) to compare examples of

value claims/alternative actions and facts or factual claims. After they have completed the sheet, go over it in a large group to be sure students are recognizing factual claims from value claims. At the overhead projector, summarize the characteristics of each. Include the following:

Value Claims	Factual Claims
1. Judgments about worth of something	1. Statements can be determined true or false by:
2. Reflects desirability or undesirability of something	Making sensory observations
3. Includes value terms:	Being clear about meaning of words in statements

3. Includes value terms:

ought	best, worst
should	desirable
worthwhile	undesirable

9. Discuss how families and individuals can create a chart of reasons to decide what it is best to do. By collecting facts regarding possible consequences and contextual factors, controversial value issues can be reduced to a factual problem. Using these facts as evidence in support of each alternative, decisions can be made and tested to decide if they are ethically and morally justifiable.

10. Have the students use practical reasoning. Let them work in small groups as in a family. (Note how easily you could adapt this to a cooperative learning approach.) They should select a controversial problem on their own, from the list on the chalkboard, or from the bulletin board. They should use the activity sheet, "Decide . . . with Practical Reasoning" (at the end of this chapter) to guide their decision-making process. When they have finished making their decisions, have each group share its process with the class. As each group makes its report, make sure to clarify whether they:

- Used decision tests for each alternative value claim.
- Decided which alternative is justifiable using the decision tests.
- Compiled a list of reasons for each alternative.
- Listed the facts.

Bring the lesson to a close by explaining that during the next lesson they will learn about values, "Why I Am What I Am" and "Why I Do What I Do."

Note: In the Ohio program, students go on to learn the management process involved in decision making in a lesson entitled "Getting It Together" and then apply the management process in daily living situations in the lesson "Making It Happen." The introduction to practical reasoning concludes with a lesson about interpersonal and communication skills, "Is Anybody Listening?"

How to Get Started

Contact the Division of Vocational Education in your state Department of Education. Ask permission to borrow the *Ohio Consumer/Homemaking Curriculum Guide.* It comes in seven volumes: *Practical Action, What to Do Regarding Economics and Managing Resources, What to Do Regarding Creating a Living Environment, What to Do Regarding Feeding and Nourishing the Family, What to Do Regarding Meeting Personal and Family Textile Needs, What to Do Regarding Coordinating Work and the Family,* and *What to Do Regarding Nurturing Human Development.*

If they do not have it, ask them to contact their counterpart in the Ohio State Department of Education, Division of Vocational Education, Home Economics Section, 65 Front Street, Room 912, Columbus, Ohio 43215.

If that does not work, contact the Instructional Materials Laboratory, Ohio State University, 1885 Neil Avenue, Townshend Hall, Room 112, Columbus, Ohio 43201.

ENERGIZE . . . WITH PRACTICAL REASONING ACTIVITY SHEET

Decisions! Decisions! How you make decisions or help others make decisions can make a difference in the well-being of you and others.

The four energizers of practical reasoning can help you make the best decision and take the best action. Study this list as you make a decision and

CHECK (✓) YOURSELF!

DO YOU:

1. Gather adequate, reliable information to help make your decisions.

    _____ a. Goals and values of those involved were considered.

    _____ b. Situational factors were considered.

        _____ Personal factors of all involved.

            _____ Resources: skills, knowledge, money, other

            _____ Developmental needs

        _____ Environmental factors

            _____ Laws—national, state, local

            _____ Governmental agencies

            _____ Economic resources

            _____ Social relationships

            _____ Cultural factors—mores, taboos, social values

    _____ c. Alternative actions or choices were considered.

    _____ d. Consequences of actions or choices were listed.

© 1993 by The Center for Applied Research in Education

2. Question, test, use careful in-depth thinking about what is best or ought to be done.

    ____ a. Facts to support my action were collected.

    ____ b. Decision was based solely on value claims.

    ____ c. Information sources are reliable.

    ____ d. Reasons support conclusion or decision.

    ____ e. Choice of action workable considering the personal and environmental factors.

    ____ f. Action is morally defensible.

3. Justify decisions or choices of action with adequate and reliable reasons.

    ____ a. Adequate information to support decision present.

    ____ b. Reliable information and sources used for the situation.

    ____ c. Consideration shown for the well-being of people involved.

4. Dialogue and collaborate with others to decide what is best.

    ____ a. Listen and ask questions to understand reasons behind position.

    ____ b. Meanings and ideas compared.

    ____ c. Ideas and feelings shared openly.

    ____ d. Support others, recognizing feelings, strengths.

    ____ e. Cooperate and expect others to cooperate.

    ____ f. Ask questions to gain and clarify meanings.

    ____ g. Negotiate to create alternative action for well-being of all.

© 1993 by The Center for Applied Research in Education

Name: _____   Date: _____

FACTS? OR VALUE CLAIMS?
ACTIVITY SHEET*

Directions: Compare the examples of statements below. Write a "V" for value claim and an "F" for fact or factual claim in the blanks at the left. Describe the characteristics of value claims and factual claims in the chart at the bottom of the page.

_____ 1. People should not be allowed to marry before age 18.

_____ 2. The age for marriage without parental consent in many states is 18.

_____ 3. People should be allowed to marry before age 18.

_____ 4. Everyone ought to eat an adequately balanced diet.

_____ 5. Eating a nutritious diet is unimportant, not worthwhile.

_____ 6. Optimum health requires a balanced diet of carbohydrates, fats, protein, vitamins, minerals, and water.

_____ 7. Anything that eases distress and anxiety ought to be undertaken.

_____ 8. Alcoholic drinks give a false sense of easing distress and anxiety and actually increase distress and anxiety in many instances.

_____ 9. We should help others deal with distress.

Summarize the Characteristics:

Value Claims	Facts Or Factual Claims

KEY: VC = 1, 3, 4, 5, 7, 9
    FC = 2, 6, 8

*Adapted from F. Hultgren, and M. Goosens-Conlon, with T. Shear, *What to do Regarding the Parenthood Decision?* University Park, PA: The Pennsylvania State University, 1981.

© 1993 by The Center for Applied Research in Education

Name: _____ Date: _____

DECIDE . . . WITH PRACTICAL REASONING*

Step 1: Identify the problem. (Ask yourself some questions on the topic.)

Step 2: Suggest possible solutions and consequences.

Solutions	Consequences
1.	1a.
	b.
2.	2a.
	b.
3.	3a.
	b.
4.	4a.
	b.

Step 3: Identify and Examine Personal and Environmental Factors.

Identify Values   **Identify Goals**   **Identify Situational Factors**

Step 4: Decide on one solution from step 2 and justify your decision with adequate and reliable reasons.

Solution   **Reasons This Solution Was Chosen**

Step 5: Reflect and evaluate. (Is this solution a good one?)

Ask yourself these questions throughout your decision-making process:

1. Do I have *facts* to support my decision?
2. Are my sources of information *reliable?* Explain why.
3. Do I have *enough relevant information* to justify my decision?
4. Will the consequences of my solution/action be for the well-being of myself and others?
   a. What if everyone acted in this way or selected this solution?
   b. If I were the people around me, how would I feel about this solution/action?
   c. Would I do this same thing in a new or another situation? Why or why not?
5. How can I better prepare myself for this or a similar situation again?

_____

*Developed by Heather Boggs and Sue Saravalli, Springfield South H.S., and Janet F. Laster, The Ohio State University.

© 1993 by The Center for Applied Research in Education

© 1993 by The Center for Applied Research in Education

PRACTICAL REASONING

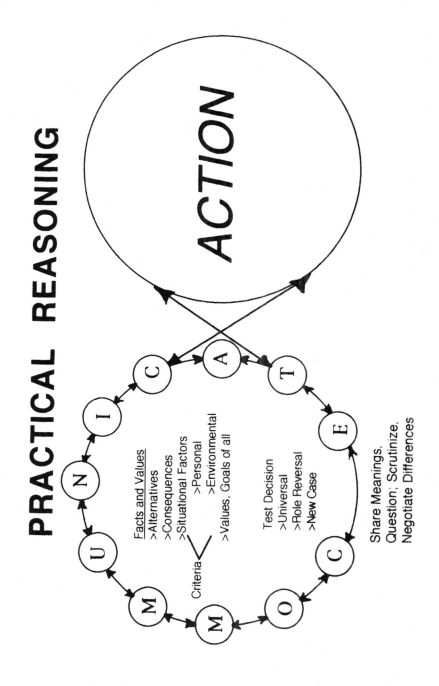

ACTION

C O M M U N I C A T E

Facts and Values
>Alternatives
>Consequences
>Situational Factors
  >Personal
  >Environmental
Criteria
>Values, Goals of all

Test Decision
>Universal
>Role Reversal
>New Case

Share Meanings,
Question; Scrutinize,
Negotiate Differences

PART TWO
MANAGING YOUR JOB AND STAYING SANE

- *Knowing Where to Find It*
- *Managing Your Time*
- *Getting the Home Ec Message Across*
- *New Technology in the Home Ec Classroom*

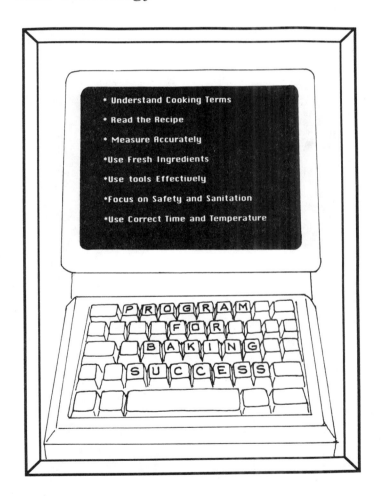

* Understand Cooking Terms

* Read the Recipe

* Measure Accurately

* Use Fresh Ingredients

* Use tools Effectively

* Focus on Safety and Sanitation

* Use Correct Time and Temperature

PROGRAM FOR BAKING SUCCESS

CHAPTER 5
KNOWING WHERE TO FIND IT

COPING WITH THE RESOURCE EXPLOSION

New subject matter, new technologies, new teaching materials, new priorities, new teaching methods, new research—new, new, new, new—the information explosion has hit home economics! Not a day goes by that most of us don't receive a ton of mail about one or more of these topics. Knowing what to do with it so that you can find something when you want it is a survival skill now more important than ever. This is another area of your job that requires you to use management skills.

One management skill often taken for granted is filing. This chapter shows you how to set up a practical filing system for vendor information for the books, supplies, and equipment you use to teach; curriculum information for the subject area content included in your courses; and general information for the day-to-day operation of your program. A starter list of curriculum sources is included.

Knowing where to find the useful but unusual is useful! An annotated list gives unusual sources of information useful to home economics teachers.

A VENDOR INFORMATION FILING SYSTEM

Setting Up the System

Simple systems work best for busy people. Therefore, base your filing system upon something you are already familiar with—the alphabet. Follow these steps:

1. Arrange a set of alphabetical dividers in the filing cabinet. Make sure you provide enough room for each section to file the information you will accumulate. Two or three drawers should be sufficient.

2. Decide what types of vendors to include in your system, for example, text and reference books, supplies, equipment, computer software, kits, audio-visual materials, and professional books.

143

3. Because some vendors sell more than one product, you need a coding system to identify what the vendor sells. For example, code text and reference books with red, supplies with blue, equipment with yellow, computer software with green, kits with black, and audiovisual materials with purple. Enter the codes with Magic Markers® or with colored press on dots.

4. Write the name of the company on the tab of a file folder and with a Magic Marker® make a large dot to indicate what the vendor sells. For example, if the company is Nasco, place red, blue, yellow, green, and purple dots on the tab. This tells you at a glance that Nasco sells text and reference books, supplies, equipment, computer software, and audiovisual materials.

5. Place the completed file in the correct alphabetical location making sure you alphabetize within the section. For example, Nasco would probably be the first catalogue in the N section since the second letter is "a."

There are some other decisions you need to make that are a matter of personal choice. Will you save all the brochures or catalogues you receive? If not, how will you decide what to keep and what to throw away? Will you purge your system each year so that it contains only current information? It is wise to think these things through while setting up the system rather than risk a major reorganization later because you are overwhelmed with the quantity of advertisements, for example.

A CURRICULUM INFORMATION SYSTEM

Setting Up the System

When you want to know where to get information about some topic in our curriculum, you want to know now, not after spending a couple of hours paging through a bunch of file folders or calling someone you know. Take the time to set up a curriculum information system. A simple alphabetical system works best.

A curriculum information filing system should be in two parts. The first part is a file for the names and addresses of sources of curriculum information and the second part is a system to file the actual curriculum materials.

There are two ways to organize the sources of curriculum information. The first is a simple alphabetical arrangement of the organizations and agencies that provide curriculum information for home economics. The second way is to create an alphabetical arrangement by curriculum topic and then file the sources alphabetically within each topic.

Each entry in the source file should include the name, address, regular phone number, 800 telephone number, and fax number. Use something as simple as 3" × 5" cards in a box or go high tech and set up a computer database to keep your information ready to use. Remember, good managers practice self-discipline and add information to their database when they get it, not when they get around to it. When new sources of information are identified, get them in the system.

It doesn't take long to accumulate a lot of curriculum information. Knowing where to put it so it can be found is the challenge. One way to do that is to organize the system around the five major areas of home economics content: foods and nutrition; housing, furnishings, and equipment; human growth and development; management and consumerism; and textiles and clothing. Within each of these areas place a file folder for each course you teach that includes content from the area. Provide for a general file in each major area to file information not directly related to the courses in your curriculum. This is a spot to include ideas for possible new units or courses.

If one filing system is to serve a multiteacher department, make certain everyone knows of the system's existence. There are several ways to keep the file up to date. First, have everyone file information as they receive it. Second, rotate the filing task according to a schedule—by the month, the marking period, or semester. Or have one person assume the responsibility to keep the filing system up to date in exchange for other department members picking up some other duty for the filer.

A Curriculum Information Filing System Example

Here is an example of a curriculum information filing system.

Home Economics Department
Curriculum Information Filing System

Foods and Nutrition

Life Arts
Eighth-Grade Home Economics
Baking Basics
Specialty Foods
Baking with a Gourmet Touch
Cultures and Cuisines
Nutrition
Independent Living
Family Living
Senior Foods
Lifeways
General

Housing, Furnishings, and Equipment

Independent Living
Family Living
Lifeways
General

Human Growth and Development

Eighth-Grade Home Economics
Understanding Young Children
Cultures and Cuisines
Independent Living
Family Living
Lifeways
General

Management and Consumerism

Eighth-Grade Home Economics
Sewing and More
Specialty Foods
Baking with a Gourmet Touch
Independent Living
Family Living
Creative Clothing Construction
Nutrition
Senior Foods
Lifeways
General

Textiles and Clothing

Life Arts
Eighth-Grade Home Economics
Sewing and More
Creative Clothing Construction
Needlecraft
Independent Living
Family Living
Lifeways
General

A Starter List of Curriculum Resources

Here is a starter set of sources for curriculum information. As discussed earlier, curriculum information sources can be arranged in a simple alphabetical system or arranged according to topics. Alphabetical topical arrangement makes it easier to find sources quickly.

Adolescent Suicide

The American Association of Suicidology
  Central Office
2459 South Ash Street
Denver, CO 80222
(303) 692-0985

Fairfax County Schools
Belle Willard Administration Center
10310 Layton Hall Drive
Fairfax, VA 22030

Indiana State Board of Health
1330 West Michigan Street, Room 232
Indianapolis, IN 46206-1964

South Bergen Mental Health Center, Inc.
646B Valley Brook Avenue
Lyndhurst, NJ 07071
(201) 460-3510

Aging

Alzheimer's Disease and Related Disorders Association
70 East Lake Street
Chicago, IL 60601
(800) 631-0379

American Association of Retired Persons
1225 Connecticut Avenue, N.W.
Washington, D.C. 20036

American Geriatrics Society
10 Columbus Circle
New York, NY 10019

American Red Cross
17th and D Streets, N.W.
Washington, D.C. 20006

Cornell Cooperative Extension Education Center
239 Wisner Avenue
Middletown, NY 10940

Family Service Association of America
44 East 23rd Street
New York, NY 10010

National Council of Senior Citizens
1511 K Street, N.W.
Washington, D.C. 20005

National Council on Aging
1828 L Street, N.W.
Washington, D.C. 20006

Superintendent of Documents
U.S. Government Printing Office
Washington, D.C. 20402
(202) 783-3238

AIDS

American Council of Life Insurance/Health Insurance
    Association of America
Department 190
1001 Pennsylvania Avenue, N.W.
Washington, D.C. 20004-2599

Channing L. Bete Company, Inc.
200 State Road
South Deerfield, MA 01373

National School Boards Association
1680 Duke Street
Alexandria, VA 22314

Sex Information & Education Council of the United States (SIECUS)
32 Washington Place, Fifth Floor
New York, NY 10003

The Center for Population Options
1012 14 Street, N.W.
Washington, D.C. 20005

Alcoholism

Al-Anon Family Group Headquarters
P.O. Box 862
Midtown Station
New York, NY 10018-0862
(800) 356-9996 or (212) 245-3151 in New York

Cambridge & Somerville Program for Alcohol & Drug Abuse Rehabilitation
(CASPAR)
226 Highland Avenue
Somerville, MA 02143
(617) 623-2080

Hazleden Educational Materials
Pleasant Valley Road
Box 176
Center City, MN 55012-0176
(800) 328-9000 or (800) 257-0070 in Minnesota

Johnson Institute
7151 Metro Boulevard
Minneapolis, MN 55435
(800) 231-5165

National Association of Children of Alcoholics
31706 Coast Highway, Suite 201
South Laguna, CA 92677-3044
(717) 499-3889

Birth Defects

March of Dimes
Check the telephone directory for the local branch's address and telephone
number.

Easter Seal Society
Check the telephone directory for the local branch's address and telephone
number.

Careers

American Home Economics Association (AHEA)
2010 Massachusetts Avenue, N.W.
Washington, D.C. 20036-1028
(800) 424-8080 or (202) 862-8300

Home Economists in Business
301 Maple Avenue West, Tower Suite 505
Vienna, VA 22180
(703) 939-3666

Child Abuse

Daughters and Sons United
840 Guadalupe Parkway
San Jose, CA 95110

The National Committee for Prevention of Child Abuse
Box 2866
Chicago, IL 60690

Conflict Resolution

Educators for Social Responsibility
23 Garden Street
Cambridge, MA 02138

National Association for Mediation in Education
The Mediation Project
University of Massachusetts-Amherst
139 Whitmore Street
Amherst, MA 01003

Consumer Information

The Consumer Information Catalog
Consumer Information Center
Pueblo, CO 81009

The Food and Drug Administration
Office of Consumer Affairs (HFE-88)
5600 Fishers Lane
Rockville, MD 20857

Consumer Complaints

Chief Inspector
U.S. Postal Inspection Service
475 L'Enfant Plaza West, S.W.
Washington, D.C. 20260-2112

The Council of Better Business Bureaus
1515 Wilson Boulevard, Suite 300
Arlington, VA 22209

The Federal Trade Commission
Office of the Secretary
6th Street and Pennsylvania Avenue, N.W.
Washington, D.C. 20580

The Food and Drug Administration
Office of Consumer Affairs
HFE-88
5600 Fishers Lane
Rockville, MD 20857

Date Rape

Project on the Stature and Education of Women (PSEW)
1818 R Street, N.W.
Washington, D.C. 20009

King County Rape Relief
1025 South 3rd
Renton, WA 98055
(206) 226-5062

Food Additives

Institute of Food Technologists
221 LaSalle Street
Chicago, IL 60601
(312) 782-8424

International Food Additives Council
5775-D Peachtree-Dunwoody Road
Atlanta, GA 30342

U.S. Department of Health and Human Services
Food and Drug Administration
5600 Fishers Lane
Rockville, MD 20852

Food Product Development

Institute of Food Technologists
221 North LaSalle Street
Chicago, IL 60601
(312) 782-8424

Grants

Apple Computer, Inc.
Education Grants
MS-38J
20525 Mariani Avenue
Cupertino, CA 95014
(408) 974-2974

Carnegie Foundation
437 Madison Avenue
New York, NY 10022
(212) 371-3200

Exxon Education Foundation
225 East J. W. Carpenter Freeway
Irving, TX 75062
(214) 444-1000

IBM Educational Systems
P.O. Box 2150
Atlanta, GA 30055

Lily Endowment Fund
2801 North Meridian Street
P.O. Box 88068
Indianapolis, IN 46208
(317) 924-5471

Mattel Foundation
5150 Rosecrans Avenue
Hawthorne, CA 90250
(213) 978-5477

Milken Family Foundation
15250 Ventura Boulevard, Second Floor
Sherman Oaks, CA 91403
(818) 784-9224

National Science Foundation
1800 G Street
Washington, D.C. 20550
(202) 357-7880

Tandy Educational Grant
Tandy, Inc.
1600 One Tandy Center
Fort Worth, TX 76102
(817) 390-3832

The Ford Foundation
320 East 43rd Street
New York, NY 10017
(212) 573-5000

The John D. and Catherine T. MacArthur Foundation
140 South Dearborn Street
Chicago, IL 60603
(312) 726-8000

United States Department of Education (USDE)
Fund for the Improvement and Reform of Schools and Teaching
400 Maryland Ave., S.W.
Washington, D.C. 20202

United States Department of Education (USOE)
Division of Vocational-Technical Education
400 Maryland Ave., S.W.
Washington, D.C. 20202

Homeless

Housing Now
425 Second Street, N.W.
Washington, D.C. 20001
(202) 347-2405

National Coalition for the Homeless
1439 Rhode Island Avenue, N.W.
Washington, D.C. 20005

National Housing Task Force
1625 Eye Street, N.W.
Washington, D.C. 20006

UNCHS (HABITAT)
DC2, Room 946
United Nations
New York, NY 10017

Insurance

Money Management Institute
Household Financial Services
2700 Sanders Road
Prospect Heights, IL 60070

Office of Agricultural Publications
47 Mumford Hall
University of Illinois
1301 West Gregory Drive
Urbana, IL 61801

The American Council of Life Insurance Information
1001 Pennsylvania Avenue, N.W.
Washington, D.C. 20004-2599

The Council of Better Business Bureaus
1515 Wilson Boulevard
Arlington, VA 22209

Latchkey Children

Project Home Safe
American Home Economics Association
2010 Massachusetts Avenue, N.W.
Washington, D.C. 20036
(800) 424-8080 or (202) 862-8377

Missing Children

Child Find, Inc.
P.O. Box 277
New Paltz, NY 12561

The Adam Walsh Child Resource Center
Mercede Executive Park, Suite 306
1876 North University Drive
Ft. Lauderdale, FL 33322

Dee Scofield Awareness Project, Inc.
4418 Bay Court Avenue
Tampa, FL 33611

Cobra Connection
P.O. Box 1958
Station A
Canton, OH 44705

Money Management

American Bankers Association
1120 Connecticut Avenue, N.W.
Washington, D.C. 20036

Ethel Maddux
Cooperative Extension Service
The University of Georgia
College of Agriculture
Athens, GA 30602

Money Management Institute
Household Financial Services
2700 Sanders Road
Prospect Heights, IL 60070

Superintendent of Documents
U.S. Government Printing Office
Washington, D.C. 20402

National Futures Association
200 West Madison Street, Suite 1600
Chicago, IL 60606
(800) 621-3570 or (800) 572-9400 in Illinois

Networking

FORECAST Magazine
Scholastic, Inc.
730 Broadway
New York, NY 10003

Nutrition

The American Cancer Society
Contact your local office. They are listed in your phone directory.

The American Diabetes Association
2 Park Avenue
New York, NY 10016
(800) 232-3472

The American Dietetic Association
216 W. Jackson Boulevard, Suite 800
Chicago, IL 60606-6995
(800) 366-1655

The American Heart Association
7320 Greenville Avenue
Dallas, TX 75231
(214) 373-6300

The American Medical Association
Food and Nutrition Program
535 North Dearborn Street
Chicago, IL 60610
(312) 645-5000

The Arthritis Foundation
1314 Spring Street, N.W.
Atlanta, GA 30309
(404) 872-7100

Human Nutrition Information Service
U.S. Department of Agriculture
HNIS, Room 325A
6505 Belcrest Road
Hyattsville, MD 20782

Penn State Nutrition Center
417 East Calder Way
University Park, PA 16801-5663
Phone: (814) 865-6323
Fax: (814) 865-5870

U.S. Department of Agriculture
FSIS Publications Office, Room 1163 South
Washington, D.C. 20250

Also contact your local Cooperative Extension Service.

State Departments of Education

Alabama
Department of Education
State Office Building
501 Dexter Avenue
Montgomery, AL 36130

Alaska
State Department of Education
Goldbelt Building
P.O. Box F
Juneau, AK 99811

Arizona
State Department of Education
1535 West Jefferson
Phoenix, AZ 85007

Arkansas
State Department of Education
Four State Capitol Mall,
    Room 304A
Little Rock, AR 72201-1071

California
State Department of Education
P.O. Box 944272
721 Capitol Mall
Sacramento, CA 95814

Colorado
State Department of Education
201 East Colfax Avenue
Denver, CO 80203-1705

Connecticut
State Department of Education
P.O. Box 2219
165 Capitol Avenue
State Office Building
Hartford, CT 06145

Delaware
State Department of Education
P.O. Box 1402
Townsend Building, #279
Dover, DE 19903

Florida
State Department of Education
Capitol Building, Room PL116
Tallahassee, FL 32301

Georgia
State Department of Education
2066 Twin Towers East
205 Butler Street
Atlanta, GA 30344

Hawaii
Department of Education
1390 Miller Street, #307
Honolulu, HI 96813

Idaho
State Department of Education
Len B. Jordan Office Building
650 West State Street
Boise, ID 83720

Illinois
State Department of Education
100 North First Street
Springfield, IL 62777

Indiana
State Department of Education
Room 229, State House
100 North Capitol Street
Indianapolis, IN 46024-2798

Iowa
State Department of Education
Grimes State Office Building
East 14th and Grand Streets
Des Moines, IA 50319-0146

Kansas
State Department of Education
120 East Tenth Street
Topeka, KS 66612

Kentucky
State Department of Education
1725 Capital Plaza Tower
Frankfort, KY 40601

Louisiana
State Department of Education
P.O. Box 94064
626 North 4th Street, 12th Floor
Baton Rouge, LA 70804-9064

Maine
State Department of Education
State House Station No. 23
Augusta, ME 04333

Maryland
State Department of Education
200 West Baltimore Street
Baltimore, MD 21201

Massachusetts
State Department of Education
Quincy Center Plaza
1385 Hancock Street
Quincy, MA 02169

Michigan
State Board of Education
P.O. Box 30008
608 West Allegan Street
Lansing, MI 48909

Minnesota
State Department of Education
712 Capitol Square Building
550 Cedar Street
St. Paul, MN 55101

Mississippi
State Department of Education
P.O. Box 771
550 High Street, Room 501
Jackson, MS 39205-0771

Missouri
Department of Elementary and
    Secondary Education
P.O. Box 480
205 Jefferson St., 6th Floor
Jefferson City, MO 65102

Montana
Office of Public Instruction
106 State Capitol
Helena, MT 59620

Nebraska
State Department of Education
301 Centennial Mall, South
P.O. Box 94987
Lincoln, NE 68509

Nevada
State Department of Education
Capitol Complex
400 West King Street
Carson City, NV 89710

New Hampshire
State Department of Education
101 Pleasant Street
State Office Park South
Concord, NH 03301

New Jersey
Department of Education
225 West State Street, CN 500
Trenton, NJ 08625-0500

New Mexico
State Department of Education
Education Building
300 Don Gaspar
Sante Fe, NM 87501-2786

New York
State Education Department
111 Education Building
Washington Avenue
Albany, NY 12234

North Carolina
Department of Public Instruction
Education Building
116 West Edenton Street
Raleigh, NC 27603-1712

North Dakota
State Department of Public
    Instruction
State Capitol Building, 11th Floor
600 Boulevard Avenue East
Bismarck, ND 58505-0440

Ohio
State Department of Education
65 South Front Street, Room 80B
Columbus, OH 43266-0308

Oklahoma
Department of Education
Oliver Hodge Memorial Education
    Building
2500 North Lincoln Road
Oklahoma City, OK 73105-4599

Oregon
State Department of Education
700 Pringle Parkway, S.E.
Salem, OR 97310

Pennsylvania
Department of Education
333 Market Street, 10th Floor
Harrisburg, PA 17126-0333

Rhode Island
Department of Education
22 Hayes Street
Providence, RI 02908

South Carolina
State Department of Education
1006 Rutledge Building
1429 Senate Street
Columbia, SC 29201

South Dakota
Division of Education
Department of Education and
    Cultural Affairs
700 Governors Drive
Pierre, SD 57501

Tennessee
State Department of Education
100 Cordell Building
Nashville, TN 37219

Texas
Texas Education Agency
William B. Travis Building
1701 North Congress Avenue
Austin, TX 78701-1494

Utah
State Office of Education
250 East 500 South
Salt Lake City, UT 84111

Vermont
State Department of Education
120 State Street
Montpelier, VT 05602-2703

Virginia
Department of Education
P.O. Box 6-Q, James Monroe
    Building
Fourteenth and Franklin Streets
Richmond, VA 23216-2060

Washington
Super. of Public Instruction
Old Capitol Building
Washington and Legion
Olympia, WA 98504

West Virginia
State Department of Education
1900 Washington Street
Charleston, WV 25305

Wisconsin
State Department of Education
General Executive Facility 3
125 South Webster Street
Madison, WI 53707

Wyoming
State Department of Education
2300 Capitol Avenue, 2nd Floor
Hathaway Building
Cheyenne, WY 82002

Violence

Curriculum Development Center
Kentucky Prevention of Family
    Violence Curriculum
2024 Capital Plaza Tower
Frankfort, KY 40601
(502) 564-2890

Education Development Center, Inc.
55 Chapel Street
Newton, MA 02160
(800) 225-4276

Society for Prevention of Violence
3109 Mayfield Road, Room 207
Cleveland Heights, OH 44118
(216) 371-5545

Violence Prevention Project
Health Promotions Program for
    Urban Youth
Dept. of Health and Hospitals
818 Harrison Avenue, NEB 112
Boston, MA 02118
(617) 424-5196

How to Obtain Information

If this is your first contact with an organization, ask for a catalogue or brochure about their publications. Be as specific as possible concerning the topics in which you are interested. If you know the publication you want, just request it. A phone call is often the quickest way to get action.

Sample Requests

Bluff City Senior High School
135 Keystone Way
Bluff City, Nebraska 98541

January 6, 199X

Penn State Nutrition Center
417 East Calder Way
University Park, PA 16801-5663

Hello,

I am in the process of revising my curriculum and would like to receive your latest catalogue of nutrition materials. Should there be a charge for the catalogue, please include an invoice, and I will see that it is paid promptly. Thank you.

Regards,

Melanie Smith
Home Economics Department
(402) 653-4489, Ext. 45

When you write to a state department of education, add Home Economics Department to the addresses given if you are writing for a curriculum guide, and you will get a faster response.

Bluff City Senior High School
135 Keystone Way
Bluff City, Nebraska 98541

January 6, 199X

Florida State Department of Education
Curriculum Services—Home Economics Education
Capitol Building, Room PL116
Tallahassee, FL 32301

Greetings,

My department is in the process of undergoing a comprehensive
curriculum review. I learned that Florida mandates a home economics
course called "Life Management." Would you please send me the
course outline and/or a copy of the curriculum guide if one is
available?

If there is a charge for these items, please include an invoice, and I
will see that it is promptly paid. Thank you for your assistance.

Sincerely,

Melanie Smith, Coordinator
Home Economics Department
(402) 653-4489, Ext. 45

A FILING SYSTEM
FOR DAY-TO-DAY OPERATIONS

Life doesn't get any easier. It seems every year there are new forms and procedures that require your response. The procedures in this book emphasize getting organized. If you are to survive the deluge of paperwork without a lot of headaches, you need a filing system for day-to-day operations. Once again, keep it simple. Here is a suggested system:

Accident Reports

Advisory Committee

Awards

Calendar

Committees

Conferences

Course Registration

Curriculum Guides

Equipment

FHA/HERO

Finances

   Amortization Schedule

   Budget

   Purchase Orders Completed

   Purchase Orders Pending

   Requisitions

Forms

General Correspondence

Governmental Agencies

Organizations

Programs and Events

Program Review

Publications

Public Relations

Student Referrals

Travel

OTHER CURRICULUM RESOURCES

Here is a list of curriculum resources you might not have thought about. They are useful when you revise existing courses or plan new ones, and they can be used by students as references in daily lessons.

Information for Consumers

Consumer Complaints

Consumer's Resource Handbook, U.S. Office of Consumer Affairs. This work is published annually and is available free by writing to Handbook, Consumer Information Center, Pueblo, CO, 81009. It includes brief information about how to make a complaint, lists of better business bureaus, consumer offices, federal agencies, lawyers, and counseling services.

Consumer Sourcebook, Gale Research, Inc., Book Tower, Detroit, MI 48266. Published annually, this work is edited by Robert Wilson. It is a subject guide to 7,000 federal, state, and local government agencies and offices; national, regional, and grass-roots associations and organizations; information centers; clearinghouses; and related consumer resources in these fields: General Consumerism, Aging, Children and the Family, Education, Employment, Energy and the Environment, Finance and Money Management, Food and Drug Safety, Funerals, Government Accountability, Handicapped, Health Care, Health Promotion, Housing and Home Improvements, Insurance, Legal Services, Mass Communications, Occupational Safety and Health, Products and Product Safety, Real Estate, Recreation and Leisure, Trade and Commerce, Transportation, Travel and Tourism, Utilities, and Veterans.

Legal Aspects

Eiler, Andrew. *The Consumer Protection Manual,* Facts on File Publications, New York, NY, 1984. This book tells how to assert your rights under consumer protection laws. It describes how to plan an effective negotiating strategy and make a convincing case. It tells what you need to know about the legal system, how to fight deceptions and frauds, your rights and obligations when buying products, about warranties, how to protect yourself through different payment methods, how to sue in small claims court.

Osborn, Susan. *Dial an Expert,* McGraw-Hill Book Company, New York, NY, 1986. This book lists sources for free and low-cost expertise by phone. Topics include everything imaginable from Aeronautics and Space Exploration to Volunteering.

Shopping Sources

Palder, Edward L. *The Catalog of Catalogs II,* Woodbine House, Rockville, MD, 1990. A directory for obtaining catalogues and information from over 12,000 catalogue and travel information sources in over 600 subject areas.

Miller, Lowell, and Prudence McCullough. *The Wholesale-By-Mail Catalog,* St. Martin's Press, New York, NY, 1987. This book is periodically updated. It lists firms selling 30% below list or comparable retail and includes all the vital information needed to shop by mail or phone, plus notes on store locations and hours.

Gottlieb, Richard, ed. *The Directory of Mail Order Catalogs,* 4th ed., Grey House Publishing, New York, NY, 1990. Lists names and addresses of mail order companies arranged by type of product.

Official Outlet Directory, Outlet Directory, Lititz, PA annual.

Buying Guides

Consumer Reports, Buying Guide Issue, annual. Rates products by brand names, and provides general buying guidance.

Consumer Digest, Special Buying Guide Issues, appear semiannually as part of regular monthly issues.

Health Information

National Health Directory, Annual, Science and Health Publications, Washington, D.C.

Hadden, Susan G., *Read the Label,* Westview Press, Boulder, CO, 1986.

Personal Finance

Andersen, Carl E. *Andersen of Financial Planning,* Dow Jones-Irwin, Homewood, IL, 1986.

Downes, John and Jordon E. Goodman. *Barron's Finance and Investment Handbook,* Barron's, New York, NY, 1991.

Financial Sourcebooks Sources, Financial Sourcebooks, Naperville, IL, 1987.

Wasserman, Steven et al. *Financial Planners and Planning Organizations Directory,* Omnigraphics, Detroit, MI, 1990.

General Curriculum Information

Professional associations produce curriculum reports, engage in research, and sponsor Member of the Year awards. Write to AHEA each year for the names and addresses of the Teacher of the Year winner and runners-up. Contact them for more detailed information.

Database Information

ERIC is a database produced by the U.S. Office of Education's Educational Resources Information Center. The database's main emphasis is on educational topics. However, it is useful in other subject areas, including psychology, social sciences, health and nutrition, work and leisure, education legislation, communication, and professional development. It contains over 760,000 records.

ERIC is available in print, CD-ROM, and on-line. Several state university libraries offer ERIC as an on-line database service available to off-campus users. For example, The Pennsylvania State University offers ERIC as part of its LIAS (Library Information Access System). See Chapter 8, "Managing the New Technology," for a complete description. At Penn State, ERIC is available on-line to off-campus individuals who are registered with the library. Contact your state department of education or state university to see if this service is available to you.

Information About Grants

Listed here are several reference books useful in locating possible sources of funding. Your public library or nearby college or university library probably have copies of these references. If not, ask your librarian to borrow a copy from your state library via interlibrary loan.

Foundation Directory and National Directory of Corporate Giving. Foundation Center, 75 Fifth Avenue, New York, NY 10003. Cost is $115 and may be ordered by calling (212) 620-4230. The Foundation operates libraries in Cleveland, New York, San Francisco, and Washington, D.C., and maintains collections in 170 libraries across the country. Call (212) 620-4230 or (800) 424-9836 for the locations of the collections in your state.

Directory of Grantmakers Interested in Precollegiate Education. Published annually by The Council of Foundations, 1828 L Street, N.W., Washington, D.C. 20036; (202) 466-6512.

Giving USA and Giving USA Update. American Association of Fund-Raising Counsel Trust for Philanthropy, 25 West 43rd Street, Suite 1519, New York, NY 10036; (212) 354-5799.

Corporate 500: The Directory of Corporate Philanthropy. Public Management Institute, 358 Brannan Street, San Francisco, CA 94107; (415) 896-1900.

Corporate Giving Watch, Corporate Giving Directory, and *Directory of International Corporate Giving in America.* The Taft Group, 12300 Twinbrook Parkway, Suite 450, Rockville, MD 20852; (301) 816-0210.

The Sloane Report, P.O. Box 561689, Miami, FL 33256; (305) 251-2199.

The Survey of Corporate Contributions, The Conference Board, 845 Third Avenue, New York, NY 10022; (212) 759-0900.

CHAPTER 6
MANAGING YOUR TIME

WHERE DID THE TIME GO?

How often have you heard, "A home ec teacher's life is like a three-ring circus. There is something going on all the time!" It's true, isn't it? Just consider—committee meetings, lesson plans for four or more preps a day, setting up labs, doing the laundry, shopping for food's lab, correcting papers, curriculum review, meeting with parents, bus duty, cafeteria duty, FHA/HERO, report cards, attending conferences, Back to School Night, staff meetings, working on an advanced degree, professional association activities, helping students after school, making arrangements for sewing supplies for student projects, and on and on and on. The list never ends. To top it off, there are your family responsibilities to consider! Is this the time to say, "Stop the world, I want to get off!" Not quite. What follows in this chapter offers you help to manage time better on the job.

TIME MANAGEMENT
FOR HOME ECONOMICS TEACHERS

If, after work each day, you find yourself saying—"I never seem to get finished. There is always more to do. Where does the time go?"—this chapter is for you!

Dr. Ester McAfee Maddux, Extension Home Economist in the College of Agriculture at the University of Georgia, notes in *How to Find Time . . . to Do the Things You Want to Do:*

> We have enough time to do what is important in our lives. After all, we have 24 hours a day and 168 hours a week. However, we don't all have the same demands on our time. The way we use our time depends on each individual and changes throughout the different stages of the life cycle.

165

We can't store time to use another day. If we waste it today, we can't get it back. It's a valuable human resource that just keeps on moving forward. Since we can't replace, store or reverse time, we either have to use or lose it.

Using time wisely really means managing yourself. You don't actually manage time. You manage yourself with respect to the clock and time. Developing good time management habits means disciplining and controlling yourself.

A Preliminary Time Management Step—Keeping a Log

One way to begin to use time more effectively is to examine in detail how you use your time. To take a snapshot of how you are using your time, complete a daily log of activities. Immediately write down what you do as you go through an entire day. Since any one day may not be "typical," it is generally more useful to keep a record for several different days. Some time management consultants recommend keeping a log every day for two weeks. Choose a length of time that seems manageable to you. Pick days at random or days you feel give you a cross-section view of your job. A sample "Log of Daily Activities" form is provided at the end of this chapter.

If a log is to be worth the effort, it is important that you write down *everything* you do, even minute details. This shows you the number of different things you do in a day and how frequently you repeat them. When logging activities, record the time you begin and end each activity. This is used later to figure out how much time you spend on certain activities that are repetitive.

After you complete a log, analyze how you spent the time you had available. When surveyed, teachers like you listed the following activities as time wasters. How many of your daily activities fall into these categories?

- Paperwork—completing forms
- Too many meetings
- Unclear meeting agendas
- A cluttered desk
- Classroom interruptions via PA announcements and messengers
- Misplaced priorities—working on tasks unimportant at the time
- Changing school procedures requiring learning a new system
- Distributing information
- No set priorities
- Doing part of task and going on to something else
- Postponing decisions
- Insufficient or inappropriate delegation
- Poor filing system
- Overcommitment to outside activities or committees

- Responding to requests for information
- Not carefully reading memorandums or written directions
- Poor communication
- Making decisions without sufficient information
- Overreacting to situations

As you think about this list and analyze your log, did you notice that some demands on your time are caused by forces—people, processes, events, things—not directly under your control? Think of these as "outside" forces affecting your time management. Examples might include telephone calls, mail, meetings, and visitors.

Did you also notice that some demands on your time are related to your style of operation or your personality—how you do, or do not, organize your life? Think of these as "inside" forces affecting your time management. Examples could include how you communicate with others, your planning skills, your willingness to delegate, and your level of procrastination.

ADOPTING OUTSIDE
AND INSIDE TIME FINDERS

Having taken the first step by completing a log, you go about identifying ways to save time by studying the "Outside Time Finders" and "Inside Time Finders" lists that follow. They contain suggestions to deal more efficiently with the outside forces affecting your time management and how to make changes in your lifestyle to alter the inner forces that affect how you use time. As you study the lists, place a checkmark beside those descriptions that seem to describe your situation. Then, go back and determine whether they merit serious consideration for change.

Outside Time Finders

Telephone

The telephone can be boon or bane. It can consume a lot of time. Let's look at ways to use it more efficiently.

1. Have the main office take your calls and answer as many questions as possible. For example, if students are required to have project materials in class by a certain date, let the secretary know about the due date so that he or she can answer questions from parents.
2. When making a call, get to the point and get off promptly.
3. If you know you are a long talker, try standing rather than sitting.

4. Establish telephone hours to avoid interruptions of other tasks.

5. If someone calls at an inconvenient time, don't hesitate to tell them you are busy and will call them back.

6. If you make a complicated call, jot down a brief outline of what you are going to talk about beforehand so you don't wander and spend more time than necessary.

7. School intercoms can be as disruptive as the telephone. Ask the office please not to interrupt your classes but to leave a note in your mailbox and you'll get back to them when possible.

8. If you are the department head or coordinator with a phone in your office next door, and you have an unbreakable "need" to answer those incoming calls, get an answering machine. Set it to pick up after two rings, and most of the time you won't even know the calls are coming in!

9. If you have trouble disciplining yourself about how much time to spend on a call, use a stove timer to set a time limit.

Meetings

Meetings, is there no end to them? No doubt about it, they can be time wasters as well as productive tools. Look at your involvement in meetings to see if any of these suggestions will help you better manage the time you must devote to them.

1. If you are in charge, make sure you provide the participants an agenda with an indication of the approximate amount of time each item will take. Make sure the objectives of the meeting are clear to everyone. If others are to contribute, make sure they are clear about their responsibilities. Have someone keep minutes and distribute them promptly. Assign your paraprofessional, if you have one, to the task.

2. If you are not in charge of a meeting and the chair does not provide participants with an agenda, diplomatically suggest this as a way for the group to be more productive. The same thing goes for minutes.

3. If you are part of a group that seems to wander off track, consider asking someone to monitor the group's attention to task. Have that person give a prearranged signal when the group strays. Make a "T" with hands, for example, to get the group back on task.

4. The same technique can be used to monitor the time spent on each item on the agenda. When the time has been used, the monitor gives the prearranged signal, and the group decides whether to give more time to the topic being discussed or go on to the next item.

5. Start the meeting on time and end it on time. Do not reward negative behavior by waiting to start a meeting until the latecomers arrive. Make it known that meetings will start and stop on time and that latecomers will be responsible for learning what took place before their arrival.

6. If you start a meeting with a social time (beverage and snack, for example), make sure not to run overtime. Have the participants bring their snack to the meeting table. And, if you take a snack break, announce how much time is available and stick to it!

7. At the close of the meeting, summarize what actions were taken and review any assignments for the next meeting. Communicate these clearly.

Mail

The mail keeps piling up at school just as it does at home. Some is junk, and some must be attended to. Here are hints to help you manage your written communication tasks.

1. If a phone call will do, never write a memo. Bureaucrats write memos. Too often they serve only to justify their existence or to make themselves feel important.

2. If you haven't joined the information revolution, get with it! Learn the simple rudiments of word processing on one of your school's microcomputers. The couple of hours you invest in this task will pay great dividends. Standardize as many letters that you must write as possible. Then in the future, all you need to do is change names, addresses, and dates. You can also streamline test, study guide, and substitute lesson plan revision.

3. Don't let your mail accumulate. Set a few minutes aside each day to go through it. Handle each communication only once. If you find yourself looking at the same stuff over and over again, something is wrong.

4. If some of your mail requires a large amount of time to answer, do a little each day or each time you pick it up. Get it done, one step at a time. Always remember what procrastination does for you—it wastes your time; make no mistake about it!

5. Recognize junk mail for what it is—junk! Get rid of it. Use the round file.

6. If your school has a fax machine, send as much of the information people want this way as possible. You can take care of many vendor questions with this technology.

Visitors

Visitors offer a refreshing break in an otherwise hard day on the job or their presence wastes time when you can least afford it. When this happens, you must be able to get rid of them without hurting the relationship. Here are ways to avoid unwanted visitors gracefully.

1. Tell them you are working under a deadline to finish a job. Ask, "Can I get back to you?"

2. Find a quiet place where you can work unnoticed or where it is difficult for someone to interrupt you. Use the department office with the door closed, the library, a conference room, or the nurse's office if it is vacant.

3. When someone approaches you and asks, "Have a minute?" Say something like, "I'm working on my lesson plans, but I can take five minutes. What's up?"

4. If you are sitting down when someone approaches, stand and start to move toward an object in the room, a book or student project, for example, to make it appear you are about to start an important project.

5. If you are working in your office and someone comes to the door, don't invite them in to sit down. Meet them at the door.

Waiting

There are times when you find yourself waiting. Your principal may be a few minutes late for a meeting, for example. Use this time to your advantage. Have something with you to work on:

- A draft of a letter or memo
- Your budget requests
- The agenda for a meeting
- Lesson plans
- Papers to correct

Get the picture? Do something, don't just sit there.

Confusion

If we don't keep our work space organized and arranged in some semblance of order, we waste time looking for the material we need.

1. Keep the papers on your desk organized. Have an "In" and "Out" section along with a "Projects Pending" area.

2. Use a filing system in a desk drawer or a freestanding unit.

3. Try to complete one project before starting another.

4. Tidy up your work space at the end of each day.

5. Use an appointment book on your desk and in your pocket or purse to keep track of daily appointments. Check them at the beginning and end of each day.

Inside Time Finders

Procrastination

If you suffer from procrastination, it will take more than prestidigitation to get you moving. Procrastinators often lack self-discipline. Too often they say, "Oh, I'll do that tomorrow." Result? Tomorrow never comes, and it never gets done. If procrastination is a problem for you, it will take a lot of self-discipline to correct a bad habit. These suggestions may help you:

1. Use a Critical Work Activity (CWA) system to monitor major projects. A CWA system is simply a way to break a project down into the subsets of tasks necessary to complete it. What are the tasks to be completed? Who is responsible for completing the task? When is the last date for completion? This process works for all types of tasks, not just major ones.

2. Mark the deadlines identified in your CWA in your calendar on a date several days before due.

3. Keep "To Do" lists. They should be short, medium, and long-range lists. On the short list, include those things you want to get done tomorrow, on the medium-range list include those due in the next week or two, and on the long-range list those due in more than two weeks. It is helpful to make a list at the end of each day of the tasks you want to accomplish tomorrow. Put it in a highly visible place on your desk and then review it the first thing in the morning when you arrive at work.

4. Most important of all, practice saying over and over again, "Don't put it off, DO IT NOW!" and then DO IT!

Communication

Communication is another of the forces over which you have direct control. When you fail to communicate to others or accept responsibility to understand what is communicated to you, time is wasted. Your time is wasted and so is that of the other person. Practice communicating in these ways:

1. When you give messages or instructions to another person, include the who, what, when, where, and how. Give enough information, be specific, and be sure to include all the details needed to complete the assignment.

2. Speak and write in simple, everyday language.

3. Ask the person to repeat the message or assignment or describe what he or she thinks is to be done.

4. When someone is speaking to you, listen closely to what the person is saying. Don't be preoccupied about what your response is going to be.

5. If you don't understand or know, say so! Do this until you do know.

6. Ask questions if necessary to get the message straight.

Setting Priorities

Some people just don't know how to get started. They seem overwhelmed with the tasks they are faced with. If you are one of these people, try the following:

1. Take your "To Do" lists and prioritize the items on them. Take a few minutes to think about everything you have to do. Arrange the tasks into four categories: those that are urgent, those that are important, those that are urgent and important, and those that can be completed by someone else. Delegate those you can, and concentrate next on the urgent/important by

ranking them in order of priority. Add the remaining urgent and important items to this list in the order you need to get to them. Using a process like this enables you to get started promptly.

Delegating

No one ever said we had to do everything ourselves. Others are just as capable as we are. Delegating tasks to others is one way to work smarter, not harder.

1. Look at your "To Do" lists from the perspective of:
   - What things must I do myself?
   - What things could someone else do?
   - Could they do it as well as or better than I?
   - Is it necessary for me to do this task?
2. Delegate as many things as you can. Be careful not to exploit others or be perceived as shirking your responsibilities.

Saying No

Teachers are in a helping profession and often find it difficult to say no. You have to face it, though—you just can't be all things to all people. Superperson that you are, even you have limits. You need to face the fact that to be more productive under less stress, there are occasions when you must say "No."

1. One way to get started is to say "no" to items that cause you to become overcommitted, that clearly can be handled by others, that are not high on your urgent/important priority list, or that do not help you achieve the goals you have set for yourself, including better time management!
2. Saying no takes practice. If you are just beginning this approach, start with people you know. It might not be in your best interest to start with your boss, for example, but even he or she will understand there are occasions when you just have to say no. Phrasing is very important. For example, you can say, "No, I can't do it," or "That sounds like a worthwhile project, but it will have to proceed without me," or "I'm really interested in your project, but I can't be a part of it at this time."

Help!

Good time managers know they don't know everything, and they ask for help.

1. If you don't know, ask! Why take the time to reinvent the wheel? It takes far less time to go to someone who knows what to do than it does to look it up or learn how to do it.
2. Inservice opportunities are out there. Take advantage of them. Sharpen your skills at every opportunity.

3. Join a network of peers from your school district, other districts, or your professional associations.

4. Become active in your regional, state, and national professional associations.

5. If you are a department head or coordinator, surround yourself with successful people.

Getting Serious About a Time Management Plan

Okay, so you've kept a lot of records, done a lot of analyzing, theorized, and talked with others. Let's get to reality! What are you going to do about it? It is time for action!

Get out your log and the list of time wasters mentioned by others. Arrange these in one column. Second, get the time finders. Arrange them in a second column parallel to the log. Third, get the worksheets, "Where I Can Find Time," that are reproduced at the end of this chapter, and begin to go through your log to see the activity you engage in for each item listed. Note that "Where I Can Find Time" has two parts, one for the external forces and one for internal forces. Write down the finders you identified that might work for you. For example, did you mark the telephone? Do you take calls the main office can handle or calls at any time during the day? Can you restrict incoming calls to certain hours? Do you spend more time on a call than you should? If so, actions to save time can be taken:

1. Have the main office take calls and answer routine questions.

2. Request parents and peers to call between certain hours.

3. Set time limits for your calls. Write these ideas in the spaces provided on the worksheets.

After you complete this list of possible time-saving actions, develop an implementation plan. Use the "Plan of Action" form to list in order of priority the actions you will carry out starting *tomorrow!* As time passes and you figure out the effectiveness of these steps, alter your plan—delete, change, or add other time finder procedures. As your time management skills improve, make this process a part of your style. Every couple of months, engage in an informal checkup, and every two or three years, complete a formal review as described.

Going Further—A Life-Cycle Approach

To go further and develop a life-cycle time management plan, you will need to add some steps to those already discussed.

1. Decide what you need more time for in your life. Make a list of these things. Do you need more time to spend with your family? For recreation?

Physical activity? Social contacts? Complete the worksheet, "What I Need Time For," found at the end of the chapter.

2. Establish a set of goals or reasons for wanting to find more time. These goals are related to your values. Start the process by thinking about what is important to you. A list of important areas of your life to consider is found in the worksheet entitled "What's Most Important to Me?" Go through the list and circle the number that most closely represents your feelings.

3. Next, write down a set of life goals for the areas of life listed on the "Life Goals" worksheet. Remember that goals will vary in length. Short-term life goals are the things you want to accomplish in the next week, next month, or next year. Intermediate goals may take one to five years and long-term goals from five to ten years. Your life should have balance and so should your list of goals. Whatever form you choose, remember to write down your life goals so they include the physical, social, spiritual, mental, financial, career, and family aspects of your life as listed on the worksheet.

4. Make a time management plan. Use the Critical Work Activity system approach. A sample form, "Implementation Plan—Critical Work Activity System" is provided.

Where to Get More Information

1. *When There's Not Enough Time,* by Mary Ann Paynter. Part of a series *Parenting on Your Own.* A practical guide to time management for single parents.

   Write to:

   > Illinois Cooperative Extension Service
   > University of Illinois
   > 122 Mumford Hall
   > 1301 West Gregory Drive
   > Urbana, IL 61801
   > (217) 333-4780

2. *How to Find Time to Do the Things You Want to Do,* by Esther McAfee Maddux. Single copy free.

   Write to:

   > Cooperative Extension Service
   > U.S. Department of Agriculture
   > Attn: Secretary
   > Hoke Smith Annex
   > University of Georgia
   > Athens, GA 30602

3. *Time Management for Teachers,* by Cathy Collins, West Nyack, NY, © 1987, Parker Publishing Co.

TIME MANAGEMENT
LOG OF DAILY ACTIVITIES

© 1993 by The Center for Applied Research in Education

Time Started	Activity	Time Started	Activity
6 A.M.		1 P.M.	
7		2	
8		3	
9		4	
10		5	
11		6	
12		7	

TIME MANAGEMENT
WHERE CAN I FIND TIME?

Part One—External Forces

TELEPHONE

MEETINGS

MAIL

VISITORS

WAITING

CONFUSION

© 1993 by The Center for Applied Research in Education

PROCRASTINATION

COMMUNICATION

SETTING PRIORITIES

DELEGATING

SAYING NO

ASKING FOR HELP

© 1993 by The Center for Applied Research in Education

TIME MANAGEMENT

PLAN OF ACTION

My Time Management Priorities

_____
Name

Priority #	Action
1	
2	
3	
4	
5	
6	
7	
8	
9	
10	

© 1993 by The Center for Applied Research in Education

TIME MANAGEMENT
WHAT I NEED TIME FOR

_____
Name

I would like to have time available to do the following:

1.

2.

3.

4.

5.

© 1993 by The Center for Applied Research in Education

TIME MANAGEMENT
WHAT'S MOST IMPORTANT TO ME?

_____
Name

Value	Not Important	Important	Very Important
education	(1)	(2)	(3)
status	(1)	(2)	(3)
family	(1)	(2)	(3)
home	(1)	(2)	(3)
friends	(1)	(2)	(3)
hobbies	(1)	(2)	(3)
children	(1)	(2)	(3)
money	(1)	(2)	(3)
new cars	(1)	(2)	(3)
personal appearances	(1)	(2)	(3)
recreation	(1)	(2)	(3)
material possessions	(1)	(2)	(3)
love	(1)	(2)	(3)
sex	(1)	(2)	(3)
job	(1)	(2)	(3)
church	(1)	(2)	(3)
health	(1)	(2)	(3)
vacations	(1)	(2)	(3)
pets	(1)	(2)	(3)
other	(1)	(2)	(3)

© 1993 by The Center for Applied Research in Education

TIME MANAGEMENT

LIFE GOALS

_____

Name

I would like to achieve the following goals in my life:	
Physical	
Social	
Spiritual	
Mental	
Financial	
Career	
Family	

© 1993 by The Center for Applied Research in Education

TIME MANAGEMENT
IMPLEMENTATION PLAN

Critical Work Activity System

_____
Name

	What	Who	When
1.			
2.			
3.			
4.			
5.			
6.			
7.			

© 1993 by The Center for Applied Research in Education

CHAPTER 7
GETTING THE HOME EC MESSAGE ACROSS

LOOKING GOOD IN PRINT

MEMO TO: ALL HOME ECONOMICS TEACHERS

FROM: PEGGY CAMPBELL

RE: SURVIVING THE PERILS OF THE WRITTEN WORD

DATE: ANYTIME AND ALL THE TIME!

"It was the best of times, it was the worst of times." "Four score and seven years ago . . . ." "Ask not for whom the bell tolls, ..." "These are the times that try men's souls." Not many of us will be a Dickens, a Lincoln, a Hemingway, or a Paine, but all of us are writers.

And you can count on it: our courses, our proposals, our teaching effectiveness, and the seriousness with which we are taken will be judged by the quality of our writing.

In this chapter you will learn:

1. How good writing and good management go hand in hand.
2. About tools that work.
3. How to write business correspondence, reports, courses of study, teaching materials, and student activity sheets.
4. How to develop your on-the-job writing skills further.

Study this chapter and learn ways to keep your writing on a par with the English department. Compete with the best. Use these pointers, and you will be taken seriously. Home economics will be a keystone in your school's efforts to teach young people the skills they need to survive life after graduation.

GOOD WRITING IS GOOD MANAGEMENT

Your writing will improve by applying home economics management skills to the writing process. Planning, organizing, and evaluating are three key elements of good writing. For example:

1. *Establish purpose.* Lessons have purpose; so does writing. Are you looking for understanding or action or both?

2. *Analyze your consumer.* Is the person to whom you are writing the decision maker or just part of a decision-making group? What are his or her concerns? How much should you say?

3. *Identify the problems.* If the communication deals with a problem, use criteria to isolate it, evaluate, and choose among alternative solutions.

4. *Develop a logical structure.* Home ec teachers break down the tasks they have to complete into the main part and the supporting parts. Good writing is no different. Every communication you make has a main point: the one concept the reader is to remember.

5. *Ask five questions.* Home economics teachers analyze things they do by addressing what, when, where, why, and how. Good writers do likewise!

6. *Develop a first draft.* Good managers develop preliminary proposals and float them out for reaction. Good writers prepare a first draft and float it out for reaction. They choose reactors who are knowledgeable and who will be frank and honest.

7. *Attend to design and style.* Good teachers know that whatever they are packaging, it must be competitive in a world full of attention-getting techniques. Good writers use a compelling format accompanied by effective exhibits. They use bullets, headings, typeface, white space, charts, graphs, and illustrations in their final product.

8. *Revise and proof.* Good managers believe in "total quality." They consistently deliver the best possible product. Good writers do likewise. Every memo, letter, report, course of study, lesson plan, or student activity sheet is carefully revised and proofed before it goes to the consumer. Careful attention is paid to organization, language, and accuracy.

The single most important way to improve writing is to *think* before writing. We need to remember that good things happen because we work to make them happen. Effective writing is no exception.

TOOLS THAT WORK

This section contains a management system to help you consistently produce high-quality written communications.

Writing Checklist

Take several recent samples of memos or letters you've written and use this checklist to analyze them. If you consistently score "no" or "not sure" on an item, it means your writing needs more thought. Continue to study the information that follows to discover ways to improve your shortcomings.

WRITING CHECKLIST

	Yes	No	Not Sure
1. Did this communication get the results you wanted?	___	___	___
2. Was the purpose clear?	___	___	___
3. Were the reader's needs taken into account?	___	___	___
4. Did the reader know the main point in the first few sentences, why he or she should care about what you are saying, and what you will do in the rest of the communication?	___	___	___
5. Can you follow the logic by skimming the topic sentences?	___	___	___
6. Would the reader be favorably impressed with you?	___	___	___
7. Does it have eye appeal?	___	___	___
8. Were the next steps established?	___	___	___

Purpose

Everything you write is written for a purpose: to get approval, to persuade, to be understood, to inform, to be noticed, to document, or to get action. Good managers always clarify purpose. Completing a written statement of purpose before beginning to write is helpful. Try using this:

My purpose is to _____ so that my reader will _____.

Reader Profile

Chances of achieving your purpose are enhanced when you analyze the person(s) who will read your communication. One way to do this is to use a Reader Profile.

READER PROFILE

1. Who will take action on this communication?
2. What question(s) did he or she ask?
3. How well does the reader know me? Do I have credibility with him or her?
4. How much does the reader know about the subject?
5. What is the reader's view on the subject?
6. How well do I know the reader? What is his or her style of operation?
7. If I am asking for a decision, will the reader make the decision alone or as a part of the decision-making process?
8. What question do I want to answer?
9. What do I want the reader to do? Will he or she feel comfortable doing it?
10. Is writing the best approach to use in this situation?

The Beginning

Readers tend to focus their attention on the beginning of a memo or report. If they don't find what they are looking for here, they go to the end. This tendency makes beginnings and endings crucial. To capture attention, focus your beginning on these questions:

1. What is the communication about?
2. What will you tell the reader and how?
3. Why is your communication important?

In addition, you should define your terms, state any criteria, establish your credibility, and set an appropriate tone.

The Ending

The ending should spell out the next steps and bring a sense of closure to your communication. If the document is lengthy, include a succinct summary of your thinking on the subject and reinforce the major points you want the reader to remember.

Charts and Tables

The use of charts and tables is a way to communicate complex information efficiently because "a picture is worth a thousand words." You can use them to dramatize major points or to help demonstrate relationships. Follow these guidelines. Make it a habit to check them off as you plan your reports.

CHART AND TABLE CHECKLIST

	Yes	No
1. The chart or table is easily understood.	___	___
2. Each chart or table conveys only one idea.	___	___
3. Tables are used to consolidate a large amount of data in a small space.	___	___
4. Charts are used to show relationships between variables.	___	___
5. The correct form of chart is employed.		
Line to show changes in variables over time.	___	___
Bar to show relationships between two or more variables at one time or at several points in time.	___	___
Pie to show the relationships among the parts of a unit.	___	___
Diagrams to show parts of a process, structures, or unit.	___	___
6. The headings convey a message.	___	___
7. The exhibits are easy to read.	___	___
8. The exhibits avoid a key by labeling important parts.	___	___

Type Style and Size

With the advent of word processors and personal computers, it became possible to change type style and size easily. You will improve your document's readability if you follow these guidelines:

TYPE STYLE/SIZE GUIDELINES

1. Use only one typeface for most communications. Use boldface, larger size, and occasional italics to add interest.
2. Use italics rarely. It is harder to read.
3. Avoid ornate type. Serif style is best.
4. Use a type size at least as large as that of a standard typewriter. This varies according to type style.

Clarification

Your choice of words can make your writing clearer. To demonstrate this, look at the following list. In the space provided, write a word to clarify the intended meaning. Check the suggested meanings given on the following page.

All of a sudden _____

Due to the fact that _____

For the purpose of _____

In lieu of _____

Ascertain that _____

In order to _____

To implement _____

In the final analysis _____

Similar to _____

Rather vague _____

Regardless of what _____

Inasmuch as _____

Enclosed herewith _____

Hereinafter _____

Listed below you will find _____

SUGGESTED MEANINGS

All of a sudden ————————— suddenly —————————

Due to the fact that ————————— because, due to —————————

For the purpose of ————————— for, so, to —————————

In lieu of ————————— for, instead, in place of —————————

Ascertain that ————————— determine, find out —————————

In order to ————————— to, so —————————

To implement ————————— to start, to do —————————

In the final analysis ————————— finally —————————

Similar to ————————— like, as, same —————————

Rather vague ————————— vague —————————

Regardless of what ————————— despite, even though —————————

Inasmuch as ————————— since —————————

Enclosed herewith ————————— enclosed —————————

Hereinafter ————————— following —————————

Listed below you will find ————————— below is —————————

Spelling

We tell our students, "Correct spelling always counts!" That goes for us, too. Look at the list of commonly misspelled words. Place a checkmark beside each one that gives you a problem. Work to master the correct spelling.

SPELLING CHECKLIST

accept	——	exceed	——	principal	——
accommodate	——	except	——	principle	——
acknowledgment	——	existence	——	privilege	——
acquaintance	——	explanation	——	probably	——
across	——	extension	——	procedure	——
affect	——	February	——	proceed	——
already	——	foreign	——	professor	——
among	——	fourth	——	quantity	——
analysis	——	government	——	questionnaire	——
apparent	——	guarantee	——	really	——
appearance	——	height	——	receive	——
arrangement	——	immediately	——	recommend	——
attendance	——	incidentally	——	reference	——
beginning	——	its	——	referred	——
benefited	——	judgment	——	referring	——
business	——	laboratory	——	restaurant	——
calendar	——	loose	——	schedule	——
canceled	——	maintenance	——	separate	——
coming	——	necessary	——	similar	——
committee	——	oblige	——	sincerely	——
commitment	——	occasion	——	stationery	——
confident	——	occurred	——	strictly	——
conscientious	——	omission	——	their	——
controversy	——	omitted	——	there	——
convenience	——	opportunity	——	too	——
criticism	——	original	——	undoubtedly	——
description	——	paid	——	unnecessary	——
difference	——	pamphlet	——	using	——
disappoint	——	personal	——	volume	——
effect	——	personnel	——	weather	——
eligible	——	possession	——	Wednesday	——
endeavor	——	practical	——	whether	——
equipped	——	practically	——		
especially	——	preferred	——		

Proofreading

Before any writing leaves your desk it should be thoroughly proofread. Check appearance, spelling, punctuation, capitalization, grammar, and content.

SAMPLE FORMATS

This section gives a sample format to use for memos, letters, reports, courses of study, lesson plans, and student activity sheets.

Memos

The first thing to decide is whether to use a modified outline format or simple prose. If the memo is long—more than one page—a modified outline may be best. If it presents arguments, documentation, or large amounts of data, the modified outline is best. Otherwise, use the simple prose method. Format memos as follows:

MEMO FORMAT

MEMO TO:

FROM:

RE: (You can use SUBJECT.)

DATE:

> The **BODY** of the memo is placed here. The body may be done in block style (no indentations to denote paragraphs) or with indentations to indicate paragraphs. If the block style is used, double space between paragraphs to indicate their presence.

Enc. (This indicates there is an enclosure.)

c.c. (This indicates a copy was sent to person listed.)

The memo is signed by initialing your name or signing your name where it is typed in after FROM. Another method is to put a signature line at the end of the memo between the body and enclosures or copies.

Business Letters

The format for a standard business letter is as follows:

BUSINESS LETTER FORMAT

HEADING (Your address, if there is no letterhead)

DATE
Double space

ADDRESS (Include title and company name.)
Double space

Re or Subject: A brief phrase to indicate subject of letter.
Double space

SALUTATION
Double space

BODY

Body of letter. Format may be block style with double spaces to indicate paragraphs, not indents, or semiblock style where paragraphs are indented, generally five spaces. Content of letter should be in this order: (1) purpose of letter and previous reference, (2) discussion, (3) request or summary, (4) personal comments, and (5) transition.

Double space

COMPLIMENTARY CLOSE (Use "Regards," "Sincerely")
Four spaces

NAME
Four spaces

Enclosures: Brief description

Copies: Identify persons receiving copies.

Reports

A common format for reports is the following:

REPORT FORMAT

TITLE PAGE: Gives the name of the organization, title of report, date, and name of writer(s).

EXECUTIVE SUMMARY: Provides an overview of the contents. It should include a statement of the problem, the major criteria, recommendation(s), and some supporting information.

TABLE OF CONTENTS: Lists the main divisions of the report with the beginning page numbers.

BODY: This should include an introduction, the findings of the study, and the conclusions. In some instances, a brief history is helpful.

RECOMMENDATIONS: A list of the recommendations.

APPENDICES AND EXHIBITS: The detailed information used to support the findings.

Course of Study

There are many formats for courses of study. This one is illustrated because it is one required by several states.

COURSE OF STUDY FORMAT

OVERVIEW: A one- or two-sentence summary of the course.

GENERAL COURSE GOALS: One or two sentences stating course goals.

WHO, HOW: A statement of who may take the course and how often it meets. You can add HOW MUCH and list the credit given for successful completion of the course.

PREREQUISITES: A statement of any prerequisites for the course.

INSTRUCTIONAL UNITS:

This section is formatted as follows.

   A. TOPIC: A statement of the unit topic.

      1. Objectives: A statement of objectives.

      2. Learning Activities: A listing of major instructional strategies.

      3. Materials and Resources: A list of instructional tools to be used.

      4. Evaluation: Types of evaluation to be employed.

      5. Mastery Level: A statement of the level of mastery that designates successful completion of unit.

Lesson Plan

Planning is one of the most important management tools home economics teachers use. Its application to lesson plan writing will help ensure total quality in the instructional process. A suggested format is shown here.

LESSON PLAN FORMAT

CONCEPTS: A list of the concepts included in the lesson.

OBJECTIVES: A statement of what the student will learn or be able to do as a result of the lesson.

TEACHER PREPARATION: A list of the activities and materials the teacher must complete or get ready to teach the lesson.

ACTIVITIES: A step-by-step description of what to do during the lesson.

Student Activities

All the admonitions regarding grammar and usage, correct spelling, formatting, and eye appeal apply to student activity sheets. They should represent your best work. A suggested format follows.

STUDENT ACTIVITY FORMAT

NAME OF SCHOOL
TOWN AND STATE

Name: _____   *Date:* _____

TITLE OF LESSON

DIRECTIONS: A statement of directions students are to follow to complete the activity sheet.

BODY: The step-by-step activities students are to complete.

NEXT STEPS: A statement of additional activities students are to complete.

SOME MEMO AND LETTER EXAMPLES

This section contains examples of memos and letters for typical home economics situations.

How to Say "Yes"

```
                              TIPS
1. Rephrase the request.
2. Say "yes."
3. Indicate any action you have taken, if appropriate.
4. Note any qualifiers.
5. State next step.
```

WORLD CLASS HIGH SCHOOL
ANYWHERE, USA

October 23, 19XX

Ms. Mary Smith
Child Development Council
1314 Sheridan Road
Anywhere, USA

Dear Ms. Smith,

In your letter of October 18, 19XX, you asked for student volunteers to assist with child care activities during the Focus on the Family Conference, November 18 and 19, 19XX. I am pleased to be able to say yes to your request. Six students from my Understanding Young Children classes have volunteered to help you.

From our past discussions, you know I am always looking for opportunities to involve students in real-life experiences. Please call me to finalize the details for our participation.

Regards,

Peggy Dougherty

How to Say "No"

TIPS

1. Offer thanks for the writer's interest or agree with some part of what he or she said in the request.

2. State reasons for saying no.

3. State your refusal.

4. Offer an alternative or a suggestion that is helpful to the reader.

HOME ECONOMICS DEPARTMENT
WORLD CLASS HIGH SCHOOL
ANYWHERE, USA

MEMO TO: Ms. Karen Russ, Chairperson

FROM: Peggy Campbell

RE: Request to provide refreshments

DATE: September 15, 19XX

The Home Economics Department shares your interest in making this year's Back to School Night a success. We discussed your request of us to provide cookies for the social hour. Since it does not coincide with our cookie baking unit, it places us in the quandary of having to omit something from our curriculum to provide the time to bake the cookies. After careful consideration, we have concluded that to do so would not be in the students' best interest. Therefore, we cannot provide you with the cookies this year.

Perhaps, as in other years, the PTO can purchase the refreshments, and then ask people for a small donation to help defray the cost.

We are looking forward to an exciting year. Be sure to stop and see us when you make your rounds!

How to Say "Thank You"

TIPS

1. State what the thank you is for.
2. Comment upon the helpfulness/appropriateness of what was received.
3. Be brief and sincere.
4. If appropriate, offer something in return.

HOME ECONOMICS DEPARTMENT
WORLD CLASS HIGH SCHOOL
ANYWHERE, USA

May 5, 19XX

Mr. Christopher Lee
Boal Mansion
Boalsburg, PA 16827

Dear Mr. Lee,

The Home Economics Department appreciates the time you and your staff spent with us on April 14. We found the mansion beautiful and full of valuable educational resources. We plan to take you up on your offer to form a partnership.

After our curriculum review process gets underway, we will identify the areas that would be enhanced by on-site experiences at the mansion. I will be in touch with you in September to set up a time to complete the details of our partnership.

Thank you very much for a worthwhile tour.

Sincerely,

Peggy Campbell

How to Inquire

TIPS

1. Make your request specific.
2. Explain your reason for the request.
3. Offer something in return, if appropriate.
4. State your appreciation for the reader's help.

WORLD CLASS HIGH SCHOOL
ANYWHERE, USA

November 19, 19XX

Ms. Jeanne Alford, Director of Public Affairs
Visa U.S.A.
3125 Clearview Way
San Mateo, CA 94402-3798

Dear Ms. Alford,

Please send me information about the new financial education
program, *Choices and Decisions: Taking Charge of Your Life,* that is
being provided to high schools this fall by Visa U.S.A. I am interested
to see if this material might contribute to the course I teach to seniors
entitled "On Your Own."

Thank you very much for your assistance. I look forward to receiving
additional information.

Sincerely,

Ellen Fitzgerald
Home Economics Teacher
(814) 456-6789

How to Order

TIPS

1. State order clearly and accurately—title, copyright date, model number, unit cost, color, size, quantity, shipping charges, and so on.
2. Include purchase order number if one is included.
3. Include name and address of person to whom order is to be shipped.
4. Give billing instructions.
5. State any deadline after which order is to be canceled.

HOME ECONOMICS DEPARTMENT
WORLD CLASS HIGH SCHOOL
TOLUME, WA 88888

November 5, 19XX

United Textbooks, Inc.
3456 Adrian Way
Prairie View, TX 99999

Dear Sir or Madam,

Please send me 24 copies of GOURMET COOKING, by Marcel Moison, 1991 edition. As per our telephone conversation, the cost is $28.95 each, plus shipping of $2.00 per unit for a total of $742.80. Delivery is to be within 30 days of receipt of order or the order is canceled.

Please ship the books to my attention, Home Economics Department, World Class High School, Tolume, WA 88888, and bill the Mt. Appleton School District, 2345 Scudder Drive, Tolume, WA 88888. Thank you.

Sincerely,

Patricia Millward
(814) 456-6789

How to Make a Complaint

TIPS

1. State specifically what is wrong. Include purchase order and invoice number, if appropriate.
2. In a reasonable manner, explain why you are dissatisfied.
3. State the adjustments or corrections acceptable to you.
4. Set a time limit for action.

Captain Philips High School
Home Economics Department
1456 Pioneer Way
Scotts Run, NE 56789

November 16, 19XX

Kwick Kit Company
4589 Douglass Drive
Dushore, SD 87432

Dear Sir or Madam,

I am writing about order PO#5609-J for 126 sewing kits. We still have not received them.

When I placed the order with you on October 8, you promised delivery in 30 days. Please note our purchase order is dated October 9, 19XX, 38 days ago.

It is urgent that we learn the status of our order. If we do not receive the kits by December 1, 19XX, we will have to cancel the order.

Regards,

Bonnie Benning
Team Leader
(814) 456-7890

How to Return Something

TIPS

1. State specifically what you are returning. If a purchase order and/or invoice is involved, give number.
2. Explain your reasons for return in a reasonable manner.
3. State your expectations for refund or credit.
4. End with a show of appreciation.

PARK FOREST JUNIOR HIGH SCHOOL
HOME ECONOMICS DEPARTMENT
2200 SCHOOL DRIVE
SEMINOLE, FL 09876

April 14, 19XX

Hitech Computer Company
2467 Laser Drive
Universal City, GA 87654

Dear Sir or Madam,

I am returning the enclosed computer software, "Nutrition Analysis," recently ordered on approval. See purchase order #45821.

Upon previewing the software, we found it to be excellent. However, it does not correlate with our curriculum.

Thank you for the opportunity to preview this material without cost or obligation. As you develop new products, please let me know about them.

Sincerely,

Samantha Davis
Department Chair
(967) 456-7890

How to Make a Request

```
┌─────────────────────────────────────────────────────────────┐
│                           TIPS                                │
│                                                               │
│  1.  State your request specifically.                         │
│  2.  Explain your reason for the request.                     │
│  3.  Offer something in return.                               │
│  4.  Show your appreciation for the reader's help.            │
│                                                               │
└─────────────────────────────────────────────────────────────┘
```

MEMO TO: Dr. William Green, Principal

FROM: Patricia Maguire

RE: Central Region Home Economics Association Conference

DATE: January 22, 19XX

I am requesting permission to attend the Central Region Home Economics Association Conference, "Focus on the Family." The conference is being held March 13–15, 19XX, at Kane University.

A major goal of curriculum review this year is to upgrade the Family Living course. I have marked on the enclosed program the sessions I believe are helpful to this process. I am particularly interested in attending the sessions led by Dr. Shirley Grafton, a national leader in the field of child abuse. I believe her presentation and workshop will be invaluable to our work.

It occurs to me that I will learn things at the conference that could be shared with the staff during the inservice session in April, and I will set up a meeting with you to discuss this possibility.

Thank you very much for your consideration of this request. I look forward to your favorable reply.

How to Say "Congratulations"

TIPS

1. State the reason for your congratulations.
2. Link the person to the occasion.
3. State your expectations for continued success.

---

146 Highland Drive
Pulaskie, PA 67543
April 24, 19XX

Mr. Jason Russ
345 King Street
Pulaskie, PA 67543

Dear Jason,

Congratulations upon being selected as a National Merit finalist! You should be very proud to have been selected for such a prestigious award.

I remember our discussions in Senior Foods class when you were concerned about how hard you were working. As I recall, you were sure all work and no play was going to make Jason a "dull boy." Well, the hard work is paying off, and I doubt you're a dull boy!

I sincerely hope Jason Russ becomes a full-fledged National Merit Scholar in the near future. My best wishes for your continued success.

Sincerely,

Peggy Campbell

How to Say "I'm Sorry"

TIPS

1. Apologize at the outset of the letter.
2. Explain what went wrong and your determination not to let it happen again.
3. Close on a positive note.

PORT HURON HIGH SCHOOL
1416 OCEAN BOULEVARD
SEAVIEW HEIGHTS, SC 89765

October 3, 19XX

Ms. Marjorie Dunn
Mount Maple High School
4343 Stewart Lane
Mount Maple, SC 98761

Dear Marjorie,

I am very sorry some of our FHA members were not on their best behavior when they visited your school yesterday. As I mentioned on the phone last night, we had carefully reviewed the guest-host relationship and thought everyone understood what was expected. The fact that a few students chose not to obey the contest rules made an otherwise delightful school exchange less positive than it could have been. I very much appreciated your assistance in getting things settled at the time.

The officers of our club met today and asked me to extend their sincere apologies to you. They will personally contact your officers to apologize and to set a positive tone for our next event.

I am looking forward to seeing you at our next countywide inservice day in December. Please accept my apology for what transpired yesterday. Hopefully, with the additional steps I intend to take, we will avoid a repeat performance.

Sincerely,

Sally Best

How to Get Parental Permission

TIPS

1. Briefly, but clearly, describe the activity.
2. Ask permission last, and provide a space for signature.
3. In some situations it may be necessary to indicate an alternate activity is available for those students who are not given parental permission.

Name: _____ *Period:* _____

Dear Parent or Guardian,

Your son or daughter is currently enrolled in a Home Economics course. During the semester we take walking field trips to Weis Market on Westerly Parkway to research products, gain shopping experience, and make price comparisons.

Please sign below to give your child permission for the semester to participate in these excursions. Thank you for your cooperation.

Sincerely,

Evelyn Wilmartin
Home Economics Department
Wachula Area High School

_____
Parent or Guardian

CHAPTER 8
NEW TECHNOLOGY IN THE HOME EC CLASSROOM

COMPUTERS ARE EVERYWHERE!

We live in the information age, the age of high technology. It is the age of "smart" machines in the home and in the workplace. Home economists are involved in the introduction of high-tech machines into many aspects of family life. With this background, it is natural that they use computers in their classrooms.

This chapter suggests ways for home economics teachers to use a personal computer to increase personal and departmental productivity and to use them in their classrooms for instructional purposes.

WHAT IT'S ALL ABOUT

Microcomputers are "smart" machines that can help you in two major areas of your life. First, they can help you more efficiently complete many of the tasks associated with the teaching process. This is commonly referred to as increasing your productivity. For example, word processing makes many of the tasks associated with writing much easier. You can use a microcomputer to set up a test item bank or a substitute lesson plan bank. You can use it to keep track of your inventory and help you decide when to replace equipment. Second, computers can be used in the classroom for instructional purposes. Students can use them to complete projects involving the manipulation of large amounts of data. For example, they can conduct a consumer survey in the school or community, enter the information into a database, tally the results, and then synthesize the information to reach conclusions. You can let students use a computer to analyze their personal diets and nutritional habits, learn the parts of a sewing machine, or participate in a simulation to solve a family crisis.

A WORD ABOUT SOFTWARE

In addition to a computer, printer, and modem, you need software to perform the applications described in this section. You first must decide whether to purchase a separate software package for each application—word processing, database management, communications, spreadsheet, and filing, for example—or purchase software where these functions are integrated into a single application program—commonly referred to as "(SOMETHING)Works" or "ClarisWorks," for example. A variety of both types are available to choose from. Get a catalogue and do some comparison of features, cost, upgrade policy, and so on. Check with neighboring school districts to see what they are using and ask them why they chose it. Ask to see it demonstrated. Ask if there is a preview policy. If not, purchase your selection on an approval basis so that if you find it does not meet your needs, you can return it. Public domain software is also available. But be wary. Make sure what you choose is free of virus and bugs and will do what you want it to do. Check with your local computer users' group for sources.

PRODUCTIVITY

Word processing, database management, desktop publishing, and telecommunications can help home economics teachers increase their productivity.

Word Processing

What It Is

It is a tool to improve written communication. It uses a programmed set of instructions to let you type in text from a keyboard; make deletions and insertions; move text about the page; revise the text; save it to a disk for future revision, use, or reference; and print out draft or final copies of your work. It frees you from much of the drudgery of writing—erasures, recopying a draft, worrying about penmanship. You can automatically check spelling, use an electronic thesaurus, or check grammar. You can experiment with your writing until you get it the way you want it—and all with a few easy-to-learn keystrokes.

What You Need to Get Started

All you need to get started are a single computer, a printer, and word processing software.

How to Get Started

It's easy. Most word processing comes with a built-in tutorial. This shows you step by step how to produce your first document. If it does not contain a tutorial, ask a friend to tutor you, study the instruction manual, or buy a "how to" book at your local bookstore.

What It Can Do for You

Here are practical suggestions for using word processing in the home economics department.

1. Prepare all your letters, memos, and reports. Save them for reference and possible future use.

2. Prepare student activity sheets. Identify them at the bottom with teacher name, course, and school year. Save the activity sheets to a special disk named "Activity Sheets." Suggest that other department members enter their activity sheets to establish a bank of activity sheets. In this case, save them to a disk named for the course. It is easy to modify the worksheets each year or semester to accommodate the differences in your classes or changes in course content.

3. Prepare invitations to periodic events. Save them to a disk named "Invitations." Each time you hold the event, you need only to change the date and time and then print the new invitation. As your expertise grows, establish a file of names and addresses using database management software. This file would include names of individuals who are always invited: your principal, the superintendent, your department chair or coordinator, and town officials, for example. The list of names and addresses is easily interfaced with your invitations to print automatically an original invitation to each person being invited. Never again will you have to type the same thing over and over! And the best news is that your students can assist you in maintaining the database.

4. Imagine having a pool of questions to use to develop a quiz or unit test. For example, create a data disk called "Gourmet Cooking Tests." Next, create a file for the heading you normally put at the top of your tests. In this file, type the Name of School, Department, Course, a line for Student Name and Period, and the Directions needed to complete the test. Name the file "Heading" or something similar. Each time you prepare a test, you copy and paste this information to the top of the new test. By creating this file, you never have to type in this information again. The next step is to create a file for the test you are writing, for example, "Soup Basics Unit Test." Make sure the name identifies the test. Type in your questions. If there is more than one teacher teaching the same course, have them enter their test items into the same file. This will create a test item bank with more items to choose from. In the future when you want to create a test for the same unit, all you need to do is access the file for the unit, scan and select the items you want, and save them to a new test file. Print a copy, send it off to have the copies you need prepared, and you're in business. You worked smarter!

5. Set up a substitute teacher lesson plan bank. Each time you write lesson plans for a substitute, do it on your computer and save your work to a special data disk you have named "Substitute Lesson Plans." Have other department members do this also. The first thing to do is to create a file, "General Information for Sub." This should include number of classes, time of class, how to take attendance, location of room(s), location of any materials needed, extra duty assignments, a list of helpful students, the name of the teacher to contact for help, and a request for the substitute to leave a written report of what was accomplished. Copy and paste this information at the top of each lesson plan before you print the copy for the substitute. For each plan you write, create a title or file name, "LP—Title of Lesson." Examples might be "LP—Dart Making," "LP—Pastry Demo," "LP—Color Analysis," or "LP—Toy Safety." Type identification information at the bottom of the plan. For example, you might include your name, the name of the course or unit, and date. Can you see what a time saver this bank could be after you have collected a selection of plans? Every time you need a sub, search the data disk for topics that might be appropriate. Copy this file along with the General Information file to a new file. Make any changes in the general information or the lesson plan. Save it as a "LP—(Title of Lesson), Revised" file. Print a copy for the substitute, and once again, you're in business. As a bonus, you can use the lesson plan bank to orient new teachers to your department. By scanning the file, they can get some insight into the topics you teach and how you teach them.

Database Management

If you haven't done much with computers you may be intimidated by the term "database management." Don't be! Here are ways to increase your productivity and save valuable time in the process.

What It Is

Simply put, "data" is factual information. It is the names of students, names and addresses of parents, supplies, for example. A "database" is a collection of this factual information organized to permit rapid search and retrieval. Some examples of databases are your grade book, a telephone book, a library card catalogue, a record of attendance, or a list of names and addresses. "Database management" is a method to maintain and manage the information. You may presently manage your data by hand, with pencil and paper. With a personal computer, you use the computer and database management software to manage it.

What You Need to Get Started

All you need to get started is a computer, a printer, and database management software.

How to Get Started

Like word processing, many database management software packages come with a built-in tutorial as part of the program disk. Those that do not have this feature will have an instruction booklet with the package. In both cases, a step-by-step procedure to create a database and manipulate the data to create different reports is explained. Technically speaking, it shows how to create a file, how to set up fields and create records, how and why to enter information consistently, and how to print a variety of informational reports. Although these terms may be unfamiliar, they are easily learned. You will be up and running in no time.

What It Can Do for You

Here's how it works. If you want to impress your principal with how well you manage resources, set up a textbook inventory system. Create a database file, "Textbooks." Then identify the information to include in the database, for example, School Location, Room Location, Title of Book, Publisher, Copyright, Quantity, Year of Purchase, Condition (Good, Fair, Poor), Replacement Cost. Enter this information. Once the data is entered, you can print out reports alphabetically, by publisher, by copyright date, by condition, by replacement cost, by year purchased, and by any other pertinent information.

With a few keystrokes you can create a list of textbooks that need to be replaced because they are in poor condition or obsolete. You instantly have a "ball park" figure that shows how much it costs to replace them. You can show this list to your principal at budget time to justify your request for new texts. The inventory can be used to determine how many additional books you need due to an increase in enrollment. Database management provides home economics teachers with the information they need to survive in a total quality environment.

Use an inventory system to manage the purchase and replacement of utensils and small equipment, audiovisual materials, computer software, textbooks, and capital equipment. The first thing to do is design a database template—an electronic arrangement of the fields of information you want to manage for each inventory. To help you get started, several examples of templates are given. Keep in mind the design of a template is determined by what information you want to be able to search and the ways you want to sort and retrieve it.

Utensils and Small Equipment		
School:	Room:	Date:
Item:		Quantity:
Date Purchased:		Cost Each:
Condition:		Action:

Audiovisual Materials

School:	Room:	Date:
Title:	Publisher:	Copyright:
Quantity:	Date Purchased:	Cost:
Condition:		Action:

Computer Software

School:	Room:	Date:
Title:	Publisher:	Version:
Quantity:	Date Purchased:	Cost:
Condition:		Action:

Textbooks

School:	Room:	Date:
Title:	Publisher:	Copyright:
Quantity:	Condition:	Cost:
Year of Purchase:		Action:

After your template is designed, enter the information. It must be entered accurately if you are to avoid garbage in, garbage out. In the examples given, "Condition" would be noted as Good, Fair, or Poor or as a number, "3" for Good, "2" for Fair, and "1" for Poor. "Action" means Replace or Add (such as purchasing more copies or items). "Cost" means purchase price unless noted otherwise.

Databases are used to keep track of equipment. You know at a glance how much you paid for it, when you bought it, the condition it's in, how old it is, where it is located, and what action is recommended. You update records annually to reflect current conditions. Then you direct the computer to prepare a printout of the items to be replaced. A simple tally shows how much it will cost. You can ask the computer to prepare a list of textbooks in the order of their copyright dates. This gives a quick assessment of how current the text materials are. You can repeat this process for audiovisual materials and computer software. By searching the records, you can ask the computer to give you a printout of the items you need more of. If you are a department chair, you can get a printout for each school to compare conditions. Does one school have more out-of-date texts than another, for example. As enrollments change, you can determine when additional purchases can be justified.

Database software can be used to set up a capital equipment replacement plan. Capital equipment generally includes only those items costing over $50. Stoves, refrigerators, sewing machines, freezers, washers, dryers, and computers are examples. Some people include groups of items that exceed $50. They group hand mixers, toasters, and irons, for example, into bundles that total more than $50. A typical template for this application follows.

Capital Equipment

School: Room: Date:
Description: Serial Number:
Year Purchased: Cost:
Replacement Year: Replacement Cost:
Salvage Value: Net Replacement:
Condition: Last Update:
Recommended Action This Date:

To complete these records, you need the serial numbers for the items to be listed, a suggested year for replacement, an estimate of its trade-in value, a determination of the item's condition, and a replacement decision. There are instances when the item is not to be replaced in the year originally entered. In this instance, the recommended action would be "DNR," Do Not Replace.

It should be apparent how such a capital equipment replacement schedule can be of benefit. It lets you establish a system to spread out the replacement of your high-cost items rather than have to replace everything at once. For example, you can establish a schedule to replace sewing machines every three years; refrigerators, eight to ten years; freezers, ten years; and computers, three to five years. You can almost instantly get a printout of the items that are to be replaced, items in poor condition, items that do not need to be replaced even though in their replacement year, and the cost of various options.

Increasingly business and industry are demanding improved management practices from schools. If home economists are to keep up with these demands, they should use new technology to manage their resources. The use of database management clearly demonstrates a commitment to increasing productivity and to managing resources efficiently so that tax dollars or tuition monies are spent wisely.

Telecommunications

Telecommunications is another marvel of the computer age. It makes computer shopping, teleconferencing, electronic mail, access to university on-line databases, bulletin boards, and commercial databases such as America Online, CompuServe, and Prodigy commonplace. Huge amounts of information are communicated electronically around the world in a matter of seconds. Home economics teachers can find many ways to increase their productivity and get students involved in the information age via telecommunications.

What It Is

The telecommunications discussed in this book is limited to the process of using a computer to interact with off-site information databases or to communicate with others via a bulletin board or electronic mail. The technology discussed here lets you comparison shop from the comfort of your home or classroom, search a university's library collection for home economics information, or send important hard-copy information to a fellow home economics teacher in Timbuktu. In short, it is instant electronic communication.

What You Need to Get Started

To take advantage of this technology, you need a computer, printer, modem, communication software, and an accessible telephone line. If you plan to use a commercial database like CompuServe, Prodigy, or America Online, you need a monthly budget to pay for the service. In most places you can access these services with a local phone number. If you cannot, then you need to budget money to pay for the long-distance phone charges. If you plan to use bulletin boards, you definitely need to budget for long-distance telephone charges and communication software.

How to Get Started

Getting started is easy. The communications software you get with your modem will explain how to set it up and test it to see if it is working properly. Should you experience any difficulty, the dealer from whom you purchased your modem and software will help you. There is also a technical assistance phone number in your software to call if you have a problem. On-line databases from colleges and universities have directions to access and use their system. Two examples are given in the next section.

What It Can Do for You

Three examples of telecommunication projects to increase your productivity follow. This is a rapidly expanding technology with more applications coming on line almost every month.

1. *Accessing a University Library Collection.* The Pennsylvania State University library system is used as an example. Penn State's system is known as LIAS, Library Information Access System. The system contains information about the books, journals, magazines, music scores, theses, and sound recordings owned by the University. Some government

documents, microforms, maps, and archives are also included. The "CARL UNCOVER" system that searches 10,000 journals published since 1988, with the ability to scan the tables of contents, is a part of LIAS. The ERIC document collection is available from LIAS to individuals registered with the library. By accessing a system like LIAS, you can complete a search to determine what is available on the topic "Home Economics—Balancing Work and Family," for instance. The LIAS system will tell you where the reference is located and whether it is available or when it is due. You can print out a hard copy of the citations you are interested in so that you can follow up at a future date. There is no charge for this service other than the phone call. Check to see if your state university, public library, or a nearby college or university has such a system. If you want to try LIAS, dial (814) 865-4820. After you connect, LIAS will display a brief greeting and directions to get information about how to use LIAS. At the bottom of your screen on the left side you will see a prompt, ⟩⟩⟩, and cursor. Type in title of book, periodical, author, or subject you want to locate or search, press RETURN, and you are on your way. Whether you use this form of computer telecommunications to help you with your degree program or to locate the latest information to use in your classes, you will soon agree that increased productivity doesn't get much easier than this!

2. *Accessing a Free Database of Interest to Home Economics Teachers.* The College of Agriculture at Pennsylvania State University has a database for persons interested in cooperative extension, agriculture, and home economics education. It is called PENpages and is available 7 days a week, 24 hours a day. There are thousands of entries that cover the gamut from complete articles, do-it-yourself guides, workshop materials, instructional materials, research abstracts, up-to-the-minute news, excerpts of articles of current interest, where to go for help, useful ideas and reports about new projects. In addition to the information provided by the University, it includes the national database "The Family and Economic Well-being" and "The International Food and Nutrition" database. You can access this information by following the directions on the next page. Pennsylvania users should call their County Cooperative Extension office to get a Username and local phone number to avoid long-distance charges or write to the College of Agriculture, Computer Services, The Pennsylvania State University, University Park, Pennsylvania 16802, for a copy of *PENpages User Guide.* Out-of-state users should check with their local extension office to see if their state is connected to the database. If it is not, they can use the system, but they will have a long-distance telephone charge. They, too, can write to the University for a copy of the *User Guide.*

If you follow these directions, step by step, you will open up a world of information useful in your classroom and in your personal life.

DIRECTIONS TO ACCESS MAPP/PENpages

1. Your communications software settings must be:

   No parity
   Full duplex
   XON/XOFF handshaking
   8 data bits
   1 stop bit

2. Dial (814) 863-4820 or your local access number. When you see "Connect," press RETURN until your screen displays the prompt *Local >* .

3. Type CONNECT PEN and press RETURN.

4. At the prompt *Username:* type PNOPTA if you are calling out of state or your local Username and press RETURN.

5. The welcome message will be displayed; press RETURN.

6. From the PENpages System Menu type 1 and press RETURN.

7. From the PENpages Main Menu type 1 and press RETURN.

8. Set your communication software to capture text.

9. At the prompt *Enter Keyword:* type KEYWORDS and press RETURN. After all the keywords have scrolled by on the screen, print the list. This list can be used to conduct future searches.

10. From the list select a keyword of interest and type it in the appropriate space to begin your search.

11. At the prompt *Enter choice:* type L and press RETURN. The computer displays the first 12 titles. Press RETURN to see the next 12 titles.

12. At the prompt *Enter title # or choice:* type the number of title you want and press RETURN.

13. To capture information and print a hard copy, follow your software directions.

14. Type @ at any prompt and press RETURN to exit from the Index-Keyword Search.

15. To disconnect from MAPP/PENpages:

    a. From the menu, type O and press RETURN.

    b. At the prompt *Local >* type LOGOUT and press RETURN.

    c. Disconnect your telephone connection.

3. *Commercial Databases.* CompuServe and Prodigy are two on-line commercial databases designed for the general public. They include an extensive selection of services of interest to home economics teachers. For example, you can perform consumer comparison shopping for a wide variety of products from electronics to shoes, to hardware, to home furnishings, to fashions. You can shop for the lowest airline fare and order your ticket for delivery to your home or office within 24 hours. Topics include classified job vacancy listings, financial planning information, news reports, an encyclopedia, entertainment, hobbies, health features, food and cooking features, housewares, movies, travel information, motel/hotel accommodations, and automobile rental anywhere in the country. Of particular interest to home economists are the bulletin boards where members can interact with people all across the country to ask questions and to read about what others are doing to solve contemporary home and family problems. You will need a start-up kit to initiate this technology. These are available at your local computer store or through most mail order vendors. If this is not convenient, call Prodigy at (800) 776-3693 or CompuServe at (800) 848-8199 for information.

4. *Electronic Bulletin Boards.* An electronic bulletin board is much like one you have at school or on your refrigerator door at home except that it is controlled by a computer. It is a place where messages from one person or organization can be posted for others to read and to respond. There are hundreds of them across the country. You can use a bulletin board to ask for information about some classroom problem you are having, to solicit information about a topic, to find persons interested in developing a cooperative unit, or to share a ride to a convention. Because bulletin boards involve long-distance phone calls, they can be quite expensive. If you use bulletin boards at school, you will need to be concerned about security to prevent someone from running up your phone bill. Your local computer user's group can provide you with information about interesting bulletin boards to consider.

Desktop Publishing

Desktop publishing is an offspring of word processing. It lets you produce school newsletters, reports to your school board, customized learning activities, or informational brochures with a professional look possible only at great expense until recently. It allows you to integrate graphics and text effortlessly and to alter layout and typography to achieve these results. The hand-typed brochure with a few cut-and-paste clip art illustrations just doesn't make it any more even though the content may be the same. Desktop publishing won't rescue inaccurate or poorly written material, but it certainly will put impact into good material.

To get started in desktop work, you will need a computer with considerable memory and a hard drive. There is software with more limited capabilities that will run on less powerful machines. You will need a mouse in addition to a keyboard. Some desktop packages include built-in word processing software; others do not. You will want a graphics program, a paint program, and a draw program. In addition, you will need to have access to a printer capable of 300 dots-per-inch resolution. If your work involves the use of text or graphics that is already on paper (a department letterhead or logo, for example), you could make good use of a scanner.

If all this hardware and software sounds overwhelming, don't panic. Many copy centers and local print shops offer desktop services. They offer technical advice and rent the necessary equipment and software to make the hard copy needed to get the work printed. This is a good way to try out the technology before you make a significant financial investment.

As for the software available, educators have found *Publish It Easy!* by Timeworks, *Springboard Publisher II* by Springboard Software, Inc., *Graphic Writer 2.0* by Seven Hills Software Corporation, *Personal Newsletter* by Softsync, Inc., and *The Print Shop* by Brøderbund as reasonable in cost and useful. Other possibilities with more capability and higher cost include *FrameMaker* by Frame Technology, *DesignStudio* by Letraset, *Aldus PageMaker* by Aldus, and *Quark XPress* by Quark.

INSTRUCTIONAL USES OF MICROCOMPUTERS

Microcomputers are being used for instructional purposes by many home economics teachers. They are used for drill and practice, tutorials, presenting text information electronically, conducting simulations, solving problems involving large amounts of data, and increasing productivity.

Basic Equipment

With one or two computers, a printer, and some software, you can establish a couple of learning centers that students can rotate through over a given time period, such as a week. If you can afford three or four computers, you can assign students to teams to work through the learning activities during a single class period. Of course, the ideal way is to be able to use a computer lab where every student has a computer. In addition to computers, you will need a printer, some software, and expendable supplies like printer paper and diskettes. Over time you will want to add more software, a modem, and perhaps a subscription to a commercial database.

In selecting the brand of computers for instructional use, keep in mind the availability of software for educational use. Determine if there is a wide selection. Has it been thoroughly tested? Did it get good reviews? Is service and technical support readily available for the machines? Do neighboring schools use the same technology so that you can establish a network support system? Another point to consider is whether the manufacturer has a special purchase plan for teachers to enable them to buy a machine at the school's price.

Software

You should approach using instructional software in the classroom with some caution. Although there is much glitz and glamour with a lot of bells and whistles, sometimes you have to look long and hard for substance. The bad news is that much of the software is just the talk and test method of teaching done by a computer. Information is presented on the screen, albeit with color, flashy graphics, and sound, and then a list of questions test the student's ability to recall the information. The good news is that some software simulates expensive and complicated laboratory procedures or involves students in open-ended problem-solving experiences that require the higher-level thinking skills of application, analysis, synthesis, and evaluation. The trick is to know the difference between the mundane and the substantive.

Your first step should be to locate resources to help you decide what you will select. *Only the Best Software* published by Educational News Service, P.O. Box 508, Saddle Brook, New Jersey 07665, and *Software for Schools: A Comprehensive Directory of Educational Software Grades K-12* by Bowker, 45 West 17th Street, New York, New York 10011 (telephone: 800 521-8110), are two examples. Several years ago the New Jersey Home Economics Association Computer Committee published a review of software. Copies are available for $6.00 by writing to the committee at 3 Hickory Road, Denville, New Jersey 07834.

A couple of pointers before you get started. Never purchase any software without previewing it. Try to have more than one person preview the software and make an evaluation. If you are a one-person department, your library media person probably has the expertise to evaluate the technical aspects of the software. Ask him or her to help you. Complete some form of formal evaluation sheet and keep it on file. Solicit advice from your associates at professional meetings. Remember, selecting computer software for use in your classroom is often like the fairy tale—you will probably run into a lot of frogs before you find the prince!

There are several other steps you can take to get started on the right foot. Write to Electronic Learning, Reader Service Management Department, P.O. Box 5288, Pittsfield, Massachusetts 01203-9826, and ask for a free subscription to "Electronic Learning." It is published each month during the school year. In it you will find feature articles about applications of computers in the classroom as well as information about the latest in productivity and instructional software. And while you are at it, don't forget *Forecast,* the magazine especially for home economics educators. From time to time it contains reports and articles about computers in the classroom. You can watch for advertisements about new software releases and reports regarding their effectiveness and applicability. Write to Scholastic, Inc., 730 Broadway, New York, New York 10003-9538, for information. *What's New in Home Economics* is a free publication that is published bimonthly

MICROCOMPUTER SOFTWARE EVALUATION

TITLE: _____

PUBLISHER: _____ COPYRIGHT DATE: _____

COURSE: _____ TOPIC: _____

LEARNING TAXONOMY (Check those that apply): Knowledge _____, Comprehension _____,
Application _____, Analysis _____, Synthesis _____,
Evaluation _____. Learning is largely in Affective Domain _____.

DOCUMENTATION INCLUDES: Teacher's Guide _____, User's Guide _____,
Activity Sheets _____.

REQUIRED HARDWARE IS AVAILABLE: Yes _____ No _____.

RATE EACH STATEMENT BELOW: 5 = Superior, 1 = Poor

CONTENT

The content is accurate.	5	4	3	2	1 N/A
The content is free of bias.	5	4	3	2	1 N/A
The content is relevant.	5	4	3	2	1 N/A
The content sequence is logical.	5	4	3	2	1 N/A

INSTRUCTIONAL TECHNIQUE

The instructional purpose is obvious.	5	4	3	2	1 N/A
The program achieves its intended purpose.	5	4	3	2	1 N/A
The program is appropriate for the target audience.	5	4	3	2	1 N/A

TECHNICAL QUALITY

The program is reliable in normal use.	5	4	3	2	1 N/A
The user controls the program's progression.	5	4	3	2	1 N/A
The user receives friendly feedback when needed.	5	4	3	2	1 N/A
Graphics, sound, and color are used appropriately.	5	4	3	2	1 N/A

DOCUMENTATION

The program guide is clearly written.	5	4	3	2	1 N/A
Precise objectives are stated.	5	4	3	2	1 N/A
Useful strategies are suggested.	5	4	3	2	1 N/A

Recommended for Purchase: _____ Yes _____ No

Evaluator: _____ Building: _____

Date: _____

© 1993 by The Center for Applied Research in Education

throughout the school year and contains worthwhile articles about using computers in the classroom. Write to *What's New in Home Economics,* 1429 Walnut Street, Philadelphia, Pennsylvania 19102, or call (215) 563-3501 for your subscription.

Once you have your computers and software, you need to pay attention to how you organize your class for instruction. For example, if you use the team approach where more than one student is assigned to a computer, you will want to make certain all students actually get on the computer. To help with this, keep a log at each machine for students to log in and out or circulate around the room to observe who may not actually be using the computer to complete the assignment. When assigning students to groups, make sure you include those who can work independently with students who need more guidance, good readers with students who have difficulty reading, and so on. The groups should represent a microcosm of the class.

Make sure you have backup copies of your software and your data disks in case something goes wrong. Provide each student with his or her own disk, if possible. Establish some basic rules. For example, you should consider such rules as no food or drink around the machines, use fingers only on the keyboard, take your turn, no games during regular class time, treat the disks properly, and obey the copyright laws.

Computers will not rescue poorly planned lessons. Units and lessons using computer technology should be based upon clearly stated goals and objectives just as all lessons are. The teaching plan should provide for an environment where students learn knowledge, skills, and attitudes across the learning hierarchy. For example, instructional experiences should require students to apply what they have learned in real-life situations, not just recall factual information.

Getting Started

Explaining what computers can do for you in the classroom is a topic big enough for a book in itself. In the space available here, only the content areas for which instructional software is available and a few applications that use software are described.

Typical home economics content areas where instructional software is available include nutrition, parenting, clothing construction, figure analysis, food preparation, personal fitness and health, substance abuse, stress management, independent living, careers, consumer education, child care, family life, home interior design, clothing and textiles, and personal and social development.

To learn about what is available, write to the following companies for catalogues. To survive the swamp of the software selection process, don't purchase software without previewing it and trying it out in your classroom.

PUBLISHERS AND SUPPLIERS OF HOME ECONOMICS SOFTWARE

NASCO
901 Janesville Avenue
Fort Atkinson, WI 53538-0901
(800) 558-9595

EMC Publishing
300 York Avenue
St. Paul, MN 55101

MCE, Inc.
1800 South 35th Street
Galesburg, MI 49053-9688
(800) 421-4157

Macintosh Software Guide
Apple Computer, Inc.
20330 Stevens Creek Boulevard
Cupertino, CA 95120

Cotton Computer Service
Route 1, Box 34
Bristow, OK 74010
(918) 367-3067

Eve Software
Route 3
Sparta, TN 38583

Midwest
Dept. WNHE
4565 Highway 33 West
West Bend, WI 53095
(800) 523-3475

Lawrence Productions
1800 South 35th Street
Galesburg, MI 49053
(800) 421-4157

NASCO WEST
1524 Princeton Avenue
Modesto, CA 95352-3837
(800) 558-9595

Pinpoint Publishing
Box 13323
Oakland, CA 94661

Orange Juice Software
338 South Arch Avenue
New Richmond, WI 54017
(715) 246-3588

Marshware
P.O. Box 8082
Shawnee Mission, KS 66208
(800) 821-3303

The Learning Seed
330 Telser Road
Lake Zurich, IL 60047
(415) 328-5410

South-Western Publishing Co.
5101 Madison Road
Cincinnati, OH 45227

Your Image, Inc.
824 Lafayette Drive
Akron, OH 44303

Scholastic Software
Inquiry Department
P.O. Box 7502
2931 East McCarthy Street
Jefferson City, MO 65102
(800) 541-5513

Two "super" catalogues that contain brief program descriptions from over 100 publishers are available by calling Educational Resources at (800) 624-2926 or CDL Software Shop at (800) 637-0047.

A SAMPLE NUTRITION LESSON

This lesson is not designed to stand alone. It would be used as part of a nutrition unit after students have studied nutrients and their sources, completed a basal metabolism calculation, discussed eating habits, and discussed the Department of Agriculture's Recommended Dietary Allowances and the Dietary Guidelines. In this lesson, students complete a "Personal Diet" Activity Sheet, analyze their diets with dietary computer software to determine the percentage of RDAs, and in conjunction with the Eating Right Pyramid and the Dietary Guidelines, determine if their diet is balanced.

The computer takes the tedium out of this lesson because it replaces hand calculations with automatic computer calculations. Students simply type information about what they ate and how much, and the computer automatically calculates the percentage of RDA. A hard copy is printed for the student to use with other tools to reach a conclusion about the correctness of his or her diet and make any necessary alterations. Used over time, the student can track consumption to determine if eating habits are healthy.

There are numerous dietary analysis software programs. Check back issues of *Forecast* for product reviews. You should carefully preview the software as you would a textbook before investing in it. And now to the lesson.

Personal Diet Analysis

Concepts

Nutrients are used by the body for energy, growth, regeneration of tissue, and regulation of body processes. Calories are used by the body for basal metabolism, for digestion of food, and for physical activity.

Objectives

The students will:

1. Account for 24 hours of dietary intake.
2. Use computer software to analyze the amount of calories, carbohydrates, protein, fat, and cholesterol contained in 24 hours of intake.
3. Revise their diet plan to meet the Recommended Dietary Allowances for carbohydrate, protein, and fat as recommended in the Eating Right Pyramid.

Teacher Preparation

1. Become thoroughly familiar with the dietary analysis software.
2. Organize the class into pairs to complete the computer dietary analysis.
3. Schedule the school's computer laboratory or set up a schedule for students to complete the analysis with your classroom computers.
4. Prepare copies of the "Personal Diet" and "Eating Right Pyramid" activity sheets for distribution to students.
5. Prepare an overhead transparency of the "Eating Right Pyramid."

Activities

1. You will need to introduce this lesson two days before you plan to have the students use the computers to analyze their food intake for a 24-hour period. This is necessary so they can record what they eat. Begin the lesson by discussing what constitutes a balanced diet. Use the transparency of the Eating Right Pyramid to discuss each of the seven Department of Agriculture's Dietary Guidelines for food selection.

   • Eat a variety of foods.
   • Maintain ideal weight.
   • Avoid too much fat.
   • Eat foods with adequate starch and fiber.
   • Avoid too much sugar.
   • Avoid too much sodium.
   • If you drink alcohol, do so in moderation.

   Explain to the students that these guidelines combine reliable nutrition information with dietary recommendations to help them improve their food choices and preparation techniques. The Eating Right Pyramid identifies the amount of food to be selected from each food group. These two tools enable an individual to plan a balanced diet for a well-nourished body. Tell the students they are going to analyze their intake of food for a 24-hour period. To do that they will keep track of what they eat on a personal diet sheet, and then complete a computer dietary analysis of what they have eaten.

2. Distribute the personal diet sheet and show students how to complete it. For example, starting with breakfast, enter orange juice as .5. Emphasize they are to list *everything* they eat or drink, even something they sampled that someone else was eating. In case of a ham and cheese sandwich, or similar items, the ham and the cheese should be listed separately. Show them how to enter the "serving size." It should be entered as ounces, spoons, cups, or pieces. Tell them that partials must be listed as decimals

because the computer program can't read fractions. Make sure all students know what they are supposed to do.

3. On the day students analyze their diets, demonstrate how to use the computer software. You could enter your own information for the 24-hour period. Explain to the students that after they have completed the computer analysis they will make an assessment of how "right" their diet was for the 24-hour period. To do this, they complete the "Eating Right Pyramid" worksheet by entering in the appropriate spaces what they ate along with the percentage of RDA for each. Then they tally the percentages for each group and enter the information in the chart to compute their assessment. Demonstrate how to do this by using the data you obtained from the computer analysis demonstration.

   Have the students complete their personal dietary analysis at the computer. Direct them to print out three copies of their analysis, one to be stapled to the "Personal Diet" sheet, one to be turned in, and one they can take home.

4. When students have completed the computer analysis, have them complete the assessment process. If the software you are using has other features, let the students experiment. Some software includes a weight-loss planner, a menu planner, and label analyzer.

5. When all students have completed their assessments show them how the results they obtained can be used to make adjustments in what they eat. Have the students prepare a revised menu for the 24-hour period they analyzed. Bring the lesson to closure by discussing how this information can be used to plan a healthy diet. Caution them not to reach dietary conclusions on the basis of one 24-hour period. Rather, they should collect data over a two-or three-week time period before making adjustments, and then they should periodically repeat the process to monitor how they are doing.

Note

This lesson could be taught without using a computer. Students would use a nutrient composition chart to determine the nutrients in each food eaten and then perform a mathematical calculation for each one to determine the percentages of fat, protein, and carbohydrates. Students with special needs and mathematics deficiencies may not be able to complete the lesson. They would certainly experience frustration and have memories of the frustration rather than of the valuable concepts involved in the lesson. This lesson demonstrates the use of the computer as a tool that lets the student synthesize information, complete an analysis, evaluate the results, and apply the new information to make changes in personal decisions. These higher-level thinking skills might never have been reached without the computer because of the student's inability to perform basic mathematical functions successfully.

© 1993 by The Center for Applied Research in Education

Name: _____ **Period:** _____

PERSONAL DIET ACTIVITY SHEET

Directions: List each food you have eaten in a 24-hour period. Begin with breakfast and list everything. Enter the serving size as a whole number or decimal.

Food	Serving Size ·

continue on the other side

Name: _____ **Period:** _____

EATING RIGHT PYRAMID

Directions: In the spaces provided, list the foods you ate and enter your dietary analysis data from the computer printout. When this is complete, enter your totals in the chart below and calculate the difference. On reverse side of this activity sheet, revise what you ate so that your intake falls within the recommended daily allowance.

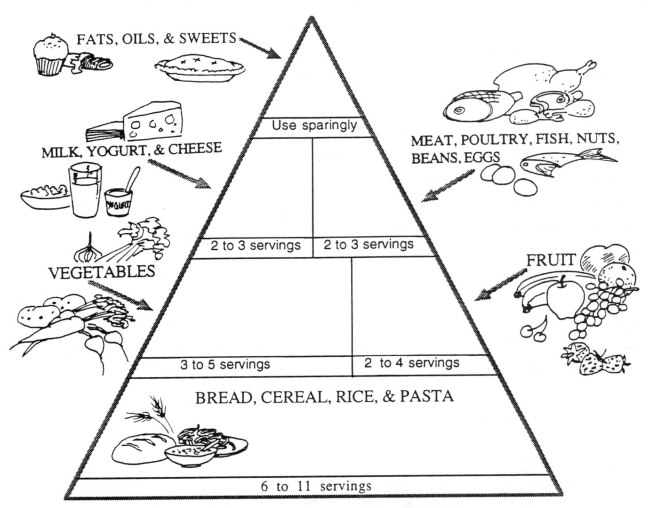

WHAT DID YOU EAT? FILL IN THE PYRAMID.

© 1993 by The Center for Applied Research in Education

	Actual	Recommended	Difference + or −
Protein		12%	
Fat		30%	
Carbohydrates		58%	

Personal Analysis

PART THREE
COPING WITH CONTEMPORARY ISSUES

- *Reviewing and Updating Your Program*
- *Selling Your Program Through Public Relations*
- *Politics and Your Program's Survival*
- *Getting Along with People*

HOME ECONOMICS FOR A BETTER WORLD

229

CHAPTER 9
REVIEWING AND UPDATING YOUR PROGRAM

THE CURRICULUM CHALLENGE—STAYING CURRENT

Like it or not, home economics is battling for its share of student enrollment and the resources needed to conduct a credible program to meet students' needs in the 1990s. To survive, you will need to engage in a curriculum review process, or you will fall by the wayside as other subject areas entice your students away from you or the school board diminishes your fiscal support in favor of other, more dynamic, up-to-date curricular offerings.

Should you accept the challenge to keep current, you will recognize there are three questions that make a systematic curriculum review necessary.

1. Am I certain the content of my courses is current and meeting the needs of students in my community?
2. Am I using the political process to gain support for home economics in my school?
3. Am I using curriculum review as a way to renew my commitment to home economics and its role in preparing young people for adult life?

The rapidly changing knowledge base that impacts upon the home economics curriculum is mind boggling: nutrition research, food technology, changing families, child development, genetics, and stress management at home and at work, among others. Never has it been more important for home economists to address systematically the Perkin's imperatives, which are:

- Managing individual and family resources.
- Managing home and work responsibilities.
- Improving responses to family crises.

- Strengthening parenting skills.
- Improving nutrition.

We need to modernize curriculum content and teaching methods. We cannot rely on a textbook-centered curriculum that all too frequently is outdated.

A thorough curriculum review offers you the opportunity to have a respected place in the school community. It gives focus and direction to your efforts. You will feel good about yourself and the importance of your work. You can concentrate on the important curricular needs of students served by home economics.

Completing a systematic review allows you to use information and the political process to influence the school district power brokers—the administration and school board. Your report to them will be a summary of the facts, not an amalgamation of opinions. Through the straightforward approach outlined in this chapter, you can substantiate your recommendations regarding the programs necessary to provide young people with the knowledge and skills to prevent them from becoming at risk when they go off on their own, which is the major mission of home economics.

HOW TO DO A PROGRAM REVIEW

The process for doing a program review is divided into four sections:

- Getting started
- Collecting the data (steps 1–11)
- Writing the report
- Getting the recommendations implemented

Reproducible worksheets that will help you in this process are grouped at the end of this chapter for easy accessibility.

Getting Started

Develop a Critical Work Activity (CWA) system as a management tool to guide your work and keep you on track. A CWA is a list of the tasks to be completed, the designation of the person(s) responsible, and an assignment of the last date for completion (LDC). Begin your CWA work by brainstorming a list of the tasks required to get you from where you are to where you want to go. When this is complete, arrange the tasks in a chronological list from the first task to be completed to the last.

A typical CWA would look like this.

CHALLENGE JUNIOR-SENIOR HIGH SCHOOL
Staying Current, Pennsylvania

Critical Work Activity System
Home Economics Curriculum Review

Task	Who	LDC
1. Identify elements of curriculum review process	Dept. Chair	8/30/XX
2. Explain process to staff	"	9/10/XX
3. Assign tasks to staff	"	9/10/XX
4. Write to the U.S. Office of Education (USOE) and state department of education for list of exemplary programs	"	9/30/XX
5. Secure copies of Middle States evaluative criteria	"	10/5/XX
6. Identify consultant	Staff	10/21/XX
7. Contract consultant	Administration	10/31/XX
8. Review info from USOE	Staff	11/7/XX
9. Complete self-evaluation	Staff	11/10/XX
10. Outline specific tasks for consultant	Staff	11/10/XX
11. Arrange on-site visit	Dept. Chair	11/15/XX
12. Forward self-evaluation and basic information about program to consultant	Dept. Chair	11/18/XX
13. Order texts for preview	Dept. Chair	12/5/XX
14. Assign selected staff to review new instructional materials	Dept. Chair	1/10/XX
15. Complete consultant visit	Consultant	1/15/XX
16. Review consultant's findings	Staff	1/31/XX
17. Prepare draft "what is supposed to be"	Staff	2/15/XX
18. Complete draft proposed home ec 7–12 program	Dept. Chair	2/28/XX
19. Prepare budget proposed program	Staff	2/28/XX
20. Prepare CWA to achieve proposed program	Dept. Chair	3/5/XX
21. Review/finalize CWA	Staff	3/10/XX
22. Prepare final report for administration	Dept. Chair	3/25/XX
23. Submit final report to school board	Dept. Chair	4/10/XX
24. Board action	School Board	6/30/XX
25. Revise/update implementation CWA	Dept. Chair	7/31/XX
26. Implement program	Staff	9/1/XX

Collecting the Data

Make a decision about the types of data you want to collect to illustrate best the home economics mission in your school. Some suggestions follow. *Remember that reproducible worksheets and examples are provided for you at the end of this chapter.*

1. Prepare a statement that summarizes the content of the five subject matter areas that make up the major mission of home economics. See the sample "Focus of Home Economics Programs."

2. Summarize your course offerings by major subject matter area. Put results in chart form. See reproducible master titled "Home Economics Program Review: Course Offerings by Major Subject Matter Area."

3. Study your school's enrollment and home economics course enrollment for at least three years. Summarize your findings in table form—one for home economics enrollment trends, one for home economics course enrollment by sex and school year, and one by enrollment in courses that stress the five major areas of home economics. A reproducible worksheet is provided for each of these areas. They are headed: "Table A: Home Economics Enrollment Trends," "Table B: Home Economics Course Enrollment by Sex and School Year," and "Table C: Student Enrollment in Human Growth and Development/Management and Consumerism/Nutrition/Housing and Furnishings/Textiles and Clothing. The directions for completing these forms are noted on the bottom of the worksheets.

4. Complete a departmental self-evaluation using a document like the one used in the *Evaluative Criteria, Sixth Edition* (published by the National Study of School Evaluation, 5201 Leesburg Pike, Falls Church, VA 22041). If your school belongs to the Middle State, New England, North Central, Northwest, Southern or Western Association, your principal probably has a copy of the criteria. Or, if your school has gone through the evaluation process recently, dust off the evaluation form, review it, and use the findings in this effort.

5. Use a consultant who is respected in home economics and has a practical approach to teaching. Esoteric and theoretical are two descriptors that should not dominate the list of qualifications of the consultant you select. Have the consultant review your curriculum and your facilities and survey your students and their parents about attitudes toward and impressions of the quality of your program. If it is not possible for you to employ a consultant, contact your state department of education, your state university, or a college teacher who is well respected in the profession. It is a good idea to conduct parent/student surveys as a part of the consultant's work. The results will provide information about what students and parents think about home economics in general and your program in particular. Too often, we assume we know how others perceive us. Using a survey, though time consuming, gets you the facts. If you use a consultant, this section of

the report could be titled "Consultant's Findings." If you do not use a consultant, but conduct a survey, call this section "Parent/Student Perceptions."

6. Prepare a chart that shows the breakdown of the types of students electing home economics in grades 9–12. By analyzing these data, you will get a profile of which students are electing your courses—college bound, vocationally bound, or others. The format you use for organizing this information will be dependent on how your school's curriculum is organized. To start, get a copy of the schedule for each student who elected home economics. Second, decide on the descriptors— college prep, general, or some other scheme. Make a tally by course and descriptor. If your school has a data processing department that completes student scheduling, check with the staff there to see if they can provide you with the summary you need. This information will help you discover the types of students electing your courses and may provide insight into why more are not—schedules too full, graduation requirements, or other problems. The worksheet "Table D: Home Economics Student Profile Grades 9–12" can be used to summarize this information.

7. Complete an analysis of your school's curriculum to determine if there are other departments offering courses that make a significant contribution to planned learning in the areas of managing individual and family resources, managing home and work responsibilities, improving responses to family crises, strengthening parenting skills, and improving nutrition. This information will enable you to determine where there is duplication and possibilities for interdisciplinary teaching. To get this information, talk with teachers in other departments. Show them your course descriptions, scope and sequence, and courses of study. Make a list by home economics course of other department's courses teaching the same things you are teaching.

8. Complete a thorough review of the literature to illustrate the sweeping changes in American life that impact what young people need to know to enjoy quality of life without being at risk. Seek out descriptions of the "new" home economics and how it can prepare young people for success in the twenty-first century. Be sure to include *Educational Leadership, Home Economics Trends Newsletter,* and *Forecast for Home Economics* among the resources you search. Although *Illinois Teacher of Home Economics* ceased publication in 1991, search back issues for usable information.

9. Preview new textbooks, filmstrips, videos, resource books, and computer software, and evaluate your current holdings. Prepare a brief summary of the status of these holdings: Are they adequate, up to date, relevant?

10. If your school district has a mission statement that outlines instructional goals, make a matrix to show where home economics courses make a direct contribution to district efforts to achieve each of the goals. See "Table E: The Interface of District Instructional Goals and Home Economics Curriculum" for an example of how this can be done.

11. Complete a study of the type and magnitude of the problems individuals and families are having in your community. Contact your local human services planning office to obtain a copy of their latest study. This type of information is a real attention getter! Your school board will not be able to turn its back on the facts. Show how your department helps ameliorate some of your community's problems. See samples in Tables F, G, and H.

Writing the Report

The process just outlined encourages you to use facts and research, a scholarly process, not hearsay and opinion. The report of your findings is the culmination of your work and should be no less scholarly than was your study. Scholarly report does not mean long and dull or dry and tedious. It means interesting, eye-catching, factual, easy to follow, grammatically correct, and representative of your best work.

A report should include the following elements:

1. Introduction—an overview of the curriculum review process, the purpose, procedure, and outcomes.
2. The Process—a detailed description of each step you used in the curriculum review process.
3. The Data—include all the information found during the data collection process, for example,
   • Home Economics Course Content
   • Enrollment Data
   • Self-evaluation
   • Consultant
   • "Types" of Students
   • Curriculum Analysis
   • Review of the Literature
   • Instructional Materials
   • Mission Interface
   • Local Problems

Here you report the data without comment. Generally there is a brief summary statement about what is contained in the section. For example, for "Enrollment Data," you might say, "The following tables contain enrollment information for the school years 19XX through 19YY. Table A shows student enrollment and home economics enrollment statistics for the three-year period mentioned. Table B shows the enrollment in home economics courses by sex and total enrollment for the time period. Table C shows student enrollment in home economics courses that contain major elements of Human Growth and Development/Management and Consumerism/Nutrition/Housing and Furnishings/Textiles and Clothing."

4. The Conclusions—present the conclusions in the order in which the data was presented. There should be conclusions for each step of the review process. For an example of how the "Conclusions" section might look, see the "Conclusions" sample at the end of this chapter. Note how the use of graphics improves the appearance by showing the information in an eye-catching way.

5. The Recommendations—include only recommendations that can be substantiated by the findings/conclusions based on the data collected. In your enthusiasm, avoid the temptation to go beyond what your data can support. Include a budget for the dollars and the time it will take to implement each recommendation. See the example of recommendations at the end of this chapter.

Getting the Recommendations Implemented

A "Next Steps" section should include a list of the next steps your department will take to make the recommendations operational. An example of such a list is found at the end of this chapter. It is helpful to your cause to translate that list into a Critical Work Activity system explained at the beginning of this chapter. An example follows the "Next Steps" list. By showing your administration where you want to go and how you propose to get there, you demonstrate your seriousness of purpose. This instills in others the confidence you need to get the approval to go ahead.

Getting changes made to improve course offerings or make conditions better in your department requires you to "play politics." Some refer to this as "exercising leadership." Call it what you will, there are things you can do to improve the chances of having your recommendations accepted. Chapter 11 suggests some ways to do this.

YOU MAY REST ON THE OARS OF YOUR PAST ACCOMPLISHMENTS OR
YOU MAY ACCEPT THE CHALLENGE TO KEEP CURRENT.

THE CHOICE IS UP TO YOU!

FOCUS OF HOME ECONOMICS PROGRAMS

Home economics programs need to reflect the interrelationships of the five subject matter areas that lead to the improvement of the home and family life. These five subject matter areas are:

Foods and Nutrition

This area prepares individuals to understand the principles of nutrition; the relationship of nutrition to health and well-being; the selection, preparation, and care of food; meal management to meet individual and family food needs and patterns of living; good economics and ecology; and the optimal use of the food dollar.

Human Growth and Development

This area prepares individuals to understand the nature, function, and significance of human relationships within the family and with other individuals. It includes instruction in various family living conditions, establishment and maintenance of relationships; and preparation for marriage, parenthood, and family life. Instruction emphasizes the uniqueness of families and individuals, the development and socialization of the individual, and meeting the needs and interests of individual and family members.

Management and Consumerism

This area prepares individuals to understand the values, needs, wants, goals, and resources that enable individuals to make rational decisions and to understand the establishment and maintenance of a satisfying home and family life. It includes instruction in budgeting, credit, investments, consumer rights and responsibilities, and the organization of activities in the home as a means of successfully combining the roles of homemaker and wage earner.

Housing, Furnishings, and Equipment

This area prepares individuals to understand the physical, psychological, and social influences on complex decisions for creating a desirable living environment. It includes instruction in the human and environmental factors influencing the form and use of housing, the varied types of housing, costs, exterior and interior design, and the selection of home furnishings and equipment that improve living space according to individual and family needs.

Textiles and Clothing

This area prepares individuals to understand the social, psychological, and physiological aspects of clothing and textiles; the nature, acquisition, and use of clothing and textile products; the selection, construction, maintenance, and alteration of clothing and textile products; and the effect of consumer choices on the individual and family as well as the clothing and textile industries.

Ready-to-Use Program Forms (pp. 239–248)

HOME ECONOMICS PROGRAM REVIEW

Course Offerings by Major Subject Matter Area

Area	Course	Year/Grade
Foods and Nutrition		
Human Growth and Development		
Management and Consumerism		
Housing, Furnishings, and Equipment		
Textiles and Clothing		

© 1993 by The Center for Applied Research in Education

Table A
HOME ECONOMICS ENROLLMENT TRENDS
19_____ to 19_____

School Year	Student Enrollment				Home Economics Enrollment			
	Grade 7	Grade 8	Grades 9–12	Total	Grade 7	Grade 8	Grades 9–12	Total
19_____								
19_____								
19_____								

Table A

1. Enter the school years included in your study in the title.
2. List the school years in the first column.
3. Enter the student enrollment figures in the spaces under "Student Enrollment."
4. Enter the home economics enrollment in the space above the diagonal line and the percentage that figure is of the enrollment in the space below the diagonal line in the column headed, "Home Economics Enrollment." To calculate the percentage, divide the home economics enrollment by the student enrollment. Enter the result to the nearest whole percentage.

© 1993 by The Center for Applied Research in Education

Table B
HOME ECONOMICS COURSE ENROLLMENT
BY SEX AND SCHOOL YEAR
19_____ to 19_____

Course	19____			19____			19____		
	M	F	T	M	F	T	M	F	T
Total									

© 1993 by The Center for Applied Research in Education

Table B
1. Enter the school years included in the study in the spaces provided in the title.
2. List the courses in the column headed "Course."
3. Enter the enrollment for each course by sex for the years included in Table B.
4. Compute the totals and enter them in the bottom spaces.

Table C
STUDENT ENROLLMENT

Human Growth and Development/Management and
Consumerism/Nutrition/Housing and Furnishings/Textiles and Clothing

19____ to 19____

School Year	Human Growth			Management			Nutrition			Textiles/ Clothing			Housing/ Furnishings			Total School Enrollment
	M	F	T	M	F	T	M	F	T	M	F	T	M	F	T	
19____																
19____																
19____																
Three-year average																

Table C

1. Enter the number of males and females enrolled in your courses that include a major amount of content in the subject matter area for each column. Study the statement you wrote that summarizes the mission of home economics to where a course's enrollment should be assigned.

2. Compute the three-year average for each column and enter the result in the space at the bottom above the diagonal line. In the space below the diagonal line, enter the percentage. For example, under Human Growth, the percentage of males for the three-year period would be calculated by dividing the three-year average male figure by the three-year average total enrollment.

© 1993 by The Center for Applied Research in Education

© 1993 by The Center for Applied Research in Education

Table D

HOME ECONOMICS STUDENT PROFILE GRADES 9–12

19 _____ to 19 _____

Home Ec Course													
Total													

Table E
THE INTERFACE OF DISTRICT INSTRUCTIONAL GOALS AND HOME ECONOMICS CURRICULUM

Course	Goal 1	2	3	4	5	6	7	8	9	10	11	12
Life Arts	X		X		X			X				X
Home Economics	X		X		X		X	X	X	X		X
Baking Basics	X		X		X			X				X
Sewing and More	X		X					X				X
Specialty Foods	X		X		X			X				X
Understanding Young Children	X		X					X	X	X	X	X
Independent Living	X		X				X	X	X	X	X	X
Family Living	X		X				X	X	X	X	X	X
Nutrition	X		X		X		X	X		X	X	X
Baking with a Gourmet Touch	X		X		X			X				X
Cultures and Cuisine	X		X	X	X			X	X			X
Creative Clothing	X		X					X				X
Needlecraft	X		X					X				X
Senior Foods	X		X		X			X				X

Note: X indicates the course content has direct application to the goal.

A copy of the Instructional Goals is on the following page.

© 1993 by The Center for Applied Research in Education

INSTRUCTIONAL GOALS

1. Quality education should help every student acquire communication skills of understanding, speaking, reading, and writing. (Primary)

2. Quality education should help every student acquire skills in mathematics. (Primary)

3. Quality education should help every student develop analytical thinking skills. (Primary)

4. Quality education should help every student acquire knowledge of different cultures and develop skills in and an appreciation for the arts and humanities. (Primary)

5. Quality education should help every student acquire knowledge, understanding, and appreciation of science and technology. (Primary)

6. Quality education should help every student learn the history of the nation; understand its systems of government and economics; and acquire the values, skills, and attitudes necessary for responsible citizenship. (Primary)

7. Quality education should help every student acquire the knowledge and attitudes necessary to promote the preservation of the environment and to conserve limited resources. (Supportive)

8. Quality education should help every student develop self-understanding and a feeling of self-worth. (Supportive)

9. Quality education should help every student understand others and appreciate the worth of all people. (Supportive)

10. Quality education should help every student acquire the knowledge, skills, and attitudes necessary for successful personal and family living. (Supportive)

11. Quality education should help every student acquire knowledge and develop practices necessary to maintain physical and emotional well-being. (Supportive)

12. Quality education should help every student acquire the knowledge, skills, and attitudes necessary to become a self-supporting member of society. (Supportive)

© 1993 by The Center for Applied Research in Education

Table F
KEY RESPONDENT SURVEY:
MOST FREQUENTLY CITED PROBLEMS FOR CHILDREN

Rank	Target Problem	Specific Problem Elements
1	Child responsibility, neglect, or abuse	Lack of parental care or control (basic needs, education, emotional needs) Physical harm to child caused by acts or omissions by parents or guardians Absence of parent(s) due to death, desertion, or divorce
2	Food	Not eating the right foods Inadequate food supply Lack of information about nutrition
3	Medical/dental/health	Costs of health check-ups and care Inability to find a doctor or dentist who will accept medical assistance Inadequate health care Lack of knowledge of proper health care and hygiene Lack of health insurance coverage Lack of dental services
4	Family conflicts	Absence of parent from home due to death, desertion, or divorce Inadequate parenting skills Inadequate communication between parent and child
5	Shelter	Lack of housing for low-income families with children Living in substandard housing
6	Clothing	Inadequate clothing for seasonal and weather changes Lack of appropriate clothes for school
7	Self-concept and personal growth	Lack of self-confidence or self-esteem Lack of skills to get along with other people

© 1993 by The Center for Applied Research in Education

Table G
KEY RESPONDENT SURVEY:
MOST FREQUENTLY CITED PROBLEMS FOR YOUTH

© 1993 by The Center for Applied Research in Education

Rank	Target Problem	Specific Problem Elements
1	Family conflicts	Inadequate communication between parent and child Parent/child conflicts Absence of parent from home due to death, desertion or divorce Inadequate family standards and expectations Inadequate parenting skills No supports for parents with problematic children
2	Drug/alcohol use	Illegal "street" drug use Alcohol abuse Lack of drug and alcohol education and information Lack of knowledge in identifying drug and alcohol misuse Lack of drug and alcohol counseling and rehabilitation
3	Self-concept and personal growth	Lack of self-concept or self-esteem Lack of emotional or social maturity Lack of motivation or self-improvement Lack of skills to get along with other people
4	Youth behavioral problems	Ungovernable or uncontrollable behavior Truancy Loitering Running away
5	Unprepared for child rearing/ family planning	Teenage problem pregnancy Lack of parenting skills Inadequate sex education and a lack of knowledge regarding birth control, pregnancy, and family planning Cannot cope emotionally, physically, or mentally with the pregnancy Unwanted children
6	Education	Inadequate reading, writing, and math skills Inadequate language and communication skills Formal education system does not adequately prepare one for jobs or further education Lack of alternative education opportunities
7	Child responsibility, neglect, or abuse	Lack of parental care or control Failure to provide basic educational or emotional needs Absence of one or both parents Physical harm to youth by parents or guardian

Table H
KEY RESPONDENT SURVEY:
MOST FREQUENTLY CITED PROBLEMS FOR ADULTS

Rank	Target Problem	Specific Problem Elements
1	Employment	Lack of jobs Current job openings not matching job seekers' training or skills Inadequate training and retraining Cost of living requiring both parents or a single parents to work Inadequate assistance or guidance in locating a job Lack of supervised or limited employment opportunities for mentally limited persons
2	Income	Insufficient money to pay routine bills Insufficient money to pay utility bills Insufficient money to buy life necessities (food, shelter, and clothes)
3	Marital conflicts	Inadequate communication between husband and wife Divorce or separation Spouse abuse
4	Drug/alcohol use	Alcohol abuse Prescription drug misuse Illegal "street" drug use Lack of knowledge in identifying drug or alcohol misuse
5	Family conflicts	Inadequate parenting skills Inadequate communication between parent and child Parent/child conflicts Overwhelmed with child caring responsibilities
6	Basic life skills	Budgeting money Household management Lack of knowledge about tax returns, rent or mortgage rebates, mortgages or loans Functional illiteracy (reading and writing skills)
7*	Self-concept and personal growth	Lack of self-confidence or self-esteem Lack of emotional or social maturity Lack of motivation for self-improvement Lack of skills to get along with other people
7*	Unprepared for child rearing	Lack of parenting skills Unwanted children Can't cope emotionally or physically with pregnancy Inadequate sex education or knowledge regarding birth control, pregnancy, and family planning

*Both problem areas received equal support—a tie for seventh.

© 1993 by The Center for Applied Research in Education

CONCLUSIONS

The Home Economics Department, after carefully studying the data presented in the former section of this report, has reached the following conclusions. The conclusions are given in the order in which the data was presented.

1. HOME ECONOMICS COURSE CONTENT

An examination of the course matrix information shows that State College area home economics courses do include subject matter from the five areas identified by experts in the field as most appropriate for secondary school students. These areas are Foods and Nutrition; Human Growth and Development; Management and Consumerism; Housing, Furnishings, and Equipment; and Textiles and Clothing. Foods and Nutrition information is found in courses at all grade levels; Human Growth and Development is found at grades 8–12; Management and Consumerism at grades 8–12; Housing, Furnishings, and Equipment at grades 11–12; and Textiles and Clothing at grades 7–12. It can be concluded that the home economics program is well rounded, albeit with one or two areas that need more emphasis.

It is also important to note that because home economics is only required at the seventh-grade level, large numbers of students may and do graduate without the benefit of planned learning experiences in Human Growth and Development; Management and Consumerism; and Housing, Furnishings, and Equipment. It appears the State College Area School District makes little or no contribution to the acquisition of the knowledge and the skills needed to perform the basic life skills needed for daily living outside of an individual's work life.

2. ENROLLMENT DATA

The enrollment data was transposed into graphic form to more clearly illustrate some interesting findings.

For example, the following graph clearly illustrates that home economics enrollment is holding steady even in the face of decreasing secondary population and the increased competition due to additional graduation requirements.

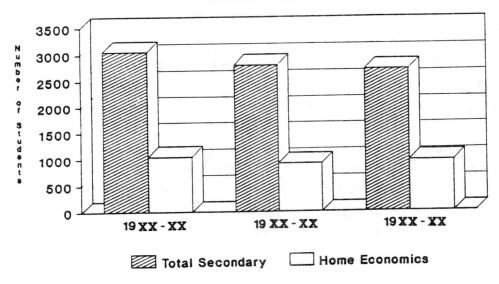

HOME ECONOMICS
Enrollment Trends
Grades 7–12

© 1993 by The Center for Applied Research in Education

RECOMMENDATIONS

After completing the curriculum review enumerated on the previous pages, the home economics department makes the following recommendations:

1. The Understanding Young Children (UYC) course is a semester course open to males and females, grades 9–12. The content of the course is currently confined to knowledge about child growth and development. The Children's Room, operated by the Child Development Council at the Senior High School, offers very limited opportunity for UYC enrollees to practice their "book" knowledge through direct contact with young children. Thus the result is like reading about how to swim, but never having the opportunity to go into the water.

   The department believes it is imperative that young people be given the opportunity to learn to manage individual and family resources, manage home and work responsibilities, improve responses to family crises, strengthen parenting skills, and improve nutrition. These skill areas are an important part of the Understanding Young Children course. The department believes these skills can best be learned through practice in a controlled environment under the guidance of skilled child care practitioners.

   It is for this reason that the Home Economics Department recommends that a full-time child care center be established under the jurisdiction of the State College Area School District's Home Economics Department and made an integral part of the Understanding Young Children course. This center should also be an integral part of a required life skills course should one be established.

2. That a required course, to be called something like "Lifeways" be established. This course would include topics from the Perkin's imperatives. The course would be a graduation requirement and would be completed by students at some point between grade 9 and the completion of grade 12.

   The department recognizes that the exact knowledge and skills involved in minimal life skill competency is yet to be identified. So, too, are the time, space, material, and staff requirements. This information would be determined and made a part of the course proposal to be made to the Board of School Directors in October 19____.

   This report presents ample evidence about the vast changes that are taking place in society, about the need for planned instruction to prepare young people with the minimal life skill competencies they need to cope successfully, and about the haphazard manner in which this instruction is being delivered to young people in this and other communities.

   The department believes this recommendation is deserving of the most serious consideration.

3. That staff members receive instruction in how to teach practical reasoning and apply it to home economics courses. This instruction should be followed by a systematic review of all courses of study to make certain practical reasoning is included where appropriate.

4. That all facilities be evaluated by a team including an architect with recent experience in designing secondary school home economics laboratories, the director of physical plant, the home economics coordinator, and a home economics consultant with knowledge about up-to-date programs and facilities.

© 1993 by The Center for Applied Research in Education

NEXT STEPS

The Home Economics Department will need to complete several major tasks outlined in the recommendations if they are to become operational. These tasks will include:

1. Complete the proposal for the Board of Education to make a decision regarding the augmentation of the Understanding Young Children course with a full-time child care center.

2. Complete the feasibility study and, if appropriate, the course proposal for a required life skills course for presentation to the Board of Education.

3. Instruct all staff members in practical reasoning skills and revise all courses of study to include same as part of instructional content and teaching strategies.

4. Complete an evaluation of home economics facilities and equipment.

5. Determine the advisability of joint instructional ventures with other departments.

6. Review consultant's recommendations.

7. Investigate ways to make home economics classes available to vocational-technical students.

8. Develop community awareness plan.

A Critical Work Activity system scheduling and assigning responsibility for the completion of the curriculum review development cycle tasks follows.

© 1993 by The Center for Applied Research in Education

HOME ECONOMICS
CURRICULUM REVIEW DEVELOPMENT CYCLE

Critical Work Activities System
19XX–19XY

Task	Who	LDC
1. Identify proposal writers.	P.C.	6/1/
2. Submit extended contract requests.	P.C.	6/1/
3. Notify proposal writers.	P.C./J.E.C.	6/7/
4. Review writing tasks, establish calendar.	P.C.	6/12/
5. Complete proposal.	Writers	8/15/
6. Review proposal.	P.C.	8/28/
7. Begin Dohner review.	Department	9/9/
8. Submit proposal to JEC.	P.C.	9/11/
9. Establish annual goals.	Department	9/15/
Etc.		

© 1993 by The Center for Applied Research in Education

CHAPTER 10
SELLING YOUR PROGRAM THROUGH PUBLIC RELATIONS

TELLING THE HOME EC STORY

Declining enrollments, decreasing numbers of taxpayers with children in school, changing community demographics, lack of confidence in schools, and negative pictures painted by the media are making it difficult for elective courses to survive. Home economics teachers need to "Tell the Home Ec Story" to students, parents, the community, and the power brokers who make decisions about their subject area. What people think about home economics depends upon what they know, and too frequently they have little firsthand information. Whether you are Ms. Smith, Home Economics Department Chairperson, or Ms. Jones, food and clothing teacher, it is important that you understand an ongoing public relations plan is an essential survival skill for today's conditions.

The information in this chapter will help you establish a public relations program or suggest additional ideas to include in your existing program. Reproducible masters and samples are provided for logos, brochures, letters, flyers, and planning worksheets. You may use these as they are or modify them to fit your situation.

ALL ABOUT NEWS RELEASES

News Release Format Guidelines

You will improve your chances of having news about your program published if you follow these commonly accepted principles for writing effective news releases:

1. Make your releases easy to read, edit, and verify. Short sentences averaging 15 to 20 words are best. The use of active verbs and short words

will help maintain reader interest. Use a variety of sentence lengths and paragraphs no longer than two to five sentences.

2. Hook the reader by making your most important point immediately. Most readers scan the opening sentences to decide if it is worth reading.

3. Arrange your points in descending order of importance. This is important because editors cut stories from the bottom up to fit the space available.

4. Home economics is about people. Use personal words like people's names or pronouns like "we" or "you." Don't forget to use quotes.

5. Type your release on paper with a preprinted masthead with your school's name and address or your department's logo, for example.

6. Type the release double- or triple-spaced on one side only of 8" × 11" paper.

7. Keep copy to a single page whenever possible. Brevity is a virtue!

8. Include good-quality black-and-white photographs, if available. Identification should be done by pasting a separate sheet of paper with the identification typed on it directly to the back of the photograph. Make sure you include signed releases for any students who appear in the photographs. If you do not have photographs available, mention photo opportunities in the news release. Allow 10 days' to two weeks' lead time.

9. Be sure to include the name, title, address, and phone number of the contact person.

10. Personal contact makes an impression. Deliver your release in person, if possible. If not, send it through the mail directed to a specific person you have identified in advance as your best contact.

A SAMPLE NEWS RELEASE

CONTACT: Peggy Davis
Coordinator of Home Economics
Glenolden Area High School
239-1162

FOR IMMEDIATE RELEASE

GLENOLDEN: If you haven't visited a home economics classroom lately, you are in for a surprise. Peggy Davis, Glenolden Area School District department coordinator, recently discussed why eleventh- and twelfth-grade students ought to enroll in a newly approved course called *Lifeways*.

As Davis put it, "Home economics instruction today is a whole lot more than stitching and stirring. Our department learned from the Human Services Planning Office that individuals and families in our community have difficulty with family conflicts, financial matters, child rearing, and getting along with others at work. When we looked at the school's curriculum, we could not find where students were being adequately prepared to cope with these issues. We decided to do something about it."

After careful study, *Lifeways* was approved by the school board in February. When making the motion to approve the course, board member Charles Right said, "I think all parents ought to discuss taking this course with their youngsters. It is so important we probably will consider making it a graduation requirement in a few years."

Ms. Davis and staff will appear on local cable, Channel 24, to discuss what will be taught in the course. The program airs Friday, March 12, 19XX, at 7:30 P.M. Viewers may call in questions. The school district has a brochure that describes the course. Students learn how it helps them make the transition from high school to college or work. Practical ways to manage time and money, how to eat to stay healthy, how to prevent family conflict, and how to make a wise decision regarding marriage and parenthood are just a few of the topics included. The brochures will be distributed before course registration time. Interested citizens may call Ms. Davis at 239-6211 to receive a copy of the brochure.

GUIDELINES FOR EFFECTIVE DISPLAYS

You can prepare an attractive display that gets your message across effectively without much special training if you follow a few simple guidelines.

1. Keep your display simple. Avoid information overload—too much to read, too many colors, too many mediums. A display should be *eyecatching*, get people's attention, and get a short message across quickly.

2. Use bright colors, strong lines, and large professional-looking letters and include as few elements as possible.

3. If the display contains exhibit objects, avoid clutter. Display the items at different heights, use spotlights and striking background materials, and include caption cards near the object to help tell the story.

4. Size is very important for photographs. A good rule of thumb is to include no photograph less than 11" × 14". Use flat or matte photographs to avoid annoying reflections from nearby objects or windows. Prints look much better when mounted on large white mats.

5. The use of professional-looking letters is the single most important guideline for effective displays. If professional lettering is not possible, use commercially made or computer-generated letters.

GUIDELINES FOR SLIDE/TAPE PRESENTATIONS

The easiest format for the production of an audiovisual presentation is a series of slides with a sound track on cassette. It can easily be revised by pulling out an old slide and inserting a new one. Experts in the field recommend using a seven-step procedure.

1. *Planning:* Identify the topic or problem and the desired result.

2. *Writing:* Develop the content outline using a storyboard. A storyboard is a series of small cards on which to sketch the visuals and make notes. As storyboarding progresses, the script will unfold. Remember effective length for each visual. The script should tell the story in a progressive manner.

3. *Artwork:* Artwork may be anything from a simple pen and ink sketch to a refined chart, graph, or illustration using many colors. Artwork should be 6" × 9" to match the ratio of 35mm slides. Lettering must be legible. Use letters approximately 1/25th the height of the information area. Pica or elite type is too small unless enlarged. Keep print no longer than 40 letters and spaces.

4. *Photography:* Basic rules of good photography apply. If you don't trust your picture-taking ability, ask another staff member. Do not skimp on the number of pictures you take. Take them from different angles and distances. Remember, if you use pictures of students, you should get parental permission.

5. *Sound:* Sound is made up of narration and music. Listen carefully to the way people speak on television and the radio. Narration is often exaggerated speaking. Practice the narration until it flows naturally. Use music that is copyright free. Have your music department provide simple music for the program.

6. *Evaluation:* Have someone preview the presentation to make sure that it is high quality to another's eyes and that it achieves your objective.

7. *Revision:* Revise your presentation when the previewers make suggestions or when it becomes out-of-date.

RADIO SCRIPTS

Local radio lets you reach people on the move—those who travel around the community doing their job, listening to their car or truck radios. Take advantage of the situation. Provide community service announcements, do some advertising, or take a position on a topic of local concern or interest. Get your name to the motoring public.

If your community has a local talk show, don't overlook the opportunity to have the show originate live from your classroom or when your students are putting on a demonstration at the mall or in a downtown department store. Often this can be combined with another activity you are conducting such as an ethnic food fair or pie baking contest.

To be effective, radio scripts should be crafted according to recognized techniques. Some to consider are:

1. Use short sentences and short words. Long sentences and multiple-syllable words quickly cause the audience to lose interest.
2. Write the script the way you talk. You need to sound natural to be believable. Read the script aloud to another to get help in fine-tuning.
3. Start with the punch line! Get the most important information in first and develop it as you continue.
4. Avoid the passive voice.
5. Try to sound friendly but authoritative.
6. Give real-life examples to which listeners can relate.
7. Give the sources for the information you quote or describe.
8. Talk directly to the listener. Personalize the message to local residents, if possible.
9. Don't be afraid to ask the pros at your radio station for help.

TIPS FOR GOOD WRITING

Good writing is good writing no matter what the subject. Whether you are composing a memo to students or a report to the principal, the purpose of the document is to communicate, not demonstrate your intellect or eloquence. Having a coworker look it over before you send it is a good suggestion to follow.

1. Prefer the plain word to the fancy. Telling a mother her son or daughter created a debacle in class may make you sound scholarly, but she'd know better what you meant if you said the student created a disturbance in class.

2. Prefer the familiar word to the unfamiliar. If you need a Thesaurus to find a word, don't use it. The words you choose should come naturally. They should be familiar to the reader, not just the writer. Know your audience and don't overestimate their reading level or their desire to plow through your prose.

3. Never use a long word when a short one will do: *transformation* means "change," *innovative* means "new," *consummate* means "finish." Words of three syllables or more raise your *Fog Index*.

4. Simple declarative sentences are the best communicators. Master their use and use them often.

5. Keep it simple. Never use two or more words when one will do. Carefully examine the phrases you use. For example, replace "due to the fact" with "because." Eliminate needless sentences and paragraphs as well. If it doesn't add to your meaning, you don't need it. Some writers think that the longer the message, the bigger impression it will make. Most often that thinking is wrong. Long sentences and paragraphs intimidate people, and often muddle the meaning.

6. Revise. Rewrite. Have an associate edit your work. Better yet, get a friend in the English Department to do it for you. Make it a golden rule that whatever leaves your desk represents your very best.

SOURCES OF
PUBLIC RELATIONS INFORMATION

For additional information about public relations for home economists, contact the following:

California State Department of Education
721 Capital Mall, 4th Floor
Sacramento, CA 95814

Florida Department of Education
Department of Home Economics
Capitol Building, Room PL116
Tallahassee, FL 32301

American Home Economics Association
1555 King Street
Alexandria, VA 22314-2716

Glencoe Publishing Company
Bennett & McKnight Division
809 West Detwiler Drive
Peoria, IL 61615

FORECAST
Scholastic Publishing Company
730 Broadway
New York, NY 10003-9538

National School Public Relations Association
1501 Lee Highway
Arlington, VA 22209

DEVELOPING A PLAN OF ACTION

A public relations program that will "Tell the Home Ec Story," enhance your image, improve your program, or attract more enrollment will not just happen. You will need a plan of action. The activities suggested here can be used by an individual teacher, a group of teachers working together informally, or a department chairperson as a formal department activity. Completing these activities in the order suggested is a concrete, sequential approach to problem solving, a model you may wish to follow in other areas of your work. Its use will almost guarantee your success.

How to Develop a Plan

1. Complete the "Assessing Needs and Past Experiences" form. If you are a department chairperson, have all your department members complete it individually or put it on a department meeting agenda for group discussion and completion. Use the top of the form to list the reasons why you want to establish a PR program and the bottom of the form to list your past PR experiences. This information is used in the next step.

2. The next step is to identify the publics you want to reach and decide upon the activities you will carry out the first year. Use the following "First-Year Public Relations Plan" worksheet. List the publics you want to reach and rank them in their order of importance to your public relations needs. Then, make a list of first year PR ideas appropriate for these publics. A good place to start is with the list of things you identified as successful. Are any of them worthy of repeating? Next, look at the 100 suggestions listed elsewhere in this chapter. From these and other ideas you might think of, list possibilities for the first year. Review the list and mark the ones you believe you have the time and resources to complete. When you finish this step, you will know what you are going to do.

3. Now that you know what you are going to do, you need to decide when you are going to do it. Lay out a first-year calendar. See the "First-Year Public Relations Plan" worksheet. Follow the directions to complete it. When you have finished this step, you will have completed the CWA (Critical Work

Activity) system discussed earlier. If you practice this approach in your endeavors, you will be amazed at how the quality of your work will improve and how much more will get completed in a timely, less stressful manner.

4. It is important to remember your PR program will be cumulative. Complete a three- to five-year plan to help you achieve your goal to "Tell the Home Ec Story." Ideas carried out the first year may be repeated in subsequent years. By taking a three- to five-year approach to your planning, you will end with a comprehensive program.

ASSESSING NEEDS AND PAST EXPERIENCES

In the space provided, list the reasons you believe it is important to communicate with others about the home economics program. Your statements should include the audience you want to reach—parents, students, administration, and community. In the space to the left of your list, assign a rank order number to each item you listed. Use "1" for the most important, "2" for second most important, and so on.

_____ _____

_____ _____

_____ _____

_____ _____

_____ _____

In the space provided, list the public relations activities or methods you have used in the past. Make special note of the media you used. For example, radio/TV, newspaper, slide show, demonstrations. Place an asterisk in the space to the left for those that were especially successful.

_____ _____

_____ _____

_____ _____

_____ _____

_____ _____

_____ _____

_____ _____

_____ _____

© 1993 by The Center for Applied Research in Education

FIRST-YEAR PUBLIC RELATIONS PLAN

In the column marked "Public," list those with whom you want to communicate. Your list might include parents, school board, students, community at large, senior citizens, and others. Then prioritize the list. In the space provided, place a "1" before the most important public, "2" for second most important, and so on.

Next, list the public relations ideas you want to consider the first year. Make sure you only list ideas that are appropriate methods to reach the publics you have identified. Place an "X" in the space provided to mark those you will carry out the first year.

Priority	Public	Priority	PR Idea
_____	_____	_____	_____
_____	_____	_____	_____
_____	_____	_____	_____
_____	_____	_____	_____
_____	_____	_____	_____
_____	_____	_____	_____
_____	_____	_____	_____
_____	_____	_____	_____
_____	_____	_____	_____
_____	_____	_____	_____
_____	_____	_____	_____
_____	_____	_____	_____
_____	_____	_____	_____
_____	_____	_____	_____
_____	_____	_____	_____

© 1993 by The Center for Applied Research in Education

CALENDAR OF EVENTS

DATE	TASK	WHO

JULY

_____

AUGUST

_____

SEPTEMBER

_____

OCTOBER

_____

NOVEMBER

_____

DECEMBER

_____

JANUARY

_____

FEBRUARY

_____

MARCH

_____

APRIL

_____

MAY

_____

JUNE

_____

© 1993 by The Center for Applied Research in Education

100 IDEAS TO PROMOTE HOME ECONOMICS

1. Develop a logo for the home economics department. Have a contest through classes, club, FHA/HERO, or schoolwide. Invite community leaders to serve as judges. Announce winner in local newspaper, radio and television, daily bulletin, school board, or other available sources.

2. Make one phone call a week to a parent to say something positive about his or her child.

3. Write one note a week to say something positive to a student.

4. Hold periodic luncheons for community VIPs, school board members, senior citizen groups, taxpayer groups, civic organizations, or business and industry moguls.

5. Establish an advisory committee to help evaluate your program, figure out community needs, and suggest possible new course content. Include students, former students, parents, and home economics–related professional people. Meet two or three times a year. Always have a meaningful agenda. Make these people feel they are a part of your team.

6. Use volunteers in your classroom.

7. Have outstanding students recognized at school board meetings.

8. Develop a home economics department slogan via a staff or student contest.

9. Display the department logo and slogan in the most visible spot in all home economics classrooms.

10. Have art students paint/letter the department logo and slogan in the corridors outside the home economics classrooms.

11. Conduct demonstrations in local shopping malls. Arrange with an appliance store to provide the necessary appliances and provide a "door" prize.

12. Use your personal computer and clip art to enliven your correspondence with others. DreamMaker Software, 3G Graphics, Inc., T/Maker, Metro Image Base, Desktop Graphics, and Adobe are some publishers that provide clip art useful to home economics teachers. In addition, you can purchase clip art very inexpensively from Public Software Library, P.O. Box 35705, Houston, Texas 77235-5705. Call them at 1-800-242-4775 for a free catalogue. Check computer magazines for advertisements about public domain shareware. Many have free catalogues.

13. Have T-shirts made with department slogan/logo and wear them once a month.

14. Have community people serve as consultants by serving on panels or being guest speakers.

15. Have students serve as hosts for consultants and make certain they receive "red carpet" treatment.

16. Use a *Good News from the Home Economics Department* memo to congratulate students, parents, school staff, community members, administration, and school board members and recognize their achievements. See the blackline master in Letterheads, Headings/Memos of the Samples and Examples section.

17. Write occasional letters to the editor of your local newspaper about creative and innovative classroom experiences. Have students write also.

18. Prepare and display special exhibits about home economics activities in local malls, storefronts, and other areas.

19. Prepare a periodic newsletter for parents and send it to administrators, school board, and news media.

20. Arrange periodically to place a display in the display cases near the main office.

21. Volunteer to speak at local civic groups about key topics of current concern to home economists, for example, selecting appropriate child care service, precautions for latchkey children, managing family crises, and time management in the home.

22. Develop brochures that explain your program in laypeople's terms and provide them to parents at Back to School Night, to visitors, to the media, service clubs, senior citizen centers, doctor's offices, and the like. See examples in Samples and Examples section.

23. Send birthday or greeting cards to board and administration members from the students or classes.

24. Hold "Dialogue Days" during which specific groups are invited to meet with students and staff to discuss current issues affecting the home and family.

25. Celebrate excellence by holding an annual student recognition banquet or program.

26. Review your course descriptions in student registration information to make certain they are current, upbeat, attractive, and appealing.

27. If you are in a school district with a central administration building, arrange to have student projects placed on display there.

28. Publish departmental information distributed to students' homes in various languages to reflect community demographics.

29. Use special printed thank you notes frequently.

30. Work with your school media person to produce an informational slide/tape show about course offerings and successful graduates, for example.

31. Create an attractive poster, "What's Cooking" to be placed on the door to show what is going on that day or week. Use pictures of students and

the products they prepared in the prior year to liven up the poster. See sample in Advertisements/Posters section.

32. Develop a package of material about the home economics program to distribute to new residents by Welcome Wagon.

33. Have a standard telephone answer message that changes monthly. For example, "Good morning, this is the home economics department, where we teach life management skills. May I help you?"

34. At course registration time, wear a sandwich board advertising home economics course offerings.

35. Conduct a Focus on Tomorrow—A Home Economics Career Symposium. Have local business and industry leaders present to discuss career opportunities, and invite the entire school to participate.

36. Sponsor/conduct community workshops on topics for which home economists are well qualified. For example, select topics from Managing Work and Home Responsibilities, Improving Nutrition, Strengthening Parenting Skills, Managing Individual and Family Resources, and Improving Responses to Family Crises. Choose topics currently discussed in your local media.

37. Include intergenerational activities in your courses.

38. Have your child care classes develop a parenting guide for students in the district or county teen parenting program.

39. Send special "Did You Know?" memos to counselors and administrators about special happenings or changes in your courses. See master in Letterheads/Headings/Memos section.

40. Get outrageous! Dress up as a special "Character of the Month," Minnie Mouse, for example. Announce to the school during morning announcements that "Minnie Mouse takes home economics courses. Have you seen her in our school today?"

41. Prepare a "Hats Off!" display case, bulletin board, or announcement in the daily bulletin to express appreciation or congratulations to students and staff.

42. Send notes to students, parents, staff, and administration, "I've been reading about you in the newspaper" to acknowledge a good deed or achievement. Attach a copy of the article with a personal message of recognition, like "Keep up the good work! We appreciate your efforts." See master in Samples and Examples section.

43. Prepare a special display about home economics activities to be displayed near the polling place if your school is used for voting on election day.

44. Conduct Home Economics Awareness Week.

45. Develop and sell a cookbook of students' and teachers' favorite recipes. If your school serves a specific ethnic group, consider having the subject be favorite ethnic recipes.

46. Sponsor a monthly food drive for the local food bank.

47. Have "stick 'ems" that say "Home Ec's for You," "Take a Home Ec Course," or "See You in (course)."

48. Check to see if your school subscribes to ED-Line, a public relations database operated by the National School Public Relations Association, 1501 Lee Highway, Arlington, Virginia 22209. If it does, you can access a database of information about schools. Check it periodically to see if there is information about home economics you can use.

49. Have buttons made with department logo/slogan.

50. Establish an Evaluation Committee composed of present and former students and parents to give you periodically feedback about the relevance of your program.

51. Arrange with local fast-food restaurants to develop placemats that include special information about your course offerings/department. For example, have a section that includes a highlighted message, "The World Class High School Home Economics Department—Teaching Life Management Skills That Last a Lifetime. For more information, call 865-8889 Monday through Friday."

52. Have a "Guest Day" in your classes when students may invite a guest to a special entertainment.

53. Write to your state organization for multiple copies of brochures they may have that help "Tell the Home Ec Story." For example, the Pennsylvania Home Economics Association recently made available to its members a brochure entitled "Home Economics Critical Thinking for Life." This brochure is reproduced in the Samples and Examples section.

54. Prepare special radio spots for use on local radio stations. See examples in Radio Spots, Samples and Examples section.

55. Send a welcoming note to families of new students introducing your department's staff and course offerings. Encourage calls to find out more information. Follow up with a phone call. See sample letter in the Samples and Examples section.

56. Prepare articles for your state and regional Home Economics Association newsletters.

57. Prepare a brief annual report for your principal, and forward a copy to the superintendent. Include information about number of students enrolled, parental contacts, student and staff honors or awards, special units, community contacts, guests, and any other information that puts your program in a special light.

58. Enter your state's "Teacher of the Year Contest."

59. Volunteer to serve on any committees in your school that will be investigating curricular matters.

60. Your state professional association is always looking for conference program ideas. If you've done something you think others would be interested in, *volunteer* to be a presenter! Make sure your local news media know about it.

61. Involve parents and FHA/HERO clubs in building a float to enter in a community parade at Halloween, Christmas, Homecoming, and other occasions.

62. Have students conduct surveys about individual and family issues of current interest to your community. For example, availability of affordable child care, homelessness, aid to dependent children, latchkey children, and so on. Publish or display the results through your school's daily bulletin, display cases, or public bulletin boards.

63. Invite parents to culminating activities where students have the opportunity to demonstrate their newly learned skills.

64. Develop letterhead stationery for the home economics department. See sample in Letterheads/Headings/Memos section.

65. Use large footsteps leading to the home economics department during open house or parent visitation events.

66. Video tape guest consultants and send a copy of the tape to his or her organization with a "Thought You'd Like to Know" note.

67. If you have a college or university that sponsors or conducts meetings related to home economics topics, volunteer to have some of your students help with registration. Perform a similar service for any meetings conducted in your community by your professional associations.

68. Conduct consumer surveys in local malls or school cafeterias. You could cosponsor this with local businesses. Cookies, ice cream, pizza, hand lotions, and soft drinks are easy-to-compare products. Your students can conduct the survey in highly visible spots, compile the results, and share the results via local media, school bulletins, or daily school announcements.

69. Participate in departmental exchanges. For example, have the guidance department present lessons on peer pressure or work with the computer lab staff to have graphics for your worksheets and publications prepared and the business education staff on personal finance, work experience on balancing work and family responsibilities, and so forth.

70. Hold a recognition breakfast for the football team during homecoming week. Invite officers of the booster club, coaching staff, and administration. This idea could be used at other times during the year to recognize National Merit finalists, faculty scholars, and others receiving honors.

71. Invite students to attend professional meetings at the local, regional, and state level. Notify local news media of this event. Better yet, send them a news release.

72. Use business cards with your logo. Including your department's logo or that of your state or AHEA will professionalize your card.

73. Let others in the school use your facilities whenever it does not interfere with your classroom program. Operate your facilities using an open-door policy. You probably will need to be careful of exploitation, however. For example, the staff may use your equipment to prepare refreshments for a meeting, and before you know it ask you to do their job, or they may leave your facilities in a mess for you to clean up.

74. Use student buttons or tags that have a message—"Home Ec Is a Life-saver," "Ask Me About Senior Foods," or "I Like Lifeways."

75. If any local service or benevolent organizations recognize students of the month or year, make sure home economics students are considered.

76. Encourage outstanding students to speak before civic groups about their awards and achievements.

77. Purchase an advertisement in the yearbook for FHA/HERO. If you can, include photographs of members in the advertisement. It guarantees student interest.

78. Make presentations to your sending elementary schools' staff about what home economics classes are doing to address the issues covered by the Perkin's imperatives. If you are in a public secondary school, do not forget the private elementary schools that send students to your school.

79. Circulate articles to your administration that emphasize the value of home economics.

80. Ask your school board or administration to send officers of FHA/HERO to annual state home economics association meetings.

81. Cooperate with your media resource center to conduct a Consumer Fair during National Consumer Education Week. Write to the United States Office of Consumer Affairs, Washington, D.C. 20201 for a free copy of *How to Run A Consumer Week*.

82. Cooperate with the community education staff that use your facilities after school hours. Work with them to develop a mutual set of guidelines for using your equipment. Not only will you protect your facilities and equipment, you will gain much goodwill.

83. Conduct special demonstrations for parents at course registration time. For example, if your school has an evening meeting for parents to discuss course selection for the coming year, hold a fashion show or conduct a bread-making session, sewing demonstration, or round-table student discussion of child care class topics.

84. Make sure your school newspaper and yearbook staff know about all upcoming home economics activities.

85. Sponsor "Wellness Tips" in the daily bulletin, morning announcements, district staff newsletter, and parent/community newsletter.

86. Establish a scholarship for graduates going into a home economics–related field. Involve the membership of your local home economics–related organizations.

87. Sponsor a schoolwide food drive for the needy at holiday time.

88. Cosponsor a Skills Festival with the industrial arts, art, agriculture, and business education departments where students display projects and conduct demonstrations. This activity is best held toward the end of the first semester. Take this opportunity to distribute brochures or other information about your course offerings.

89. During the Skills Festival or during Course Registration Fairs, sponsor a contest or quiz with a prize. For example, have the students complete a quiz about some area of home economics. Prizes can be items produced by your students, a fancy decorated cake, for example. The activity is designed to keep participants in your area longer to capture their interest.

90. Sponsor a fall countywide apple pie contest open to all students at designated grade or school levels. Use administrators and community leaders as judges.

91. Design and display a special bumper sticker on your car.

92. Cosponsor an ethnic foods demonstration or fair with the foreign language department.

93. Sponsor a school recycling program. Make sure this is accompanied with much fanfare at school and in the local news media.

94. Hold an Appreciation Tea for staff during National Education Week.

95. The newspaper *USA Today* has an article related to home economics almost every day. When one catches your eye, call your local newspaper and mention you saw an article in *USA Today* and you thought he or she might be interested in knowing what your department is doing about it.

96. Sponsor a toy selection seminar for parents at holiday time.

97. Write to your legislators about what you are doing concerning some current home economics–related issue, for instance, child abuse, child care, or the homeless.

98. Conduct parent information sessions in your feeder elementary schools.

99. Investigate *Forecast's* professional public relations tapes. Inquire at 730 Broadway, New York, New York 10003-9538.

100. Remember, good news travels by word of mouth! An interesting, well-taught lesson is the best public relations you can devise.

SOME PUBLIC RELATIONS SAMPLES
AND EXAMPLES

This section contains some samples that you may duplicate to use in your public relations program. It also contains some examples of ideas others have developed that with some modification can be adapted to your situation.

You have now come face to face with an area where a personal computer with word processing, paint and draw software, and a collection of fonts will enable you to do all sorts of things not possible with a typewriter. The process is called "desktop publishing." If you are not familiar with these procedures, someone in your school will be—if not a staff member, then a student—or both! Don't be intimidated by the computerese. Search out the hackers in your school, talk over your ideas with them, enlist their help, and along the way pick up many skills that will enable you to do much of your own work in the future. Some additional information can be found in Chapter 8. For more help, visit your local computer store or buy a couple of issues of a monthly computer or desktop publishing magazine at your local newsstand. Another source of help is your local copy store or printing shop. Most of them now offer a wide range of desktop publishing services from layout to illustrations to text selection.

Set up a public relations idea file. Develop a PR eye. Look for eye- or ear-catching ideas everywhere you go. When you see or hear one, make a note and put it in your file. *Forecast* regularly includes public relations ideas others have successfully used. Clip these articles and put them in your file where you can review them when you plan your annual PR activities.

Sample Logos

Using a logo for your correspondence, your business cards, and the covers of any reports you prepare will definitely add a touch of class. Here are some sample logos you may use. You can alter the size by making copies on a copy machine that allows you to increase or decrease the copy size. If your school has a computer lab with a scanner, you can have the logo scanned and then altered to suit your needs. If you have a local copy or print shop that does desktop publishing, you can have it altered there to your specifications.

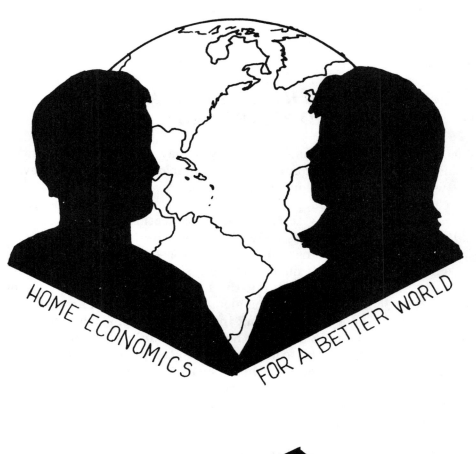

HOME ECONOMICS FOR A BETTER WORLD

© 1993 by The Center for Applied Research in Education

HOME EC
PROVIDES
FOOD FOR
THOUGHT

HOME ECONOMICS
IS FASHIONABLE

PANTHER
HOME ECONOMICS

© 1993 by The Center for Applied Research in Education

Bumper Stickers

America is big on bumper stickers. Page 275 is an example you can reproduce as is or modify. One modification you might want to consider is to include your school name on the sticker. Don't be shy about asking others to use the stickers!

Recognition Ideas

It is good to recognize those who have done you a favor, have completed a task outstandingly, or are celebrating a special occasion. The accompanying reproducible masters on pages 276–283 can be used for these occasions.

© 1993 by The Center for Applied Research in Education

HOME ECONOMICS

Lights Up Your Life!

THANK YOU

*FROM PANTHER
HOME ECONOMICS*

THANK YOU

place school logo here,
in a lighter shade of grey

*FROM THE HOME
ECONOMICS DEPT.*

© 1993 by The Center for Applied Research in Education

© 1993 by The Center for Applied Research in Education

Certificate
of
Appreciation

Thank You

_____

for being a Guest Speaker in the
Home Economics Department

_____

Teacher

Date_____

Certificate
of
Appreciation

Thank You

_____

for being a Classroom Volunteer in the
Home Economics Department

_____
Teacher

Date_____

© 1993 by The Center for Applied Research in Education

HOME ECONOMICS

AWARD

This Certifies That

is Awarded this Certificate for

_____

Teacher

Presented _____ 19 ___

© 1993 by The Center for Applied Research in Education

HOME ECONOMICS

Certificate of Achievement

This Certifies that

is Awarded this Certificate for

Teacher

Date

© 1993 by The Center for Applied Research in Education

© 1993 by The Center for Applied Research in Education

HAPPY BIRTHDAY

from the

Home Economics Department

_____
Teacher

_____
Date

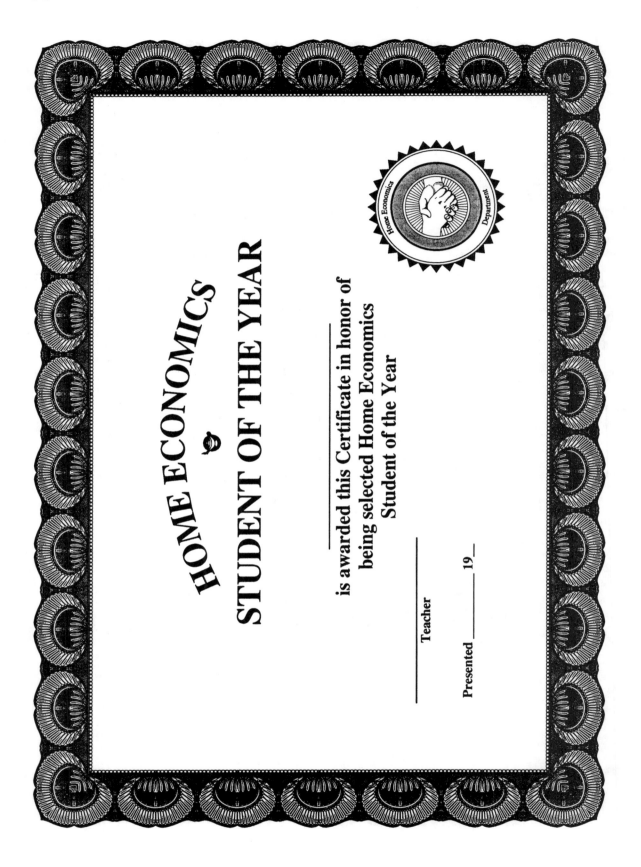

HOME ECONOMICS
❧
STUDENT OF THE YEAR

is awarded this Certificate in honor of
being selected Home Economics
Student of the Year

_____
Teacher

Presented _____ 19__

© 1993 by The Center for Applied Research in Education

© 1993 by The Center for Applied Research in Education

HOME ECONOMICS
STUDENT OF THE YEAR

is awarded this Certificate in honor of
being selected Home Economics
Student of the Year

_____
Teacher

Date _____

Brochures

Brochures are good advertising. They are useful to inform students, parents, the community at large, and visitors about key aspects of your program and the mission of home economics education. "Critical Thinking for Life" was produced by the Pennsylvania Home Economics Association several years ago and made available to the membership for mass distribution. It is reproduced on pages 286–287 with permission. Check with your state association to see if it has such a brochure available. If not, encourage them to produce one.

This is another area where desktop publishing can be of assistance. The production of outstanding brochures requires expertise in layout and design that you may not possess. If that is so, seek out your art department, media person, or the school or district printing department, or go to a commercial copy store, advertising agency, or print shop and ask them for their help. If you have a county or regional vocational-technical school see if they can help you.

A sample layout for a brochure is shown on page 285.

Flyers/Handouts

There are occasions when you can tell part of your story by distributing a flyer or a handout. Back to School Night, course registration fairs, budget hearings, school board meetings, conferences, county fairs, and visitors can be target audiences.

A selection of reproducible masters is provided on pages 288–292. These may be used as is or altered to fit your situation. Check the Advertisements/Posters section for additional ideas that can be turned into flyers or handouts.

© 1993 by The Center for Applied Research in Education

FACTS ABOUT THE
HOME ECONOMICS
PROGRAM

COURSE
DESCRIPTIONS

FOLD HERE

SCHOOL NAME
HOME
ECONOMICS

SCHOOL LOGO

Critical Thinking For Life

SOURCES USED:

Home Economics Education Association,
Publication A261-08466, "Communicating The
Contributions of Home Economics Education", 1985.

Illinois Home Economics Association,
Position Paper, "Education For What?", 1985.

Illinois Teacher of Home Economics, "Home
Economics Education: An Undergraduate's
Philosophy", September/October 1986.

Journal of Home Economics, "Marketing
Professional Home Economics", Winter 1987.

Pennsylvania
Home
Economics
Association

*AFFILIATED WITH
THE AMERICAN
HOME ECONOMICS
ASSOCIATION*

Reproduced by permission from the Pennsylvania Home Economics Association.

© 1993 by The Center for Applied Research in Education

HOME ECONOMICS

Education can be enabling and preventative. Home Economics is both. The focus of Home Economics is to contribute to the well-being of individuals and families. Home Economics is the only profession and body of knowledge that formally prepares individuals for family life. We contribute knowledge that society needs and we contribute services that demand specialized training. We help individuals and families to function in their own strengths.

Educates to Prevent Problems

Classes in Human Relationships, Parenting, Marriage, Family Life, Child Development, Resource Management, Housing, Nutrition, Foods, and Clothing enable students to develop critical thinking skills and address a wide variety of situations and identify positive ways to handle potential problems. Research indicates that "Home Economics courses produce better problem solving ability than do courses in Algebra," according to Robert Hempel in the May, 1983 issue of *The Phi Delta Kappan.*

© 1993 by The Center for Applied Research in Education

Foods, Dietetics & Nutrition

Child Development & Family Relations

Prepares for Life

Home Economics helps students to learn about themselves, the human heritage, and the interdependent world in which they live. Courses help students explore and set personal and career goals, to develop positive self-concepts and to develop abilities in working and getting along with others. The interdependence of people is an integral part of the Home Economics program.

Addresses Contemporary Issues

National studies and reports provide statistics which confirm that many changes are affecting the American family. Home Economics courses are addressing these changes. Educating individuals and families to anticipate and deal with daily concerns is a legitimate and important aspect of any Home Economics program. Some issues include . . . developing positive self-concepts, the impact of increased fitness concerns on nutrition in the family; the impact of unemployment on home and family life; teen pregnancy; the impact of consumers' behaviors on environment; changes in family forms; caregiving for children and elderly; family economic literacy; entrepreneurship, and the impact of advanced technology on the home and daily life.

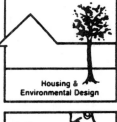

Housing & Environmental Design

Consumer Affairs & Economics

Fashion Merchandising & Textiles

Uniquely Employs Both Theory and Practice

Young men and women, both college and non-college bound, need Home Economics education. Developing positive self-concepts, good human relations, and positive attitudes toward work are taught as well as competencies for Home Economics related occupations. No other curriculum deals entirely with the improvement of the quality of life, or helps students learn how to manage the problems of daily living in a practical manner. As Eleanor Roosevelt said, "**We need to understand that the purpose of schooling is not just preparation for more schooling, but preparation for life.**"

© 1993 by The Center for Applied Research in Education

© 1993 by The Center for Applied Research in Education

HOME ECONOMICS

When you
leave school,
it's sink or
swim...

GRAB ONTO IT NOW!

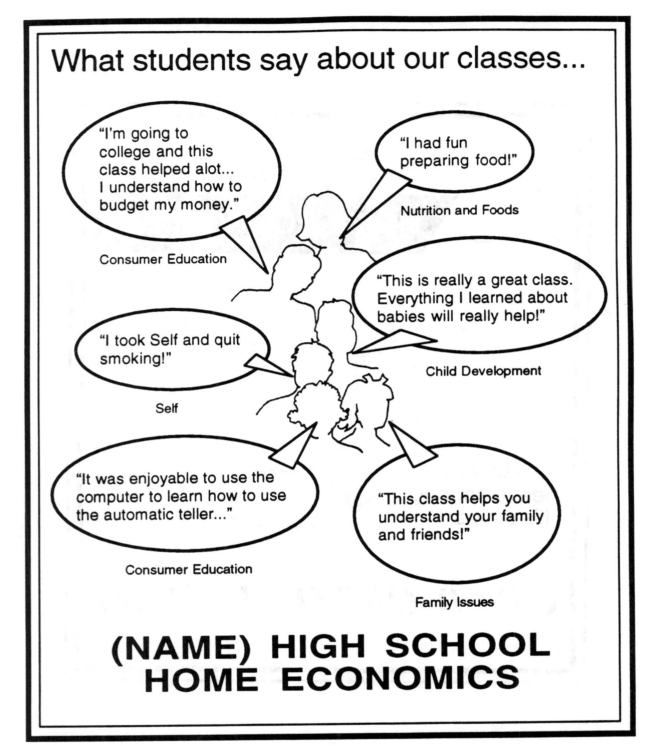

© 1993 by The Center for Applied Research in Education

© 1993 by The Center for Applied Research in Education

DID
YOU KNOW
THAT.....

- THERE WERE MORE THAN 800,000 DOCUMENTED REPORTS OF CHILD ABUSE AND NEGLECT LAST YEAR!
- 80% OF AMERICAN ADULTS FEEL THEIR FAMILY IS ONE OF THE MOST IMPORTANT ELEMENTS IN THEIR LIFE?
- RECENT STATISTICS SHOW THAT ONE OUT OF EVERY TWO MARRIAGES ENDS IN DIVORCE?
- TEENAGERS WHO MARRY ARE SIX TIMES MORE LIKELY TO DIVORCE THAN 20 TO 23 YEAR OLDS!

WE TEACH LIFE MANAGEMENT SKILLS!

(NAME) HIGH SCHOOL HOME ECONOMICS

HOME ECONOMICS

PASSPORT

TO A SUCCESSFUL FUTURE

SCHOOL NAME

YOUR NAME _____

© 1993 by The Center for Applied Research in Education

Advertisements and Posters

An idea for a poster that can be placed on the door of your classroom to attract the attention of students is shown on page 294. To get even more attention, include pictures of students in action and mount the poster somewhere in your school where there is a lot of traffic.

Consider using smaller versions of the flyers and handouts presented in the preceding section as advertisements that can be placed in the school newspaper, yearbook, parent newsletter, guidance newsletter, local bargain sheet, newspaper, or other publications. They can also be used as ideas for posters or bulletin boards to display in the home economics suite or around the school at course registration time.

A blank poster for your use is shown on page 295.

WHAT'S COOKING?

© 1993 by The Center for Applied Research in Education

TODAY'S MENU

BREAD BAKING

WHAT'S COOKING?

TODAY'S MENU

© 1993 by The Center for Applied Research in Education

Letterheads/Headings/Memos

Add a touch of class to your department by using letterhead stationery, special headings for special communications, and a customized departmental memorandum. The use of well-designed letterheads calls attention to your department as one that operates in a businesslike manner. You are special and you want others to know it.

A starter collection of reproducible blackline masters is provided on pages 297–300.

HOME ECONOMICS DEPARTMENT

© 1993 by The Center for Applied Research in Education

HOME ECONOMICS DEPARTMENT

© 1993 by The Center for Applied Research in Education

© 1993 by The Center for Applied Research in Education

GOOD NEWS

MEMO FROM THE HOME ECONOMICS DEPARTMENT

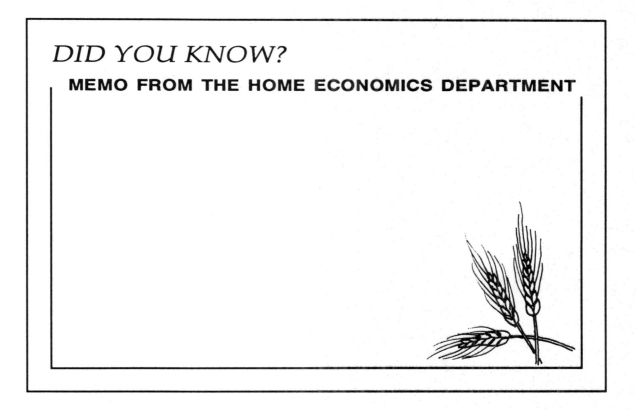

DID YOU KNOW?

MEMO FROM THE HOME ECONOMICS DEPARTMENT

MEMO FROM THE HOME ECONOMICS DEPARTMENT

© 1993 by The Center for Applied Research in Education

Buttons/Business Cards/Placemats

Buttons, business cards and placemats were mentioned in "100 Ideas to Promote Home Economics." Some reproducible blackline masters or layouts for these ideas are shown on pages 302–303.

Button

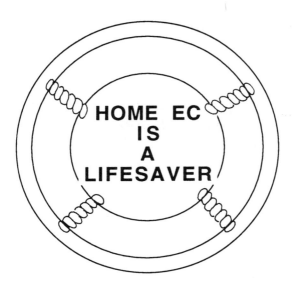

Business cards

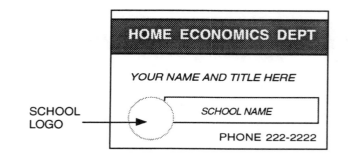

SCHOOL
LOGO

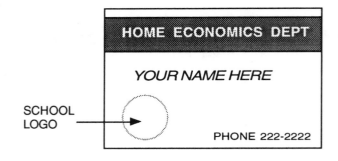

SCHOOL
LOGO

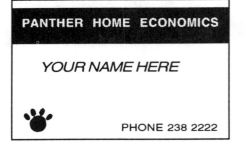

© 1993 by The Center for Applied Research in Education

© 1993 by The Center for Applied Research in Education

Placemat

BOB'S RESTAURANT

PANTHER HIGH SCHOOL
HOME ECONOMICS CLASSES
MAKE A DIFFERENCE

Radio Spots

Radio spots give you the opportunity to reach people on the move, those who drive as part of their job. They can be particularly useful at course registration and budget time. Make them short and to the point. Your state association and the AHEA can offer you assistance, and so can your local radio station.

Radio Spot 1

Are you ready for life after high school? Do you know how to live within a balanced budget? Can you prepare well-balanced meals? Are you consumer savvy? If you need help in these areas, contact your home economics teacher and take a class. You'll be preparing yourself for the rest of your life!

Radio Spot 2

Hey Gang! _____ High School has a deal you can't refuse. You can learn to manage your money, eat healthy, manage your time and energy, and look terrific. For the time of your life and the opportunity to learn the skills to last a lifetime, take a home economics course [or list special course name like Senior Seminar, for example]. You'll be glad you did! Contact your home economics department at _____ for more information or call (teacher name) at _____ for more information.

Radio Spot 3

For a sunny future after high school make sure you get your bright ideas for living now! Learn about managing your resources, using credit wisely, eating to maintain good health, parenting skills, and responding to family crises. _____ High School has a course for you! Stop by the home ec booth at the Course Registration Fair, _____, _____ (date) or contact _____.

Radio Spot 4

Does your high school student know how to balance a checkbook—select an appropriate wardrobe—cook a well-balanced meal—complete a 1040A? If not, encourage him or her to enroll in [special course name] at your local high school. Home economics courses teach skills for a lifetime. Contact your local home economics teacher for more information by calling _____.

Sample Informational Letters

No public relations program is complete without a letter to target audiences. Two sample letters are given to illustrate the type of information that can be communicated with such a letter.

HOME ECONOMICS DEPARTMENT

_____ (Date) _____

Dear Parent or Guardian,

There's a very important subject taught in our school, and you should know about it! It's a course to assist young people make the transition from high school to college or work. It is called Senior Seminar—Lifeways.

The course teaches teenagers like your eleventh or twelfth grader the skills needed to manage life on their own, so important in those first years of independence. Senior Seminar teaches important life skills concerning individual and family resources, nutrition and life-styles, parenting, home and work responsibility, and responses to family crises.

I agree with the September 1991 GOOD HOUSEKEEPING article, "Are We Preparing Our Kids for the Real World?" that "we cannot afford not to teach our children to become self-reliant, independent adults." Wouldn't it be nice to know that your daughter or son has the basic life skills to cope with the many responsibilities she or he will face after graduation? Now is the time for your youngster to learn these skills. The way to learn them is to take Senior Seminar—Lifeways. It will make a difference in your teenager's future!

I urge you to encourage your daughter or son to take this important course next year. If you would like more information, please call me at
_____.

Sincerely,

_____ (Name) _____
Home Economics Coordinator

HOME ECONOMICS DEPARTMENT

___(Date)___

Dear Parent or Guardian,

Hello, I am _____, home economics teacher at _____ High School. We have begun an exciting year in home economics, and I would like to tell you about it.

Home economics includes five areas of living: Foods and Nutrition, Human Growth and Development, Management and Consumerism, Housing/Furnishings/Equipment, and Textiles and Clothing. This year we will learn about the topics mentioned in the enclosed outline.

From time to time we will have a project that may require your student to complete it at home. When that happens, you are asked to participate by giving me feedback about how well your daughter or son completed the task.

The goal of home economics in our school is to prepare students for LIFE! The skills we learn are for everyone and will serve each person for a lifetime. Your opinions about what we do are important. Please let me know if you have suggestions to strengthen our program. Feel free to call me at _____ between _____ and _____, Monday through Friday. I am looking forward to meeting you at Back to School Night, _____(Date)_____.

Sincerely,

CHAPTER 11
POLITICS AND YOUR PROGRAM'S SURVIVAL

FACING THE FACTS

Home economics is one of 17 possible subject areas demanding time, space, staff, and money during these times when schools find resources declining. To make matters worse, home economics is not found on the "in vogue" list of subjects like mathematics and science. It is an elective subject, not a regulated monopoly like the required subjects. It is not a subject required for college admission. It frequently is referred to as a "minor" subject. It's not a pretty picture, is it? Home economics education must cross many hurdles to survive in the current era.

If home economics is to survive, it is not enough for you to work longer and harder, you must also work smarter. One way to work smarter is to "be political." The phrase "be political" used here in a positive way refers to a set of behaviors, attitudes, and procedures to help you get what you need and keep what you have. How well you succeed in the competition for time, space, money, and staff will depend to a large extent on your political skill.

GETTING WHAT YOU NEED AND KEEPING WHAT YOU HAVE

Learning About What Is Going On

Smart politicians know what is going on. They have an information network. They go everywhere. They know knowledge is power. These strategies will help you be "in the know."

1. Try to get on one or two key committees. Key committees include principal's advisory, curriculum council, budget, teacher evaluation, technology, staff development—the groups that consider topics across the entire school and stay in existence from one year to another. But be careful not

to overlook the committees addressing the hot topic of the day. Those issues perceived by staff, administration, and community as very important, such as drug education, teen suicide, senior skip day, eliminating all courses with low enrollments, or setting up a computer lab.

2. If you are a one- or two-person department, form an information network with other elective departments—art, music, technology, computer education, foreign language, and the humanities, for example. Get together with them to decide how to get involved in the school to learn what is happening. Develop a way for home economics to get a member on the principal's advisory committee, music, the budget committee, art or the staff development committee. Establish a process to distribute the information learned. For example, you can circulate minutes and reports, hold briefs after or before school meetings, meet for lunch, or hold periodic joint department meetings.

3. Read the daily bulletin, school board reports, principal's advisory committee minutes, and news releases in the local paper. Try to ferret out the latest issues. What is the administration or school board considering? What problems are the school or school district facing? What is the budget situation? Are organized community groups pushing for some action? Are community social agencies identifying problems that might be addressed by the home economics department? What curricular issues are being discussed? Do enrollment projections portend increases or decreases in staffing? Are local taxpayers' groups raising questions at school board meetings, writing letters to the editor, taking out advertisements in the local papers? If so, what are they saying? Are they targeting specific groups or programs?

4. Place a "What's New?" item on department meeting agendas or regularly set aside time during common planning periods to share information about issues, concerns, and new ideas being considered in your building, and elsewhere in the district.

Being Visible to Others

If you are going to be taken seriously by the power structure in your school, you need to be visible. Your visibility needs to be more than a cardboard cutout of yourself placed in strategic locations. You need to be seen as a contributor, a worker, a person who makes things happen, a person who is part of the action. Here are ways to achieve that type of visibility.

1. Be a volunteer! Volunteer to serve on committees that have high visibility in the school and community—those that take on the hard issues, the unpopular tasks, the nitty-gritty but important jobs that keep the school running smoothly. Show your peers and the administration that home economics is interested in the life of the school and works for its betterment. Place home economics in the mainstream of the school. Become a doer.

Make yourself someone the school would be poorer without. Remember, it never hurts to stop by and ask your principal, "Can I help in any way?"

2. Do your very best work—always. Written communications, proposals, and oral presentations should incorporate the suggestions found in Chapter 7, "Managing Written Information."

3. Keep your department in the limelight. Implement a public relations plan according to the suggestions found in Chapter 10, "Selling Your Program Through Public Relations."

4. Get involved in the community. Serve as a guest speaker or board member for your school's parent/teacher organization, the community library, child care center, health organization, or service club. Spread the word about home economics through your good deeds.

5. Attend school board meetings. Take advantage of breaks in the action to speak with board members and administrators. If there is a topic related to home economics and the audience is asked for input, make a statement. If you know the board is seeking input for agenda items where home economics has expertise, prepare an oral statement and a well-written handout to be distributed to the board and audience.

6. Communicate with the power brokers. Write informal notes to your principal to let him or her know about exemplary happenings in your classes or department. Send notes, department meeting minutes, or reports to other department chairpersons, the principal's advisory council, and officers of the parent/teacher organization. Don't forget the superintendent and other central office personnel. In small districts especially, it is important that you periodically let the superintendent know what you are doing. Use common sense. Remember, administrators are busy people. Make sure what you communicate is important and worth reading. Don't overlook other central office people. For example, if you set up a new appliance selection system, local purchasing plan, or anything that increases cost effectiveness, let the business manager know! Business managers are often asked by the school board if a proposal is affordable. It will not hurt your future causes to be known by the business office as a department concerned with fiscal accountability.

7. If you are the chair of a multiperson department, spread the good news about everyone. Let everyone share the limelight. Involve everyone in the development of proposals and requests. People who have an interest in a project will work hard to ensure its success.

8. Home economics teachers are sometimes timid and often think their work is not valued by others. They act as if they don't deserve the same respect as advanced placement mathematics or honors English teachers. Nothing is farther from the truth. No other subject in the school does more to prepare students for successful individual and family life after high school. Think about it. Run those Perkin's imperatives through your mind: managing individual and family resources, managing home and

work responsibilities, improving responses to family crises, strengthening parenting skills, and improving nutrition. Can you name another subject in your school district that has an organized sequential curriculum dealing with these topics? Home economics has every right to be a proactive force in your school. Don't hesitate to speak up and express an opinion. Yes, fight for your place in the school program.

9. Get actively involved, as a department, in a schoolwide project to address a concern related to individual and family life. Some examples are peer counseling, teen parenting, child care, MADD/SADD, crisis hotline, latchkey children, or staff well-being.

Relating to Administrators

There are a few commonsense rules to help you establish a positive relationship with administrators. This is especially important at the building level because building principals often hold the key to the door labeled "money." Without your principal's support, your proposals will not be funded. Here are guidelines to establish a good working relationship with your administrator.

1. Always make an appointment to discuss a proposal or concern. Administrators do not like to be stopped in the hall or caught for a minute before a meeting.

2. Go to the meeting prepared. Have the request or key points in writing. Take two copies with you, one for you and the other for the administrator. Administrators do not like to have to take notes during this type of meeting. Prepare a written summary to take with you to the conference. Use the sample "Request to Increase the Food Budget" and the following reproducible worksheets, "Administrative Conference Worksheet" and "Summary of Administrative Request" to organize your thoughts. In the *Opening* section make a few notes about how you might start your conference. You asked for the conference, so it is up to you to get things started. Comment upon last night's school board meeting, his or her spouse's recent Jaycee award, or other accomplishment. Engage in a few pleasantries before jumping into the purpose of your appointment. In the *Request* section clearly state what you want. In the *Facts* section give some hard data to show why your request is reasonable. In *Actions Taken* briefly outline some steps you have already taken to ameliorate the condition or solve the problem. In *Effects on Curriculum/Students* spell out how your curriculum and the students have been affected by the problem or condition. In the *Justification* section summarize the facts that spell out why your request should be granted. In the *Summary* section summarize your request and thank the person for his or her consideration of your request. After you have completed your notes on the worksheet, transfer the information in its final form to the "Summary of Administrative Request" form.

A REQUEST TO INCREASE FOOD BUDGET

Re: A Request to Increase Food Budget for 19XX–XY

Request: This is a formal request to increase the food budget for the 19XX–XY school year from $2,165 to $2,780.

Facts: The food budgets, enrollments, and per-pupil expenditures for the past five years were:

Year	Budget	Enrollment	Per-Pupil Exp.
19XX–XY	$1,850	124	$14.92
19XX–XY	$2,000	130	$15.38
19XX–XY	$2,075	131	$15.84
19XX–XY	$2,075	146	$14.21
19XX–XY	$2,165	148	$14.63

Actions Taken: Bulk purchasing was started three years ago wherever feasible, recipes were altered to reduce yield, five kitchen groups were combined into four.

Effects on Curriculum/Students: Several important areas were cut out of the curriculum, including convenience food comparisons and microwave cookery. The number of hands-on lab experiences was reduced by going to more teacher demonstrations.

Justification: It is apparent our per-pupil allotment has not kept pace with the rate of inflation. We desperately need an increase in the food budget if we are to get the courses back to the level approved by the school board, that is, number and type of lab experiences. A projected enrollment of 164 students for next school year will mean added reductions in course content unless more money is provided. We simply cannot offer a quality program on $13.20 per student.

Summary: The Home Economics Department urgently requests an increase in the food budget to $2,780 or $16.95 per-pupil allotment projected. Thank you very much for your consideration of this request.

1/25/XX

© 1993 by The Center for Applied Research in Education

3. After a few opening pleasantries, state your request or make your position known in clear, easy-to-understand, open, language. No guarded phrases or "double-speak" language, please!

4. Quickly review the facts to support your case and outline the steps you have already taken and the effects being felt by students, the department and/or the curriculum.

5. If your request gives the administrator options, explain the pros and cons of each.

6. Conclude the appointment by summarizing your justification for the request and restating what action you are requesting. Ask when you can expect a reply.

7. Rehearse what you are going to say and how you are going to say it. Your presentation and demeanor should send the message that you are a team player. You need his or her help. You recognize there is a "big picture" and home ec is only a small part of it. You know there are more demands than resources, but you trust his or her judgment to do what is best for students.

8. Make sure you dress appropriately for the occasion. Treat this appointment as you would a job interview. Impeccable grooming, neat clothing on the conservative side, shoes shined and heels in good repair, and no overdone accessories are in order. If you believe in color analysis, you know that blue is believable, black is power, and green is not believable. Choose accordingly!

Home economists are skilled at building relationships. It's their business. Remember, it's politically savvy to tell your principal or superintendent what a terrific person he or she is or what a fine job they are doing when they are. Home economics teachers know—we all need hugs!

Sample Reproducible Forms

The following two reproducible masters will help improve your chances of having administrative requests approved.

ADMINISTRATIVE CONFERENCE WORKSHEET

Opening Remarks: _____

_____

_____

Request: _____

_____

_____

Actions Taken: _____

_____

_____

_____

Effects on Curriculum/Students: _____

_____

_____

_____

_____

Justification: _____

_____

_____

Summary: _____

_____

_____

_____

_____

© 1993 by The Center for Applied Research in Education

SUMMARY OF ADMINISTRATIVE REQUEST

Request: _____

_____

_____

Actions Taken: _____

_____

_____

_____

Effects on Curriculum/Students: _____

_____

_____

_____

_____

Justification: _____

_____

_____

Summary: _____

_____

_____

_____

_____

_____

© 1993 by The Center for Applied Research in Education

Taking Advantage of Opportunities

Politically smart people are always on the lookout for opportunities—opportunities to learn, to be recognized, to influence the decision-making process. As you develop your strategy for approval, consider the following opportunities.

1. Because of the individual and family living nature of home economics subjects, you have opportunities to involve power people in your program. Invite them to be guest consultants. For example, have the principal or a guidance counselor discuss how he or she copes with balancing work and family responsibilities. It is obvious why you would invite administrators; what might not be so obvious is why you would invite a guidance counselor. You would invite them because they have so many student contacts regarding course selection. Always try to groom at least one counselor to be a home economics advocate. When these people are present in your classroom, be sure they have the opportunity to interact with students so they observe firsthand how important home economics is to young people. Don't overdo inviting them to occasions where they sample the results of a cooking lesson. Too many of these invitations only reinforce the stereotype image that home economics is only a "cook and sew" course.

2. Form an advisory committee of students, parents, community leaders, and other staff. Have them help you complete an evaluation of the home economics program and identify student needs that can be addressed by the home economics program. Let them help develop proposals for new courses or grants. Getting people involved this way broadens the level of support for home economics.

When the time comes for you to make a proposal to your administration, school board, or state agency, take the advisory committee with you. Better yet, let them make the presentation. Make sure to list their names on the request. Sometimes it is helpful to attach letters of support from council members or influential citizens. Be careful about letters of support. You do not want them to be perceived as petitions. Let the person(s) involved in making the decision regarding your request know that you have support, but be careful you are not perceived as being pushy or trying to apply pressure. Never use petitions.

3. Solicit help from your feeder schools. Elementary schools are often more child- and family-centered than secondary schools. Therefore, it is easy for them to relate to home economics. Go to elementary school staff meetings and parent/teacher organization meetings to discuss your program or present proposals you are developing. Show them how what you are doing builds on what they are doing. Invite them to visit your classes. Ask for their support.

4. Home economics has a natural connection to many child/family-oriented community organizations. Youth services, law enforcement, county human services, cooperative extension offices, and a host of other private social agencies are examples. Build communication bridges to these organizations and agencies. Talk with them regularly and involve them in your classes where feasible. Call upon

them to help you develop proposals or provide justification data. If you make a presentation to the school board, add their voices to yours. Just having them present in the audience sends a message that your proposal is of interest to a constituency broader than just the home economics department.

5. Take every opportunity to share the honors. Have your principal, superintendent, or school board president give out awards at FHA/HERO ceremonies. Mention how important his or her support has been. Include administrators' and school board officers' names on programs or handouts you distribute at school and community functions.

6. Be sure to inform other departments about your proposals. If you do an end run to the administration they will find a way to shoot down your project. No one likes surprises in the workplace unless it is a surprise day off or a pay raise. Inform and involve are key actions in any strategy you use to get a project approved.

7. Sometimes the best way to succeed is to broaden the base of support for a proposal by cosponsoring an idea with another department. For example, cosponsoring a food science course with the science department might be much more palatable to the decision makers than if the proposal comes only from the home economics department.

POLITICS BEYOND THE LOCAL SCENE

Recognize that your long-term survival in the teaching profession may depend upon how important the public views family and individual well-being issues. You should be concerned about emerging state and national legislative initiatives. It is at these levels that curriculum regulations, vocational education funding, and other family and individual well-being legislation that impacts on home economics are enacted into law. Once enacted into law the effects filter down to your school. For example, if the state legislature increases the number of mathematics or science credits required for graduation, your courses will be affected because students will have fewer periods available for electives. If Congress enacts a law requiring employers to provide child care, demand for child care workers will increase, and home economics will have an opportunity to develop a curriculum to prepare child care workers.

Many ways are open to you to become meaningfully involved in the political process beyond your school and school district. Some suggestions:

1. Join professional and special interest groups interested in child welfare, the family, and home economics–related issues. Become an active member by attending meetings, doing research, preparing position statements, participating in political rallies, distributing petitions, and writing letters.

2. Contact individual legislators at both the state and national level as an individual teacher or as a department. Become proactive. Follow these guidelines.

   • Become aware of your legislators' voting record and policy position. Make sure you are on his or her mailing list.

   • Learn your legislators' committee and subcommittee assignments for clues about his or her priorities.

   • Establish an ongoing contact with his or her office staff.

   • Personal contact is important. If you are planning a trip to your state capitol or Washington, make an appointment to see your legislator. If you know when he or she is going to be in your area, invite him or her to participate in one of your classes or attend a department or advisory committee meeting.

   • Consider the timing of your contacts. Your influence will be greater when the bill is still in committee or undergoing hearings.

   • Letters are important. Write regularly, but be sure you have something important to say. Legislators are busy people and get lots of mail. Your letters will have more impact if you follow this letter writer's guide.

A LETTER WRITER'S GUIDE TO LEGISLATORS

1. Write on your personal or school letterhead and be sure to sign your name above your typed signature.

2. Make sure your correct return address is on the letter, not just on the envelope. Include your telephone number with area code on the line following your typed signature.

3. Identify your subject clearly by stating the name of the legislation you are writing about and giving the House and Senate bill numbers.

4. State your reason for writing and explain how the legislation would affect you, the home economics profession, your school, your students, or your community. Let the legislator know you have a wide audience—you lead an advisory council, you chair the regional home economics association, you are the department chair, you are an officer in your local teacher's professional association, you are an active member in a local social agency or service organization, you are a member of AHEA, for example.

5. Set a constructive tone in your letter. If you agree that a problem exists, but believe the legislation is the wrong approach, state your suggestion for the right approach.

6. Make it clear you want a reply to your letter and you want to know his or her position on the issue or legislation.

7. Don't forget to write a thank you letter when your legislator votes your way on an issue. Everyone likes to be complimented, and tends to remember it.

8. Send letters to senators to:

> The Honorable _____
> U.S. Senate
> Washington, D.C. 20510

Send letters to representatives to:

> The Honorable _____
> U.S. House of Representatives
> Washington, D.C. 20515

Sample Letter

If you are going to take the time to write to your legislators, and you should, don't waste your time sending mass-produced letters or postcards. These are weighed at the legislative offices whereas personal letters are read and responded to by someone. Petitions of 10,000 names will have some impact, but not as much as personal letters. Send a copy of your letter as a letter to the editor of your local newspaper.

This sample letter is directed to a member of Congress about Child Care Services.

PENNS GROVE HIGH SCHOOL
Home Economics Department
Penns Grove, Pennsylvania 16432

September 15, 19XX

The Honorable William J. Smith
U.S. House of Representatives
Washington, D.C. 20515

Dear Representative Smith,

I received your newsletter in which you discuss family issues in the 76th District. As Home Economics Curriculum Coordinator in the Penns Grove Area School District, I share many of the concerns you express.

In my work, I have an advisory council of parents, students, and influential citizens who help me identify community needs. Recently we studied the high cost and shortage of licensed day care centers in our community. We were particularly concerned about a disaster in a neighboring community in which three children were killed in a fire at an unregulated day care center. A copy of the newspaper report is enclosed. We have been working with staff members in our school to help them find safe, affordable child care. I serve on the board for the local Child Development Council. My work clearly indicates there is a pressing need for more child care services in the Penns Grove community where parents can be assured their children are protected. It is apparent this need cannot be met by local funding sources.

Home economists have long been champions for family and individual well-being. I strongly support House Bill 30, The Act for Better Child Care Services. I am interested in your position. Do you intend to support HB 30, and will you seek full funding for this measure? I look forward to your early reply and have enclosed a self-addressed stamped envelope for your convenience. Your response will be shared with my advisory council and the Child Development Council. Thank you.

Sincerely,

Kathryn A. Adonis
(814) 356-8973

SHOULD YOU BE CLONED?

It sounds so overwhelming! You must be saying, "How can I possibly do all this, still teach my classes, and have a life?" It really isn't that overwhelming, it certainly isn't impractical, and it certainly is necessary to survive.

Although it may help to be cloned, if you practice these commonsense political skills on a daily basis, they will soon become your standard operating procedure. You won't even think about them. In the process, your success rate will become the envy of your peers, and you will certainly survive.

CHAPTER 12
GETTING ALONG WITH PEOPLE

GETTING ALONG WITH OTHERS

An Opportunity

Whether you are a butcher, a baker, a candlestick maker, or a home economics teacher, you need to get along with people. The people you need to get along with include your friends, relatives, department members, fellow teachers, your principal, superintendent, students, parents, and yes, your spouse and children! Are you aware that teaching calls for more people contact per minute than most other professions? To be successful and keep sane on the job, you must develop and practice a set of people skills just like you do for the other skills of your job. People skills are universal. Learn them and you can apply them in every situation you face whether it be with a student in one of your classes, your spouse, your department chair, or a friend.

Getting along with other people is often viewed as a problem because we have to get along with people we find difficult, and they are not pleasant to deal with. If you take the view, however, that this is an opportunity, that it is one of the great joys of teaching, you will reap rewards—a sense of satisfaction, a feeling of self-worth, a growing self-esteem, and the knowledge that you made a difference in someone else's life.

Information gained from attendance at conferences, workshops, readings, course work, discussions with associates, and practical experience is summarized in this chapter. The information is not a do-it-yourself manual. It is an introduction to getting along with others and developing personal effectiveness and leadership skills that is intended to pique your curiosity so you want to learn more. Techniques to work with people you find difficult and the characteristic behaviors of effective people are discussed. Several strategies to improve your skills to work effectively with others are suggested.

320

Who Are the Difficult People?

In Utopia, they probably don't exist. But we live in the real world. See if you recognize these people.

The Complainers

Nothing is ever right. Everytime you see them, they give you the daily recitation of what's wrong. You get the feeling in meetings they would rather complain than work to fix a problem. They turn people off by their negativity and nit-picking. Behind their screen of complaints they often are right. They frequently try to delay action. When they do this they are called "Delayers." Have you heard this? "Well, Mr. Jones, providing double lab periods for science and home economics will ruin the social studies minicourse program my department worked on for three years. I move we have the curriculum council conduct a survey of students and parents to get their opinion before we go any further."

The "No" People

Somewhat like the complainer, they are negative and pessimistic. They are skeptical about almost everything being proposed; they resist change, are inflexible, and can quickly dampen enthusiasm in an entire department or school. In faculty meetings you hear them say, "That won't work, we tried it ten years ago."

The "Yes" People

These people agree to anything. They promise to meet a deadline, to complete a task, to chair a committee, and then rarely deliver. Afterward, they are always sorry and frequently pass the buck. "Gee, Sally, I'm really sorry we don't have our Middle States report completed as I promised, but I just couldn't get anyone to attend the meetings." You simply can't trust them to do what they say they will do.

The Despots or Dictators

They tell it like it is to the point where it's insulting. They talk in a big voice, bully, wheedle, coax, cajole, and intimidate. They are always demanding something and are brutally critical of others. In staff meetings you hear them say, "Bob, that is absolutely the worst idea we've heard today! Get real!"

The Pouters or Passives

Look across the table; you can see them—their deadpan faces and blank stares. Shake their hand, not much of a grip, eh? They sit in meetings for days and never offer an opinion or idea. They avoid controversy at all cost by not saying anything. You never know where they stand. You often hear them say *Nothing!* They are like cardboard cutouts.

The Know-It-Alls

They are the resident experts. They know everything about everything. They have an opinion on most issues. They are arrogant. When they are wrong they pass the buck or become defensive. You've heard them. "In my opinion, we ought to ask for the moon because the taxpayers in this community haven't begun to pay their fair share. My cousin's wife works in the tax office so I know whereof I speak."

The Ulterior Motive Players

They maintain a cover. They snipe, take potshots, use well-timed verbal missiles. They frequently respond during unresolved or unheeded problems. You've heard them utter in an audible voice at the back of the room, "I can't believe the administration doesn't take a turn at bus duty if this is such a big problem."

Some Clues to Working Successfully with Difficult People

The key to success with people is to find out what they really want and then help them get it. Difficult people have the need to be valued and understood. To work successfully with them, you must respond in ways that help them feel valued and understood.

Here are some ways to work with difficult people.

The Complainers

1. Listen assertively to complaints.
2. Acknowledge what is being said by paraphrasing.
3. Don't agree or apologize.
4. Reword an accusation.
5. Move to problem solving by asking specific informational questions or ask for the complaint in writing.
6. As a last resort, ask "How do you want this conversation to end?"

When Complainers Become Delayers

1. Make it easy for them to tell you about conflict, what bothers them.
2. Listen for indirect clues about what is bothering them.
3. Offer to help them solve the problem.
4. If they have reservations about you personally, acknowledge past problems.
5. Help them examine facts and put alternatives in priority order.
6. Emphasize quality product or service that will come out of what is being proposed.

The "No" People

1. Be alert to being dragged down; make optimistic statements in response to their negativity.
2. Don't argue.
3. Don't offer alternatives until the problem or issue has been thoroughly discussed.
4. When offering alternative solutions, raise questions yourself about negative aspects or possible negative consequences.
5. As a last resort, ask that a worry list be made and then let things proceed to see what really happens.

The "Yes" People

1. Structure questions to get underlying issues/causes that prevent them from taking action to fulfill their promises to the surface.
2. Tell them directly that you value them. Ask them about their family, favorite project, anything personal.
3. Ask them about things that might interfere with a good working relationship.
4. Use friendly quips to get across your message.

The Despots or Dictators

1. Give them time to run down.
2. Don't necessarily be polite; break into the conversation any way you can.
3. Get their attention and maintain eye contact.
4. If they have exploded, let them know you take them seriously.
5. Get them to sit down.
6. Strongly state your opinions.
7. Don't argue or try to put them down.

The Pouters or Passives

1. Ask open-ended questions.
2. Wait patiently/calmly for response.
3. Be attentive, but don't gush.
4. Avoid polite ending.
5. Terminate meeting, but set up another.
6. Advise them what you must do if _____ doesn't occur.

The Know-It-Alls

1. Do your homework before meeting.
2. Listen carefully and paraphrase what they say.
3. Use questions to raise problems with what they say.
4. Propose delays.
5. Help them save face.
6. Try not to openly contradict what they say.
7. Pick up on anything that makes sense.
8. As a last resort, take them aside and caution them about their behavior.

The Ulterior Motive Players

1. Smoke them out.
2. Provide sniper with a direct contest.
3. Don't capitulate.
4. Try to solve the problem out in the open for everyone to see.
5. Set up regular problem-solving meetings.
6. Stay out of middle if you are third party.

Another Way of Looking at People

Human relations experts have categorized people into different types. Among those suggested are "analyzer," "director," "relator," and "salesperson/ entertainer." The difficult people just discussed fit into these types. By looking at the characteristics of these four types and what makes them "tick," we can learn more about getting along with difficult people. For example, consider the following.

Analyzers:

Positives: Accurate, precise, organized.

Negatives: Stubborn, aloof, boring, unimaginative, autocratic.

When do they become difficult? When they are shown to be wrong or something unexpected happens.

How to communicate effectively: Go step-by-step, use facts, logic, structure, tie new ideas to old ones, remember they like to solve problems independently.

Which difficult people types are included? Know-It-Alls, Pouters and Passives, the "No" People, Complainers, and Delayers.

Directors:

Positives: Decisive, confident, get things done.

Negative: Intimidate, alienate, yell, bully, blow up, arrogant.

When do they become difficult? When someone else is in control.

How to communicate effectively: Support their goals, be businesslike, get to the point, be task oriented, assign them responsibility.

Which difficult people types are included? The Despots or Dictators and Know-It-Alls.

Relators:

Positives: Team players, steadfast, loyal, likable, patient.

Negatives: Indecisive, time wasters, gullible, submissive, passive.

When do they become difficult? When someone treats them insensitively or they are confronted.

How to communicate effectively: Be casual and sincere, listen, never lie, slow down, set goals, emphasize self-development, remember they need to be accepted.

Which difficult people types are included? Pouters and Passives, "No" People, Complainers, and Delayers.

Salespersons/Entertainers:

Positives: High verbal skills, optimistic, persuasive, people oriented.

Negatives: Egotistical, fast talkers, do not always follow through.

When do they become difficult? If ignored or put down.

How to communicate effectively: Be flexible and enthusiastic, let them talk and use demonstrations, remember they like to be recognized.

Which difficult people types are included? "Yes" People and Ulterior Players.

How to Use This Information

Recognizing the information presented does not make you an expert; it can be used to illustrate how to work better with difficult people. For example, assume you are chairing a committee that has a member who is constantly complaining. This person takes up a lot of the committee's time and, even worse, is hard on morale. How can you use the information just given to cope with this person?

You need to apply some system of analysis. One way to do this is to ask yourself these questions.

1. Determine if the Complainer is an Analyzer or Relator. Analyzers are accurate, precise, organized people who tend to be stubborn, aloof, boring, lacking in imagination, and autocratic.

   Relators are loyal, likable, patient people who are team players but who tend to be indecisive, time wasters because of their complaints, submissive, or passive.

2. After you have decided which type of Complainer you are dealing with, determine what types of situations trigger their difficult behavior. Complainer/Analyzers don't like to be shown they are wrong. They also become difficult when something unexpected happens.

    Complainer/Relators become difficult when they are treated insensitively or are confronted.

    Try to avoid the situations described to help prevent sending the Complainer into his or her difficult behavior mode.

3. Determine your responses/behaviors to maximize your effectiveness in working with the Complainer.

    Complainer/Analyzers: Take a step-by-step approach in discussions and problem-solving situations. Use facts, logic, and a structured approach. Tie in your new ideas to ones the Complainer is familiar with. Assign him or her tasks to complete independently.

    Complainer/Relators: Be casual, sincere, and take your time. Do a lot of listening. Always tell the truth. Help them set goals. Make them feel accepted.

TECHNIQUES TO DEAL WITH DIFFICULT PEOPLE

One of the best ways to deal with difficult people is to shape your communication with them so that it fits their personality and style. Here are some examples of ways to respond to difficult people in difficult situations.

1. Fogging or blowing smoke. Give attention to what the person says without agreeing or disagreeing. "That's an interesting point you are making."

2. Broken record. Keep making the same point. "I know you would like your daughter to be exempt from home economics, but it is a state requirement."

3. Share how you feel about the situation. "I would like to discuss this further, but I'm already late for a department meeting."

4. Persistence. "I know you will continue to work to achieve your best."

5. Active listening. "I hear you say that you are unhappy about your teaching assignment for the coming year."

6. Eye-to-eye. Say what you have to say without losing eye contact.

7. Compromise or negotiate. Make a statement such as, "Based upon the circumstances, what are our alternatives? What action can we take so we both feel positive about the outcome?"

8. Offer an unacceptable outcome. "You could teach six periods without a break."

9. Free information. Use your knowledge of the situation to share something you know the person would like to know. "Did you realize that _____?"

10. Stroking. "I was so pleased to hear you had been elected president of the Mid-Central Home Economics Association."

11. Tone. Use the tone of your voice to help convey the meaning you intend.

12. Body language. Be sure your nonverbal cues and body language convey the message you intend: interest-boredom, approval-disapproval, or enthusiasm-passivity.

13. Know what you want that is positive and state it. "I would like to see our department get a paraprofessional to help us with foods labs."

14. Pace your approach to the other person. Be cognizant of the person's "type" so you can pace your presentation to best meet the person's needs.

15. Backtrack and clarify. "It seems to me you have been saying . . . ."

16. State your positive intent. "I want us to achieve a solution that is in the best interest of the students in this school."

WHERE TO GET MORE INFORMATION

Keep your eyes and ears open for information concerning workshops or seminars about how to get along with difficult people. Here is an organization that conducts one-day "How to Handle Difficult People" seminars across the United States and Canada. You can write or call them for information about seminars in your area.

National Seminars Group
6901 West 63rd Street
P.O. Box 2949
Shawnee Mission, KS 66201-1349
(800) 344-4613

If you are interested in reading more about the topic, here are some suggestions:

Anderson, Karen. *Getting What You Want: How to Reach Agreement and Resolve Conflict Every Time.* New York: E. P. Dutton, 1993.

Bramson, Robert M. *Coping with Difficult People.* New York: Dell, 1988.

Dymer, Chuck. *How to Handle Difficult People* (four-cassette series). Shawnee Mission, KS: National Press Publications, 1988.

Giblin, Les. *How to Have Confidence and Power in Dealing with People.* Englewood Cliffs, NJ: Prentice Hall, 1986.

Lacey, Walt. *How to Work With People (six-cassette series).* Shawnee Mission, KS: National Press Publications, 1988.

BECOMING A MORE EFFECTIVE PERSON

MEMO TO: ALL HOME ECONOMICS TEACHERS

FROM: PEGGY CAMPBELL

RE: BECOMING A MORE EFFECTIVE PERSON

DATE: ANYTIME

If you follow only one suggestion in this book, please let it be this one. I know it will improve your effectiveness in all of your endeavors with all the people with whom you associate, be they students, coworkers, friends, relatives, your spouse, your children, or your significant other.

I suggest you study the work of Stephen R. Covey to discover how his insights into what makes an effective person can help you.

A statement on the cover of one of his books reads, "In *The Seven Habits of Highly Effective People,* author Stephen R. Covey presents a holistic, integrated, principle-centered approach for solving personal and professional problems. With penetrating insights and pointed anecdotes, Covey reveals a step-by-step pathway for living with fairness, integrity, honesty, and human dignity—principles that give us the security to adapt to change, and the wisdom and power to take advantage of the opportunities that change creates."

I suggest you approach Covey in two stages. First, study and practice the principles taught in his book *The Seven Habits of Highly Effective People.* In this book you learn about the seven habits he identified during his 25 years of experience, research, and thought. They are:

Habit 1: *Be Proactive.* By that he means taking responsibility for your attitudes and actions. You are "response able." You have the freedom to choose your responses making them more a product of your values and decisions than your mood or condition. To be proactive, Covey says you need "to be a light, not a judge; a model, not a critic; a programmer, not a program; to feed opportunities, starve problems; to keep promises, not make excuses, ..."

Habit 2: *Begin with the End in Mind.* He calls this the habit of personal leadership. You begin each day with a clear understanding of where you are going and how you are going to get there.

Habit 3: *Put First Things First.* He calls this the habit of personal management. It involves organizing tasks and managing time and events to accomplish what you set out to do in Habit 2.

Habit 4: *Think Win-Win.* He calls this the habit of interpersonal leadership. He says, "Win-win thinking begins with a commitment to explore all options until a mutually satisfactory solution is reached, or to make no deal at all."

Habit 5: *Seek First to Understand, Then to be Understood.* Covey calls this habit the habit of communication, one of the master skills of life.

Habit 6: *Synergize.* Covey calls this the habit of creative cooperation or teamwork. Synergy occurs when people value differences by bringing different perspectives together in a spirit of mutual respect. When this occurs they feel free to seek the best possible alternative.

Habit 7: *Sharpen the Saw.* This is the habit of self-renewal. The habit of sharpening the saw means having a balanced, systematic program for self-renewal in the four areas of our lives: physical, mental, emotional-social, and spiritual.

Dr. Covey found these habits to be the powerful factors in our lives that consistently and constantly express our character and produce our effectiveness—or ineffectiveness. Habits, he says, are the behavior that results from the intersection of knowledge, skill, and desire, with knowledge meaning the knowing of what and why to do, skill as knowing how to do, and desire as the wanting to do.

I followed the suggestion Covey makes about how to use his book and found it effective. I read the book in its entirety to get a picture of the whole and then went back to examine each principle and put it into practice so that my knowledge, skill, and desire to become more effective grew. I took his suggestion to make a paradigm shift from learner to teacher. I involved my husband, and as a team we studied and practiced the principles by sharing and discussing with each other what we learned within 48 hours of learning it. You could involve a friend, a member of your department, or a fellow teacher to share the excitement of becoming a more effective person. Just do it!

For Stage Two, I recommend you study Covey's book *Principle-Centered Leadership* and put into practice the principles he suggests. This guidebook will help you to develop the skill to unleash the creative talent and energy of others, to build team spirit and harmony in your department and school, to enrich your marriage and family relationships, to develop a mission statement to guide your life at home and at work, to develop win-win performance agreements, and to interact with others to internalize the principles of total quality and continuous improvement.

I recommend you use the same approach with this book that you used with *The Seven Habits of Highly Effective People*.

Getting started is easy. Call 1-800-255-0777 to request a free copy of the "Personal Leadership Application Workbook." It contains an overview of *The Seven Habits;* a self-scoring profile based on *The Seven Habits;* examples of personal, organizational, and family mission statements; worksheets to create and monitor the implementation of a mission statement; and some examples of win-win performance agreements.

Go to your local bookstore and purchase one or both of these books. Start to read immediately!

Covey, Stephen R. *The Seven Habits of Highly Effective People.* New York: Simon & Schuster, 1989. $9.95

Covey, Stephen R. *Principle-Centered Leadership.* New York: Simon & Schuster, 1991. $20.00

This is a long memo, but I believe its message is important. Home economists recognize how important it is for every human being to maximize his or her potential. By accepting my suggestion, you will not only improve your own personal effectiveness, but you will acquire the skills, the tools, and the approach to help your students develop these critical life skills. I wish you Godspeed and good luck!